Studies in Eighteenth-Century Culture

VOLUME 31

Studies in Eighteenth-Century Culture

VOLUME 31

Edited by

Ourida Mostefai
Boston College

and

Catherine Ingrassia
Virginia Commonwealth University

Published by The Johns Hopkins University Press for the
American Society for Eighteenth-Century Studies

The Johns Hopkins University Press
Baltimore and London

Printed in the United States of America on acid-free paper
9 8 7 6 5 4 3 2 1

The Johns Hopkins University Press
2715 North Charles Street
Baltimore, Maryland 21218-4363
www.press.jhu.edu

ISBN 0-8018-7256-1
ISSN 0360-2370

Articles appearing in this annual series are abstracted and indexed in *Historical Abstracts* and *America: History and Life*.

Editorial Readers for Volume Thirty-One

Contents

Editor's Note

In keeping with our tradition, the essays published in this volume are based on papers that were presented at the annual meetings of the American Society for Eighteenth-Century Studies and its affiliates. The essays selected for this volume present a variety of disciplinary and interdisciplinary perspectives and thus offer a glance at the state of scholarship in eighteenth-century studies.

The first cluster of essays deals with the question of spending. In the first essay, James E. Evans examines the depiction of gambling in comedies and periodicals in the late seventeenth- and early eighteenth-century in England. The article focuses on the shift that occurs after the Revolution of 1688 when gambling ceases to be seen as an acceptable recreation for gentlemen and ladies and is increasingly condemned as an immoral activity, a "wicked folly," and a threat to a woman's honor. This question of the dangers of gambling for women is developed in the second essay (by Beth Kowaleski Wallace) which examines a number of fashionable lady gamesters in the Restoration and the early eighteenth-century stage. Focusing on the female performance at the gambling table, the article explores the connections between the game of chance and the control of social behavior. The gaming woman emerges from this reading as a complex and potentially subversive figure. Catherine Keohane's essay examines the fear raised by women's participation in the consumer economy of eighteenth-century England. An analysis of didactic as well as fictional works reveals a growing concern about women's control of money. The author explores the relationship between charity and expenditure as well as the conflicting philosophies about spending available at the time and proposes a new "economic" argument regarding women's consumption.

In the second section questions of national and international identities are explored. Brijraj Singh's contribution offers an examination of the international collaboration among Protestants in the early part of the eighteenth century. Recreating the history of the interaction between the pietist wing of the Lutheran Church in Germany, the Church of England in Britain, the American Puritan movement in New England and protestant missionaries in south India, the author offers an international perspective on the question of ecumenism and tolerance. Historical figures are examined in the context of their religious ideas and well as their social work (in particular the establishment of orphanages and schools for the poor). Daniel J. Ennis offers a reflection on the role of poetic discourse in the formation of eighteenth-century American identity. Drawing on the discovery of a letter and a poem written by John Paul Jones and addressed to Phillis Wheatley the author explores the connections between the fugitive Scottish sailor and the former black slave and finds profound similarities in the fashioning of their respective identities as Americans. Both found similar opportunities in the writing of poetry and in the American Revolution. The third article (by Leanne Maunu) examines Frances Burney's *Evelina* in the context of the shaping of a national identity in Britain. By focusing on two colorful characters from the novel—a French woman, and a British sea captain—the author shows how Burney uses anti-French propaganda as an inspiration for her characters, expressing the contemporary fears and anxieties about the French nation as an "Other" threatening to contaminate the national character. A close textual analysis reveals both the violence of this depiction and its limits, suggesting Burney's own ambivalence.

The third cluster of essays is devoted to France's literary tradition. Reginald McGinnis proposes an examination of the negative meanings and uses of the concept of originality in France. Focusing on the social critique of originality this article presents a reading of dramatic and fictional works which offer polemical perspectives on originality. In particular, the literary quarrel between the *philosophes* and their adversaries brings into focus the relationship between originality and imitation. The second essay, by John Iverson, deals with the emergence of a new cultural practice in France: the first literary centenary held in 1773 in celebration of Molière's death. This event is seen as a key moment in the formation of a national literature and of French national identity. The article analyzes this expression of national pride in the context of France's cultural and political rivalry with England, and in the wake of France's humiliating defeat in the Seven Years' War. In the third article Joe Johnson offers an interpretation *Manon Lescaut* through the perspective of male friendship. Refocusing the reading on the male hero, the author explores the manifestations of homosocial desire in the novel. A close reading reveals the ambiguity of the concept of friendship presented in the novel. Similarly, an examination of the male characters brings to light their duality and ambivalence.

Art and music is the topic of the last section of the volume. Examining the association between women and nature, J. David Macey proposes a model for interpreting the work of eighteenth-century novelists. Through the close reading of a scene of the repainting and revising of Poussin's *Et in Arcadia Ego*, this article shows the possibility of a "disobedient" reading and revision of tradition for women. A series of intertextual interpretations offers divergent models of utopian communities. John Irving's essay examines the cultural schism in late eighteenth-century England between the partisans of ancient music and the proponents of modern music. By focusing on John Marsh, a moderate voice in this debate, this article emphasizes the question of tolerance as a central issue in this debate. A reading of Marsh's autobiography as well as his essays uncovers a new perspective on his musical theory. Finally, Amy Wyngaard's article examines the problematic representation of the French peasantry on the eve of the French revolution. This study focuses on the works of Arthur Young and Legrand d'Aussy and their reaction against the sentimentalized portrayal of peasantry prevalent in the art and literature of the period. In their depiction of the plight and the suffering of French peasants, the Englishman and the French Jesuit have different goals but they both reveal the importance of fictional representations of peasantry in the construction of French national identity.

I wish to thank my predecessor Timothy Erwin for his friendship and guidance. I would also like to thank all the members of the editorial board. I am enormously grateful to my colleague, Associate Editor, Catherine Ingrassia, for her dedication and support, and to Vickie Cutting, the volume copyeditor, for her constant care and attention.

Studies in Eighteenth-Century Culture

VOLUME 31

"A sceane of uttmost vanity": The Spectacle of Gambling in Late Stuart Culture

JAMES E. EVANS

Restoration diarist John Evelyn describes a memorable occasion at court on Twelfth Night, 6 January 1662:

> This evening (according to costome) his Majestie opned the Revells of that night, by throwing the Dice himselfe, in the Privy Chamber, where was a table set on purpose, & lost his 100 pounds: the yeare before he won 150 pounds: The Ladys also plaied very deepe: I came away when the Duke of *Ormond* had won about 1000 pounds & left them still at passage, Cards &c: at other Tables, both there and at the *Groome-porters*, observing the wiccked folly vanity & monstrous excesse of Passion amongst some loosers, & sorry I am that such a wretched Custome as play to that excesse should be countenanc'd in a Court, which ought to be an example of Virtue to the rest of the kingdome.[1]

According to *The History of Gambling in England*, "Play at Court was lawful, and encouraged" between Christmas and Epiphany: "When the King felt disposed, and it was his pleasure to play, it was the etiquette and custom to announce to the company, that 'His Majesty was out'; on which intimation all Court ceremony and restraint were set aside, and the sport commenced."[2] Restored along with the Stuart monarchy, this custom was not limited to holidays. A few years after the Restoration the French ambassador wrote about the court of Charles II: "There is a ball and a comedy every other day; the rest of the days are spent at play."[3] High stakes gambling, which became one of the ubiquitous recreations of late seventeenth-century England at palaces, the groom-porter's, and private houses, epitomized the Carolean carnival that followed the Cromwellian lent. "At no time probably in the history of England," asserts Cyril Hughes Hartmann, "has the passion for gambling reached a greater height or spread over a larger section of society" than during the late seventeenth and early eighteenth centuries.[4]

Nowhere did the rage for gambling remain more evident than at court, where the King's mistresses and numerous others wagered enormous sums. In January 1685, near the end of Charles's reign, Evelyn once again depicts the gamblers: "I saw this evening such a sceane of profuse gaming, and luxurious dallying & prophaneness, the King in the middst of his 3 concubines, as I had never before." Among those present, Evelyn adds, he was "witnesse" of

> the King, sitting & toying with his Concubines . . . whilst about 20 of the greate Courtiers & other dissolute persons were at Basset round a large table, a bank of at least 2000 in Gold before them, upon which two Gent: that were with me made reflexions with astonishment, it being a sceane of uttmost vanity; and surely as they thought would never have an End: six days after was all in the dust.[5]

The rhetoric of Evelyn's diary frames these occasions in such language as "observing the wiccked folly," "a sceane of profuse gaming," and "a sceane of uttmost vanity." However, between the two passages, separated by more than twenty years, there is an important shift in perspective. On the first evening, the persons observed retain their power; depicted in active verbs, the King opens the gambling, the ladies play, the Duke wins. During the second visit the spectator assumes greater authority over those observed. He sees the King "in the middst" and the courtiers "at Basset." Given additional force, at the time of writing, by his knowledge of the reign's imminent end, Evelyn emphasizes the observers' "astonishment" and moral outrage rather than lamenting the negative influence of the court.

Using Evelyn's texts as a starting point, this essay examines a similar shift in the discourse of gambling--from a social spectacle representing the uneasy privilege of the aristocracy during the Restoration to a spectacle recreated in comic plays and periodicals after the Revolution of 1688. Early in this period, for example, Charles Cotton's *The Compleat Gamester* (1674), a manual describing "all manner of usual and most Gentile Games either on CARDS or DICE," includes an apology for "the lawfulness of recreation" and promises "delight to such who will pass away their spare minutes in harmless recreation if not abus'd."[6] Looking backward in *Memoirs of the Lives, Intrigues, and Comical Adventures of the Most Famous Gamesters and Celebrated Sharpers in the Reigns of Charles II, James II, William III and Queen Anne* (1714), Theophilus Lucas laments that "diversion and entertainment" are "the great excuse which gentleman have for losing their money: Every-body pleads privilege for recreation." To him, gambling is "an enchanting witchcraft, begotten by those devils, avarice and idleness."[7] The differences between Cotton's book, with its accounts of twenty "Principal Games at Cards," six "Games within the Tables," and seven "Games without the Tables," and Lucas's "Secret History" of twenty-six gamblers illustrate the change in the cultural signification of gambling.

According to Lawrence Stone, high stakes gambling in the seventeenth century was one form of "conspicuous expenditure," which was "deeply ingrained in this idle and exhibitionist society." In a century during which "insecurity caused a struggle for status," gambling served "a social function as a symbolic justification for the maintenance or acquisition of status."[8] Georges Bataille theorizes similarly about the function of "unproductive expenditure" in archaic societies: "More or less narrowly, social rank is linked to the possession of a fortune, but only on the condition that the fortune be partially sacrificed in unproductive social expenditures such as festivals, spectacles, and games." Usefully for this study, Bataille connects "a positive property of loss" to "nobility, honor, and rank in a hierarchy" and hypothesizes that wealth is "entirely directed toward loss in the sense that power is characterized as power to lose. It is only through loss that glory and honor are linked to wealth."[9] Paradoxically, then, upper class willingness to venture enormous sums, even perhaps to risk ruin, was necessary to manifest status to others and thus to maintain privilege in Restoration England.

This process may have been exacerbated by circumstance. After the Restoration, writes Christopher Hill, as "the distinction between landed and moneyed interests" became "more apparent than real," the added insecurity generated another problem for gentlemen and ladies: "The aristocrats who regained their privileged position after 1660 had no significant role to play in the reconstructed social order. Flocking to the court, they ceased even to take their traditional part in local government; and at court their role was decorative rather than functional."[10] In response to "an increasingly defensive awareness that social hierarchy was under assault," argues Michael McKeon, aristocratic conduct illustrates "the more elaborate sort of 'theatricalization' that is likely to occur whenever social convention is raised to the level of self-conscious practice."[11] This self-consciousness can be found, for example, in Obadiah Walker's *Of Education* (1673), which asserts that a gentleman "by his *Family*" is "already placed upon the *Theater*, where all his actions shall be observed . . . even more then they deserve; all mens eyes are upon him."[12] Gambling, in all its Restoration excess, contributed to the social spectacle at court and elsewhere, as some men and women risked their fortunes to demonstrate their status.

Not surprisingly, then, gambling was also integral to the reopened theater, especially to comedies of the 1660s and 1670s, including such major plays as Sir George Etherege's *The Man of Mode* (1676) and William Wycherley's *The Country Wife* (1675). Etherege, for instance, evokes "deep play" as a practice congruent with his protagonist's social identity. To the modish Dorimant, "deep" signifies high stakes, which are not, by definition, irrational or immoral.

> Emilia. There are afflictions in Love, Mr. *Dorimant.*
> Dorimant. You Women make 'em, who are commonly as unreasonable in that as you are at Play; without the Advantage be on your side, a man can never quietly give over when he's weary!
> Medley. If you would play without being obliged to complaisance, *Dorimant*, you should play in publick places.
> Dorimant. Ordinaries were a very good thing for that, but Gentlemen do not of late frequent 'em. The deep play is now in private Houses.[13]

As this passage establishes Dorimant as a skilled libertine and gambler, it expresses the values of a gentleman who prefers his pleasures apart from those who gamble for gain. According to Thomas M. Kavanagh, "The true courtier never plays *only* to win money. If he gambles, it is to demonstrate a prowess superior to that of his adversary." Consequently, the courtier's gambling, which shows his "superiority to the ever more imperious rule of money," centers "on affirming one's basic ethics and identity . . . that of the individual as one who knew, lived by, and incarnated a socialized perfection conceivable only within the context of the court."[14] In England, Stone observes, gambling was "a suitable pastime for a gentleman, one of whose functions was to live in idleness with elegance and grace. It was as important to know how to play cards or handle the dice as it was to be able to ride a horse or dance a galliard."[15] As the aristocracy persisted and "grew more and more into an actor, playing an elaborate part," V. G. Kiernan remarks, "A man had to be able to hazard his fortune on a turn of the cards as cooly as his forefathers risked their lives on the luck of the battle."[16]

The discourse that precedes Etherege's representation of the idle and elegant Dorimant began much earlier when the English began to imitate European courts of the Renaissance. According to Castiglione's seminal text, *The Courtier*, gambling is suitable as the courtier "attends sometimes to grave matters and sometimes to festivals and games, depending on the occasion." It is not a vice unless the courtier gambles "too constantly and as a result should neglect other more important things, or indeed unless he should play only to win money and to cheat the other player."[17] Numerous English texts echo Castiglione's counsel. Mary Lady Despencer expresses these values to her grandson, a future Earl of Westmorland: "Know play to make thee sociable, but sett not thy harte upon it . . . to play for gayne more then recreation illegittimates all good meetings."[18] Among conduct books repeating such advice, Richard Brathwait's *The English Gentleman* (1641) includes, among "exercises of the mind . . . Cards and Dice, a speciall *Recreation*, meerely invented and intended to passe tedious Winter nights away, and not to hazard ones fortunes at them." "Make not your *Recreation* a distemper," he adds, and advises gentlemen "never to mount your stake so high, as the losse of it may move you to choler."[19] On the other hand, in The *Gentlemans Companion* (1672), William Ramesay asserts the legitimacy of "*Recreations and Exercises within doors . . . Cards, Dice, Tables*, which many narrow-witted People too severely explode; in themselves they are honest and harmless recreations; the abuse of them must not deny the use of them." Yet Ramesay also declares that "to spend all their Life in gameing" is "very unseemly" for gentlemen.[20] Even George Savile, Marquis of Halifax, advising his daughter on "a wise and a safe method of useing diversions," writes that "To play sometimes, to entertain company, or to divert your self, is not to be disallowed; but to do it so often as to be called a Gamester, is to be avoided."[21] For all their efforts to justify gambling as aristocratic recreation, however, none of these authors condoned the deep play that became widespread in late Stuart England. The status conflicts following the Restoration assured the prominence of gambling as a form of conspicuous, unproductive expenditure. "Nothing," asserts La Bruyère, "makes a man more immediately fashionable or raises him higher in public esteem than high-stakes gambling."[22]

While *The Man of Mode* does not present the spectacle of characters gambling, Derek Hughes argues that "compulsive play" in Dorimant's world is "nothing less than a generalized model of social existence," which Etherege subjects to "sceptical analysis rather than uncritical celebration."[23]

Gambling also permeates *The Country Wife*. As John T. Harwood comments, "Horner's world is not the world of sex . . . but of gaming. Sex is sought, offered, or withheld not for its own sake but as a means of enhancing one's power over others through calculated risks."[24] The libertine Horner identifies his seduction plot with gambling even before he is invited to join "a drolling pack of ombre players" or Lady Fidget learns that he "loves play as much as you, and has money." Although Wycherley does not represent their card games, the social complicity of audience and characters in his dramatic satire makes such absence plausible. Playwrights "must follow their copy, the age," declares one of his wits; adds another "'Tis but being on the stage, instead of standing on a bench in the pit."[25] Restoration comedy, according to Peter Holland, "emphasised its close connection with its audience--and hence its claim, through its *vraisemblance* in acting and locale, to comment on its audience's morals--by placing the action principally on the forestage." As a result of familiar settings and the alignment of actors with audience, he adds, "The audience saw the actor as in a situation potentially analogous to their own, rather than in a totally fictive world."[26] It is not remarkable, then, that gambling is integral to characters' conduct without being part of the dramatic action. On a given night the audience in the well-lit theaters could contain a number of recognized gamblers; later in the period, for example, Thomas Durfey complains that the reception of *A Fools's Preferment* (1688) was marred by "the Party that was malitiously made by some eminent Gamesters of both Sexes, who thought themselves touch'd."[27]

Carolean comedies feature a variety of gamblers and gambling. In James Howard's *The English Mounsieur* (c. 1663) the protagonist Wellbred is a "*wild Gentleman*," whose gambling, "thy Extravagant humor," must change before Lady Wealthy will marry him; when she invites him to play ombre in Act 4, Wellbred, lacking funds, comically refuses to join her.[28] Prig, the humorous gamester in Thomas Shadwell's *A True Widow* (1679), evokes an ironic estimate of "the Groom-Porters, where you may play all night. Oh, 'tis a Heavenly Life! we are never idle."[29] Thomas Otway's *The Atheist* (1683) presents a generational inversion, the protagonist's "wild, extravagant, old Father," who must promise his son "to leave off Gaming."[30] Games of ombre take place offstage in Act 2 of Wycherley's *The Plain Dealer* (1676), Act 3 of Durfey's *A Fond Husband* (1676), and Act 4 of John Dryden's *The Kind Keeper* (1678). Characters in Shadwell's *Epsom-Wells* (1673) are reported to lose money at put and cribbage. There are so many allusions to "the great pleasure of gaming" in Sir Charles Sedley's *The Mulberry Garden* (1668) that it seems as much the center of characters' social existence as in *The Man of Mode*, though without much skeptical reservation.[31] When Restoration playwrights represent gambling on stage, they sometimes ridicule pretenders to privilege, antagonists of the rake hero, such as the recently titled Sir Nicholas Cully, who plays dice with sharpers at a tavern in Act 2 of Etherege's *The Comical Revenge* (1664), or the avaricious merchant Sir Cautious Fulbank, who uses his wife's body as his stake in a game of dice with Gayman in Act 4 of Aphra Behn's *The Luckey Chance* (1686). Behn's stage direction locates the satiric exposure of rake and fool in her cuckolding plot on the forestage, when Gayman "*Puts down his Hat of Money, and each of 'em take a Box and Dice, and kneel on the Stage, the rest come about 'em.*"[32]

While Dryden sometimes mocks pretenders to gentility, identifying the eponymous character of *Sir Martin Mar-all* (1667) as a gamester, two of his comedies also ridicule the "extravagant rake," a more humorous, less dangerous version of this character type.[33] In his Spanish carnival play *An Evening's Love* (1668), the English character Wildblood, who twice exits to a gaming-house, loses at dice in Act 3 to the masked Jacinta, who cheats him, then turns the event into a test of his character. When his servant advises Wildblood to "consider your condition," he laughs at himself, "for my condition is so ridiculous that 'tis past cursing," and cites his "promise to return to play."[34] In *The Wild Gallant* (1663) Dryden employs two discovery scenes of the kind that became more common in post-Revolution comedy to expose gambling as a vice. Both show the ridiculous character Justice Trice gambling alone. At the start of Act 1, scene 3, "*The Scene changes, and* Trice *is discovered playing at Tables by himself,*" as other characters "*return and see him, undiscovered by him.*" Trice invents a genteel quarrel with himself, while the others "*laugh and discover themselves.*" Trice's humor emerges again in Act 4 in another discovery ("*Table set with Cards upon it.* Trice walking"), when he plays picquet and pretends that his victorious opponent is the protagonist Jack Loveby. Already on stage, but unseen by Trice, Loveby seizes his winnings, "won fairly; a Sixieme, and Fourteen by Aces by your own confession" to conclude this "Game of Gentlemen." Well known for his own gambling debts, Loveby, nevertheless, receives a sort of comic blessing in the play's Epilogue: "The Wild Gallant *has quite playd out his game.*"[35] Unlike Cully, Fulbank, and Trice, the extravagant rakes Wildblood and Loveby gamble without threatening their aristocratic status, though their conspicuous, unproductive expenditure causes temporary, comic embarrassment.

Writing texts that remained unpublished during the Restoration, fascinated observers like Evelyn and Samuel Pepys saw another, more decadent spectacle than that represented on the stage. Pepys record of a visit to the halls of the Inner and Middle Temple during the Christmas season of 1668 emphasizes his role as spectator in a crescendo of infinitive phrases: "to see the manner of the gaming at the Groome porter's," "to see how the dice will run good luck," "to see the different humours of gamesters," "to see how persons of the best quality do here sit down and play with people of any." Pepys concludes:

> And lastly, to see the formality of the Groome-porter, who is their judge of all disputes in play and all quarrels that may arise therein; and how his under-officers are there to observe true play at each table and to give new dice, is a consideration I never could have thought had been in the world, had I not now seen it. And mighty glad I am that I did see it.[36]

Determined not to relinquish the perspective necessary to judge the disorder of the scene, Pepys even refuses the opportunity to gamble with another's money.[37]

Critiques such as this are more common after the Revolution of 1688, when reform-minded writers routinely link gambling to other libertine conduct as a legacy of the Restoration. The diarists' dismay becomes received wisdom in texts like *The Tatler*, where Richard Steele mocks a character who spends his days "in the common Diversions of Men of Fashion; that is to say, in Whoring, Drinking, and Gaming."[38] In Susanna Centlivre's *The Busybody* (1709) a father complains that "gaming, whoring, and the pox, are requisites to a gentleman."[39] Though high stakes gambling continued to flourish during the reigns of King William and Queen Anne, more authors wrote critically of gambling as a recreation in the decades when Societies for the Reformation of Manners spoke for the new morality encouraged by the last Stuart courts. Colley Cibber's *The Lady's Last Stake* (1707), for instance, includes this declaration: "'tis amazing, that so many good Families shou'd daily encourage a Diversion, whose utmost Pleasure is founded upon Avarice and ill Nature: For those are always the secret Principles of deep Play."[40] Linking "Covetousness" to "this Diversion," Jeremy Collier argues that "playing deep" exposes the passions: "Cards and Dice, &c. command the Humour no less than the Moon does the Tide."[41] Integral to such judgments was the altered perspective that made gambling a dramatic and literary spectacle.

In the theater and in print this change increased the authority of the spectator at the expense of gamblers and demonstrated authorial confidence in a post-Revolution epistemology which, according to Rose A. Zimbardo, "takes it as a given that vice can be distinguished from virtue."[42] By making the discovery scene central to dramatic actions, Mary Pix's *The Beau Defeated* (1700), Centlivre's *The Gamester* (1705) and *The Basset Table* (1705), and Cibber's *The Lady's Last Stake* expose as false the connection of gambling to status. Adopting the perspective of the observer to discredit gambling, Ned Ward's *London Spy* (1698-1700), Tom Brown's *Amusements Serious and Comical* (1700), and Steele's and Joseph Addison's *The Tatler* (1709-1711), *The Spectator* (1711-1712, 1714), and *The Guardian* (1713) take advantage of the emerging role of periodicals in the bourgeois public sphere to accomplish their critique. Both periodicals and comedies participate in the rhetoric found in texts like *The Country Gentleman's Vade Mecum*, an anonymous series of letters to a friend, that "discovers to him most of the Humours, Tricks and Cheats of the Town"; in Letter XI such attributes of the Groom Porter's, ordinaries, and gaming houses are "*briefly exposed*."[43]

Two recent dramatists prepared the way for the campaign of exposure in the humane comedies of Pix, Cibber, and Centlivre. In *A Fool's Preferment* (1688) Durfey's satire of gambling (anachronistically focused on basset, "the most Courtly, the most Grand, the most Graceful Game," according to one character) includes this stage direction for the discovery scene opening Act 2: "*Discovers the* Basset-Table; Aurelia, Clermont, Longville, Bewford, *and other Gentlemen and Ladies sitting round at Play,* Winnall *is dealing; several are standing by, and others walking about; Acting the several Humours of Winners and Losers*."[44] To create such a tableau, more common in Restoration tragedies than comedies, writes Holland, "the shutters, large flats which moved in grooves across the stage to join in the center, open and actors are discovered behind, set against a further piece of scenery." "Restoration practice," he judges, made such upstage action "equivalent to a stronger divorce from reality and a weakening of the claim on the audience to see the actors as individuals similar to themselves."[45] Durfey's scene, which includes more farce than usual in such discoveries, presents the spectacle of a country gentleman's town house turned upside down by his own aspirations to be a courtier and the ruinous gambling of his wife, part of the project, stated in the Dedication, of exposing vice.

Less farcical and didactic are gambling scenes in two of Thomas Southerne's comedies. While Durfey ridicules those who imitate aristocrats and their games, Southerne satirizes the adulterous world of upper class marriage rather than gambling per se. *The Wives' Excuse* (1692), which opens with the spectacle of "*Several Footmen at Hazard, Some rising from Play*," includes one of the most ingenious uses of scenery for the discovery of gamesters, the after-dinner card game at the Friendalls' house in Act 4. As characters talk of play, a stage direction indicates "*Scene draws, shews*

Tables and Cards"; after several characters speak, "*They go in to play. The Scene shuts upon 'em.*" Two characters remain on stage for a brief dialogue until "*The Scene opens, the Company rises from play, and comes forward.*"[46] Like Etherege and Wycherley, Southerne is not interested in reforming gamblers, but in examining a way of life that features gambling among its extravagant recreations. The link between libertinism and gambling recurs vividly in Act 1 of *The Maid's Last Prayer* (1693), when the audience views two perspectives on an evening of basset. While Scene 1 begins at Lady Trickitt's house with "Gayman *and* Granger, *from Play*," Scene 2 presents the spectacle the gentlemen have been discussing: "*Scene drawn, shows Lady* Trickitt, Maria, *and* Garnish, *making up the Bank, Cards scatter'd about.*"[47] Through this representation of gambling Southerne introduces "the human competitiveness" central to his play, which Hughes describes, as "not of the Hobbesian wilderness but of the drawing room . . . not expressions of some deeper and more atavistic urge to dominate;they are the thing itself."[48]

Unlike the satirical comedies of Southerne, the humane comedies of Pix, Cibber, and Centlivre use discovery scenes to represent the need for reform to the audience. Nowhere is the bourgeois ideology underlying the reforming impulse more explicit than in *The Beau Defeated*. Mrs. Rich, the widow of a prosperous London merchant, regularly gambles with Lady La Bassett and Mrs. Trickwell, cheats whom she wrongly assumes to be ladies of quality. Her motive is the ridiculous dream she expresses: "may I hope to play at Court? I have a great ambition to play at Court: Oh my Stars! I shou'd torment our City Ladies to death, to talk of Honours done me at Court." Pix's plot eventually compels Mrs. Rich to renounce gambling and subscribe to middle class values offered by other characters. In Act 2 Pix utilizes the scenic stage, the large area behind the proscenium arch, to represent her character's folly: "*Scene draws and discovers Mrs.* Rich, Mrs. Trickwell, *and Lady* la Basset, *Rising from Play.*" Having turned this conduct into comic spectacle, Pix ironically permits the beau, Sir John Roverhead, to comment on it and to uncouple status from recreation; "in the last Generation, and this," he observes, "Sharpers, had their Cullies; Gamesters, their Fools . . . Courtiers Promises, and Bullies Oaths, ever made a great Noise, and signify'd nothing." The tableau receives final, more authoritative commentary from Mr. Rich, who advises his sister-in-law to "retrench all this Greatness and Folly."[49] Pix leaves no doubt that families of respected merchants should not aspire to the vices of aristocrats. Even Sir James Bellmont, the genteel protagonist of her later comedy *The Different Widows* (1703), abandons gambling ("that Scandalous Diversion . . . the Shame of Gentlemen, the Destruction of Families, and the last refuge of the Prodigal"), reforming four acts after he provides his own "Harangue against Gaming."[50]

Cibber uses the discovery scene even more effectively than Pix. If gambling threatens Mrs. Rich's respectability, his Lady Gentle faces peril to her virtue in *The Lady's Last Stake*. Identified as "the Perfection of a good Wife," except for "her Over-fondness for Play," the lady's gambling is finally observed in Act 5: "*The* SCENE *opening discovers Lord* George *and Lady* Gentle *rising from Play.*" When the lord convinces the lady to wager once more, her body against her debts, she loses (though a gift of 2000 pounds rescues her). At the end of the scene Lady Gentle reflects on her experience: "This Vice of Play . . . appear'd at first an harmless, safe, Amusement; but stealing into Habit, its greatest Hazards grew so familiar, that ev'n the Face of Ruine lost its Terror to me."[51] As Laura J. Rosenthal points out, Cibber sought "to specularize anxieties about the mobility of property and the instability of gender"; once Lady Gentle enters the "unstable economy" of gambling, the play presents "a lesson about the extraordinary risk."[52] In his Dedication Cibber is explicit about the purpose of this spectacle:

> Gaming is a Vice, that has undone more innocent Principles, than any one Folly that's in Fashion; therefore I chose to expose it to the Fair Sex in its most hideous Form, by reducing a Woman of Honour to stand the presumptuous Addresses of a Man, whom neither her Virtue or Inclination wou'd let her have the least Taste to.[53]

Cibber employs the discovery scene to parallel Lady Gentle's progress, in his post-Revolution epistemology, from appearance to truth. Not a recreation to be associated with honor, gambling potentially involves women, even more than men, dangerously in vice. To Cibber, it is no longer a matter of conspicuous or unproductive expenditure. According to *The Ladies Library*, "if Gaming is a Vice in Men, it is much more so in Women; for that one of its Consequences is often the Loss of what is much more valuable than Gold or Diamonds, their Reputation, if not their Honour."[54]

Centlivre's two comedies represent her characters' problematic gambling even more extensively. To Valere, the extravagant protagonist of *The Gamester*, gambling is "my dear Diversion . . . the genteelest Way of passing one's Time . . . as much in Fashion here as 'tis in France." In his humorous obsession with play and his reform prior to marriage, he resembles Wellbred in *The English Mounsieur*. Unlike Howard, Centlivre represents her genteel character's gambling on stage, near the end of Act 4, when the "SCENE *discovers a Gaming-Table, with* Valere, *Count* Cogdie*, and other Gentlemen at Hazard, with several Rakes and Sharpers, waiting round the Table; a Box-Keeper, and Attendants.*" She sets Valere's deep play in a gaming house, where the heroine Angelica appears in masculine disguise to test him. After he loses a token of their love to her in a dice game, he must "behold what a Monster this darling Sin has made me." In order to earn Angelica's forgiveness, Valere finally discards his unproductive expenditure as immoral. Near the play's conclusion, Angelica's question opposes claims of status to the privileges of recreation: "Can you upon Honour . . . forsake that Vice that brought you to this low Ebb of Fortune?"[55] Centlivre's spectacle exposes the post-Revolution truth about gambling to protagonist and audience alike. Her gentleman must redefine the relationship of honor to diversion.

A fifth act repentance and reconciliation also conclude Centlivre's *The Basset Table*, in which the young widow Lady Reveller believes it is not "possible to pass the evenings without diversions" like gambling. Although one admirer calls her "an exact model of what all women ought to be," this comedy begins at 4:00 a. m., following all-night gambling at her lodgings. Her admirer, Lord Worthy, admits "I love her person, but hate her humours," which he associates with her foolish "passion for gain." Once again Centlivre uses the final scene of Act 4 to stage the spectacle of gambling--"LADY REVELLER, MRS. SAGO *and several gentlemen and ladies round a table at basset*." As in Cibber's play, the Lady's losses put her virtue in jeopardy to pay off debts of honor by borrowing money from a gentleman, Sir James Courtly. Unlike Cibber's Lord George, however, Sir James plots to assist Lord Worthy's pursuit of this humorous character. In Act 5, when he seems to demand her last stake, Sir James asks Lady Reveller: "Can a lady that loves play so passionately as you do, that takes as much pains to draw men in to lose their money . . . can you, I say, boast of innate virtue?" When she learns to moderate the carnivalesque behavior her name suggests, Lady Reveller qualifies to enter the domestic sphere as a wife; her change concludes, for the audience, the process Sir James describes to his friend, "to be spectator of the very diversion you hate, gaming."[56]

While the humane comedies of Pix, Cibber, and Centlivre exploit late Stuart theater design, especially its increased emphasis on the picture stage, to represent gambling as folly or vice rather than as aristocratic recreation, the periodicals deploy their emerging role in print culture for a similar critique. As the titles of *The London Spy* and *The Spectator* indicate, the authors control readers' perspective in order to present gambling and other aspects of urban life as spectacle. Scott Black's description of Steele's "new kind of representation, one that provided a way to depict the modern public sphere in its indigenous terms," applies to some extent to his less genteel predecessors, Ward and Brown, who, using periodical publication, also "mapped an imagination defined by London's social geography."[57] In *The London Spy*

Ward creates a rural persona "to Expose the *Vanities* and *Vices* of the *Town* . . . that the *Innocent* might see by *Reflection*, what I should gain by *Observation* and *Intelligence*." Taking advantage of an outsider's sense of "*Wonder* and *Amazement*" to evoke distance, Part VII includes a visit to the Temple and the sight of "Merry" gamesters, whose "whole *Lives* are a *Lottery*, they read no *Books* but *Cards*, and all their *Mathematicks* is to truly understand the *Odds* of a *Bet*."[58] Brown's *Amusements Serious and Comical*, on the other hand, presents a dual perspective, that of the author and a non-English visitor, an Indian, who "has never seen anything like what he sees in London. We shall see how he will be amazed at certain things which the prejudice of custom makes to seem reasonable and natural to us." Like *The London Spy* in evoking such distance, Brown's "Amusement VIII" describes Gaming-Houses from the Indian's point of view:

> It happened, one day, that my traveller dropped into a chocolate house in Covent-Garden, where they were at this noble recreation; he was wonderfully surprized at the oddness of the sight. Set yourself now in the room of a superstitious Indian, who knows nothing of our customs at play, and you will agree that his notions, abstracted and visionary as they may seem, have some foundation in truth.[59]

The Indian's fragmentary letter is an ethnography of the disorders of gambling, which is framed and complemented by Brown's persona's more extensive reflections on the social scene they observe.

Like their Grub-Street brethren, the more polite writers Steele and Addison use their observers to expose gambling as part of their project of recovering readers "out of that desperate State of Vice and Folly into which the Age is fallen." Steele turns to gambling often in early numbers of *The Tatler*; by the time Isaac Bickerstaff assumes the title of Censor of Great Britain, he claims that he has already "taken many curious Surveys of this great City," including "your *Gamesters*." *Tatler* 15 includes Bickerstaff's account of an evening at White's Chocolate House, the periodical's setting for "*All Accounts of* Gallantry, Pleasure, *and* Entertainment," where his familiar, Pacolet, makes him invisible, "so that we could see and hear all others, our selves unseen and unheard." This report of their surveillance follows:

> The First Thing we took Notice of, was a Nobleman, of a goodly and frank Aspect, with his generous Birth and Temper visible in it, playing at Cards with a Creature of a black and horrid Countenance, wherein were plainly delineated the arts of his Mind, Cousenage and

> Falshood. They were marking their Game with Counters, on which we could see Inscriptions, imperceptible to any but us. My Lord had scor'd with Pieces of Ivory, on which were writ, *Good Fame*, *Glory*, *Riches*, *Honour*, and *Posterity*. The Spectre over against him had on his Counters the Inscriptions of, *Dishonour*, *Impudence*, *Poverty*, *Ignorance*, and *Want of Shame*. Bless me! said I, Sure my Lord does not see what he plays for! As well as I do, says *Pacolet*.[60]

Social invisibility permits their observation of conduct in need of reform and the reformist insight that accompanies it. This process contributes to Steele's and Addison's project of "reconstructing honor," as described by Shawn Lisa Maurer: "The notion of honor, customarily a genteel stronghold, was rewritten in ways that appealed to both Christian virtue and burgeoning commercial values."[61] While typical of early eighteenth-century periodicals, which, according to Scott Paul Gordon, seek to "monitor London by means of invisible rather than visible watchers," Steele's allegory also "assumes that truth lies hidden from ordinary sight and therefore equips its authorial persona to see not only everything but *into* everything."[62] Unlike the gamblers he observes here and elsewhere, Bickerstaff possesses the insight to dissociate gambling from false notions of honor.

Steele and Addison's periodicals also published letters from readers, other friendly spies who add their sightings to those of the personae in an effort to persuade readers "made to fear that any offense will be publicly exposed--to pre-emptively discipline themselves."[63] For example, in *Spectator* 140, Rachel Basto writes, "I have observed Ladies who in all other respects are Gentle, Good-humoured, and the very Pinks of good Breeding; who as soon as the Ombre Table is called for, and set down to their Business, are immediately Transmigrated into the veriest Wasps in Nature." Letters such as Josiah Fribble's about his wife's gambling debts, "as becomes a Woman of her Fashion," Clarinda's "Picture of a Life filled with a fashionable kind of Gaiety and Laziness" (on Wednesday, "*From Six to Eleven*. At *Basset*"), and "*The humble Petition of* Jeoffry Hotspur, *Esq*." after a passionate game of whist, all evidence the on-going surveillance of gambling in *The Spectator*.[64]

By the time Addison and Steele were writing *The Guardian*, they could joke about readers' fears of exposure in their periodicals. One correspondent tells the persona: "I MUST acquaint you, for your Comfort, that your Lion is grown a kind of Bull-beggar among the Women where I live. When my Wife comes home late from Cards . . . I whisper in her Ear, partly betwixt Jest and Earnest, that *I will tell the Lion of her*." Despite such expectations, Addison continues to record the spectacle of gambling in *Guardian* 120, which begins with a correspondent's complaint about his wife's "shaking her Elbow for a whole Night together, and thumping the Table with a Dice-Box." This letter prompts the Guardian to "look into the *Mind* of a Female Gamester," where he finds "a fine Woman fretting and bleeding inwardly from such trivial motives." Addison's regulation of conduct according to bourgeois standards marks the threat to a woman's honor as the most dangerous aspect of gambling, a position emphasized by this visual transformation of the gamester: "I have known a Woman carried off half dead from Bassette, and have many a time grieved to see a Person of Quality gliding by me in her Chair at two a Clock in the Morning, and looking like a Spectre amidst a glare of Flambeaux."[65] Addison's ghostly spectacle permits no leeway for gambling as genteel diversion.

I conclude this essay with a scene from George Farquhar's *Sir Harry Wildair* (1701) because his reprise of the gambler as extravagant rake represents such an anomaly in early eighteenth-century drama and literature. Farquhar introduces the second scene of Act 2 with the discovery of another apartment in the stage set and this direction: "*Enter* Lurewell, Ladies, Monsieur Marquis, *and* Fireball, *as losing Gamesters, one after another, tearing their Cards, and flinging 'em about the Room*." While the scene includes the disorder conventionally associated with gambling, it allows Farquhar to bring his popular character Wildair on stage to rejoice in his triumph over the others and to rhapsodize about the pleasures of unproductive expenditure:

> What, forswear Cards! Why, Madam, you'll ruin our Trade.--I'll maintain, that the Money at Court circulates more by the Basset-Bank, than the Wealth of Merchants by the Bank of the City. Cards! the great Ministers of Fortune's Power; that blindly shuffle out her thoughtless Favours . . . . What Adoration do these Pow'rs receive *(Lifting up a Card.)* from the bright Hands and Fingers of the Fair, always lift up to pay Devotion here! And then the pleasing Fears, the anxious Hopes and dubious Joys that entertain our Mind! The Capot at Picket, the Paroli at Basset; -- And then Ombre! Who can resist the charms of Mattadors?[66]

The spectacle of the comical Wildair, speaking in "the spirit of True born *English* Quality," seems quaintly out of place in the decade of Centlivre, Cibber, and Steele. It serves as a nostalgic reminder of the world of deep play, of the bad old days of Charles II, supposedly being reformed by authors of contemporary comedies and periodicals, and even offers an amusing rebuttal of bourgeois economic discourse, in which gambling benefits trade.

One type of pleasure to be found in the extravagant Wildair is described by Edward Hyde, Earl of Clarendon: "All Nations . . . have such natural Inclinations to Gazing and Spectacles, that they crowd to those which are not in themselves very pleasant." It is preferable, he continues, "to comply with this natural Curiosity, by providing Places for them to resort to, and to be pleased in, than by Inhibitions and Restraints to extinguish that harmless Appetite."[67] In late Stuart England the comedies of the London stage and the periodicals anatomizing London life provided sites for their audiences to "resort to" and to satisfy their inclinations by witnessing the spectacle of gambling, increasingly one filled with admonitions. Few characters like Sir Harry Wildair trod the boards of Williamite or Queen Anne theaters to proclaim the joys of aristocratic diversion, as Loveby in *The Wild Gallant* or Dorimant in *The Man of Mode* had done a generation earlier. Gambling, which some conduct books deemed acceptable recreation for gentlemen and ladies, was already theatricalized in the Restoration as an unproductive expenditure of an anxious class. Many Restoration comedies, like *The English Monsieur* or *The Country Wife*, incorporated aspects of this spectacle into representations of a Wellbred or a Horner, seen on the forestage in somewhat more proximate relation to audiences and their values, even when these characters were ridiculed. After the Revolution, however, shifts in ideology and epistemology led to a different and, in Hyde's phrase, more "harmless" spectacle. The use of the scenic stage in comedies like *The Lady's Last Stake* and *The Gamester* and the narrative perspective of such periodicals as *The Spectator* and *The London Spy* turned the formerly genteel gamester into the object of the audience's disapproving gaze. A recreation that once seemed, even when excessive, to be aristocratic folly, was increasingly represented as vice. The private disapproval of Evelyn and Pepys toward deep play during the Restoration received confirmation in the bourgeois public sphere of the early eighteenth century.

NOTES

1. *The Diary of John Evelyn*, ed. E. S. De Beer, 6 vols. (Oxford: Clarendon Press, 1955), 3: 308.

2. John Ashton, *The History of Gambling in England* (1898; rpt. Montclair, NJ: Patterson Smith, 1969), 47.

3. Quoted in R. O. Bucholz, *The Augustan Court: Queen Anne and the Decline of Court Culture* (Stanford: Stanford University Press, 1993), 15. Bucholz observes that there is "much more than a grain of truth" in the picture of "the court of Charles II as the very epitome of Stuart exuberance, extravagance, and corruption" (12).

4. Cyril Hughes Hartmann, "Introduction," *Games and Gamesters of the Restoration* (London: Routledge, 1930), ix

5. Evelyn, 4: 403, 413-14.

6. Charles Cotton, *The Compleat Gamester*, rpt. in *Games and Gamesters of the Restoration*, xxiii, xxv.

7. Theophilus Lucas, *Memoirs of the Lives, Intrigues, and Comical Adventures of the Most Famous Gamesters and Celebrated Sharpers in the Reigns of Charles II, James II, William III and Queen Anne*, rpt. in *Games and Gamesters of the Restoration*, 119, 120.

8. Lawrence Stone, *The Crisis of the Aristocracy, 1558-1641* (Oxford: Clarendon Press, 1965), 571, 185.

9. Georges Bataille, "The Notion of Expenditure," *Visions of Excess: Selected Writings, 1927-1939*, ed. Allan Stoekl (Minneapolis: University of Minnesota Press, 1985), 123, 122.

10. *Collected Essays of Christopher Hill, Volume One: Writing and Revolution in 17th Century England* (Amherst: University of Massachusetts Press, 1985), 320, 301.

11. Michael McKeon, *The Origins of the English Novel 1600-1740* (Baltimore: Johns Hopkins University Press, 1987), 151, 169.

12. Obadiah Walker, *Of Education*, English Linguistics 1500-1800, ed. R. C. Alston (Menston: Scolar Press, 1970), 53.

13. *The Man of Mode, The Dramatic Works of Sir George Etherege*, ed. H. F. B. Brett-Smith, 2 vols. (Oxford: Blackwell, 1927), 2: 228.

14. Thomas M. Kavanagh, *Enlightenment and the Shadows of Chance: The Novel and the Culture of Gambling in Eighteenth-Century France* (Baltimore: Johns Hopkins University Press, 1993), 38-39, 44.

15. Stone, 567.

16. V. G. Kiernan, *The Duel in European History: Honour and the Reign of Aristocracy* (Oxford: Oxford University Press, 1988), 153, 154.

17. Baldesar Castiglione, *The Book of the Courtier*, trans. Charles S. Singleton (New York: Anchor, 1959), 127.

18. Quoted in Stone, 569.

19. Richard Brathwait, *The English Gentleman; and The English Gentlewoman: Both in One Volume Couched, and in One Modell Portrayed*, 3rd ed. (London: I. Dawson, 1641), 109, 110.

20. William Ramesay, *The Gentlemans Companion: or, a Character of True Nobility and Gentility* (London: E. Okes, 1672), 125, 126.

21. *The Lady's New-Year's Gift: or, Advice to a Daughter*, *The Works of George Savile Marquis of Halifax*, ed. Mark N. Brown, 3 vols. (Oxford: Clarendon Press, 1989), 2: 404, 405.

22. Quoted in Kavanagh, 44.

23. Derek Hughes, *English Drama 1660-1700* (Oxford: Clarendon Press, 1996), 151.

24. John T. Harwood, *Critics, Values, and Restoration Comedy* (Carbondale: Southern Illinois University Press, 1982), 106.

25. William Wycherley, *The Country Wife*, ed. Thomas H. Fujimura (Lincoln: University of Nebraska Press, 1965), 44, 57. See Arthur H. Scouten and Robert D. Hume, "'Restoration Comedy' and its Audiences, 1660-1776," in Robert D. Hume, *The Rakish Stage: Studies in English Drama, 1660-1800* (Carbondale: Southern Illinois University Press, 1983), 46-81.

26. Peter Holland, *The Ornament of Action: Text and Performance in Restoration Comedy* (Cambridge: Cambridge University Press, 1979), 29.

27. Thomas Durfey, *A Fool's Preferment* (London: Jos. Knight and Fra. Saunders, 1688), np.

28. James Howard, *The English Mounsieur: A Comedy*, intro. Robert D. Hume, Augustan Reprint Society Publication No. 182-183 (Los Angeles: Clark Library, 1977), 26.

29. *A True Widow*, *The Complete Works of Thomas Shadwell*, ed. Montague Summers, 5 vols. (London: Fortune Press, 1927), 3: 347.

30. *The Atheist*, *The Works of Thomas Otway*, ed. J. C. Ghosh, 2 vols. (Oxford: Clarendon Press, 1968), 2: 334, 397.

31. Sir Charles Sedley, *The Mulberry Garden*, *Restoration Comedy*, ed. A. Norman Jeffares, 4 vols. (London: Folio Press, 1974), 1: 150.

32. *The Luckey Chance*, *The Works of Aphra Behn*, ed. Janet Todd, 7 vols. (Columbus: Ohio State University Press, 1996), 7: 267. Jean I. Marsden regards this scene and its sequel as "perhaps Behn's starkest representation of the objectification of women" ("Rape, Voyeurism, and the Restoration Stage," *Broken Boundaries: Women & Feminism in Restoration Drama*, ed. Katherine M. Quinsey (Lexington: University Press of Kentucky, 1996), 195.

33. See Robert Jordan, "The Extravagant Rake in Restoration Comedy," *Restoration Literature: Critical Approaches*, ed. Harold Love (London: Methuen, 1972), 69-90; Hume, "The Myth of the Rake in 'Restoration Comedy,'" *The Rakish Stage*, 138-175; Richard Braverman, "The Rake's Progress Revisited: Politics and Comedy in the Restoration," *Cultural Readings of Restoration and Eighteenth-Century English Theater*, ed. J. Douglas Canfield and Deborah C. Payne (Athens: University of Georgia Press, 1995), 141-168.

34. *An Evening's Love*, Vol. 10 of *The Works of John Dryden*, ed. Maximillian E. Novak (Berkeley: University of California Press, 1970), 264-265.

35. *The Wild Gallant*, Volume 8 of *The Works of John Dryden*, ed. John Harrington Smith and Dougald MacMillan (Berkeley: University of California Press, 1962), 21-22, 53, 54-55, 89.

36. *The Diary of Samuel Pepys*, ed. Robert Latham and William Matthews, 9 vols. (London: G. Bell, 1970), 9: 2-4.

37. Among texts critical of gambling prior to the Revolution of 1688 are Sir John Denham's *The Anatomy of Play* (1651), the anonymous *Leathermore: or Advice Concerning Gaming* (1668), and *The Gaming-Humor Considered and Reproved* (1684). *Leathermore* features a scene at an ordinary, which Cotton plagiarized in *The Compleat Gamester*.

38. *The Tatler*, ed. Donald F. Bond, 3 vols. (Oxford: Clarendon Press, 1987), 1: 413.

39. *The Busybody, Female Playwrights of the Restoration: Five Comedies*, ed. Paddy Lyons and Fidelis Morgan (London: Dent, 1991), 309.

40. *The Lady's Last Stake, Colley Cibber: Three Sentimental Comedies*, ed. Maureen Sullivan (New Haven: Yale University Press, 1973), 249.

41. Jeremy Collier, *An Essay upon Gaming, in a Dialogue between Callimachus and Dolomedes* (London: J. Morphew, 1713), 13, 17.

42. Rose A. Zimbardo, "Toward Zero/Toward Public Virtue: The Conceptual Design of Dramatic Satire Before and After the Ascension of William and Mary," *Eighteenth-Century Life* 12 (1988): 63.

43. *The Country Gentleman's Vade Mecum: or His Companion for the Town* (London: John Harris, 1699), 69.

44. Durfey, 9, 15. J. Douglas Canfield finds this play to be corrective: "On the eve of the Revolution . . . just as the aristocracy is about to lose control over at least the apex of the status hierarchy to the rising bourgeoisie--it is a satire on social climbing . . . [on] the complicity of the Country in its love affair with the Town and the Court" (*Tricksters & Estates: On the Ideology of Restoration Comedy* [Lexington: University Press of Kentucky, 1997], 229-230.

45. Holland, 33, 36. Holland describes "the retreat of comedy behind the proscenium arch" at the end of the century: "The picture stage becomes the norm for all drama" (29, 31).

46. *The Wives' Excuse*, *The Works of Thomas Southerne*, ed. Robert Jordan and Harold Love, 2 vols. (Oxford: Clarendon Press, 1988), 1: 274, 323, 324.

47. Southerne, *The Maid's Last Prayer*, *Works*, 1: 372, 379.

48. Hughes, 349.

49. *The Beau Defeated*, *The Plays of Mary Pix and Catharine Trotter*, ed. Edna L. Steeves, 2 vols. (New York: Garland, 1982), 1: 11, 12, 14. Canfield discusses the play as post-Revolution comedy in "Dramatic Shifts: Writing an Ideological History of Late Stuart Drama," *Restoration & Eighteenth-Century Theatre Research*, 2nd ser., 6 (1991): 1-9.

50. Pix, *The Different Widows*, *Plays of Pix and Trotter*, 1:59, 3. Two other contemporary gamblers in need of reform in are Clarissa in Sir John Vanbrugh's

The Confederacy (1705) and Riot in Charles Johnson's *The Wife's Relief* (1711).

51. Cibber, 196, 257, 263.

52. Laura J. Rosenthal, *Playwrights and Plagiarists in Early Modern England: Gender, Authorship, Literary Property* (Ithaca: Cornell University Press, 1996), 236, 232.

53. Cibber, 177. Cibber also uses a discovery scene in Act 2 of *The Careless Husband* (1704), exposing Lord Morelove and Sir Charles Easy in a game of piquet.

54. *The Ladies Library . . . Written by a lady*, 4th ed. (London: J. Tonson, 1732), 39.

55. *The Gamester*, *The Dramatic Works of the Celebrated Mrs. Centlivre*, 3 vols. (London: John Pearson, 1872), 1: 162-163, 176, 182, 192.

56. *The Basset Table*, *Female Playwrights of the Restoration*, 242, 277, 244, 278, 283, 244.

57. Scott Black, "Social and Literary Form in the *Spectator*," *Eighteenth-Century Studies* 33 (1999): 23.

58. *The London-Spy Compleat, In Eighteen Parts*, intro. Ralph Straus (London: Casanova Society, 1924), 2, 163.

59. Tom Brown, *Amusements Serious and Comical and Other Works*, ed. Arthur L. Hayward (London: Routledge, 1927), 10, 53.

60. *The Spectator*, ed. Donald F. Bond, 5 vols. (Oxford: Clarendon Press, 1965), 1: 44; *The Tatler*, 2: 403; 1: 16, 128-129.

61. Shawn Lisa Maurer, *Proposing Men: Dialectics of Gender and Class in the Eighteenth-Century English Periodical* (Stanford: Stanford University Press, 1998), 75. While *The Gentleman's Journal: or the Monthly Miscellany* includes pieces critical of gambling, such as "The Witchcraft of Gaming" (May 1693), it does not use the rhetoric of spectacle.

62. Scott Paul Gordon, "Voyeuristic Dreams: Mr. Spectator and the Power of Spectacle," *The Eighteenth Century* 36 (1995): 6, 17.

63. Gordon, 7.

64. *The Spectator*, 2: 54; 3: 51, 181, 182; 4: 10-11.

65. *The Guardian*, ed. John Calhoun Stephens (Lexington: University Press of Kentucky, 1982), 448, 401, 402, 403. On Addison's and Steele's "refashioning of woman," see Erin Mackie, *Market à la Mode: Fashion, Commodity, and Gender in The Tatler and The Spectator* (Baltimore: Johns Hopkins University Press, 1997), especially pp. 104-143.

66. *Sir Harry Wildair*, *The Works of George Farquhar*, ed. Shirley Strum Kenny, 2 vols. (Oxford: Clarendon Press, 1988), 1: 274, 276-277.

67. *Two Dialogues: Of the Want of Respect due to Age and Concerning Education*, intro. Martine Watson Brownley, Augustan Reprint Society Publication No. 227-228 (Los Angeles: Clark Library, 1984), 345.

A Modest Defense of Gaming Women

BETH KOWALESKI WALLACE

Nearly two hundred years after her death in 1806, Georgiana, Duchess of Devonshire, is back in fashion. As the subject of Amanda Foreman's best-selling biography, Georgiana holds much fascination for a contemporary audience.[1] Many find uncanny parallels between Georgiana and the late Princess Diana to whom she is distantly related: for example, both were exploited by and exploiters of the media. In addition, a growing popular audience for feminist history finds Georgiana an engaging case study. In an age when women were denied direct access to political power, how did they manage nonetheless to effect the course of history? A third explanation for Georgiana's popularity is the fact of the Duchess as a colorful—and sometimes sorry—spectacle. Iconographically rendered by Gainsborough, pornographically caricatured by the political cartoonists of her day, the Duchess remains a fascinating sight today.

And nothing rivets attention more than the vision of Georgiana as extravagant, reckless gambler. The sums are astounding: in 1784, her gambling debt was one hundred thousand pounds, or the equivalent of six million pounds today![2] But even more surprising is the recognition that this kind of loss did not actually destroy her marriage. When the "secret" of her indebtedness was finally revealed to her husband, he was angry for a little while, but he ultimately managed to forgive her.[3] As we contemplate this unfathomable dissipation, we are bound to disapprove. Yet at the same time, we cannot bring ourselves to look away. How could Georgiana have lost so much—and not really have lost much at all?

A quick turn back to the eighteenth-century suggests that the Duchess of Devonshire bears resemblance to the fashionable lady gamesters who walked the boards of the Restoration and early eighteenth-century stage. During this period, the lady gambler was a familiar character. In particular, Georgiana's real life escapades have their fictional counterpart in the behavior of Lady Reveller in Susanna Centlivre's *The Basset -Table* (1706), Lady Gentle in *The Lady's Last Stake, or The Wife's Resentment* (1721) by Colley Cibber, and Lady Townley in *The Provoked Husband* (1728) by Sir John Vanbrugh and Colley Cibber .[4] The subjects of my paper, these theatrical sisters to Georgiana were similarly objects of a voyeuristic gaze. Also like their real life counterpart, these dramatic characters are seen as sexually imperiled but ultimately "saved." I will argue here that more than the question of female reputation is at stake in both the plays and in our renewed fascination with Georgiana. All of these women, fictional and non-fictional alike, are not just gamesters, but aristocratic or genteel gamblers. In their proper contexts, they bring to the foreground a class-bound anxiety about the derivations, disseminations, and ultimate destination of wealth.[5] As I will suggest at the end of my paper, Georgiana's popularity today may have something to do with the persistence of that same anxiety in a modern context.

These three plays capture a moment when an older and powerful way of signifying of rank was increasingly under attack, as we can glean from Thomas Kavanagh's *Enlightenment and the Shadows of Chance*. In France up until the French Revolution, a truly aristocratic identity expressed itself through particular kinds of display and exaggerated social "performance," not only the obvious case of sartorial splendor, but also through such practices as dueling and high stakes gambling. Gaming in particular, writes Kavanagh, "became a token of class affiliation, an affirmation of the individual's superiority to any change of fortune consisting solely in a gain or loss of money."[6] Or, "the noble was noble precisely because he was beyond the power of money to make him more or less than what he was by the unalterable fact of birth."[7] The aristocratic willingness to let it all go—in this case, to dissipate vast sums at the gambling table— paradoxically proved who the man was. Kavanagh finds in aristocratic high-stakes gambling traces of a Maussian gift logic at work: such gaming was one of "the primary social practices through which nobles sought to affirm their identity within an individual and group ethos defining them as independent of the ever-increasing power of money."[8] A willingness to lose all, then, signals the imperviousness of superior birth to the power of money itself, and it forces those around the gamester to recognize true breeding for what it is. In this way, Kavanagh helps us to recognize the performative nature of this particular kind of gambling.

However, in England beginning with the Restoration, gambling increasingly comes under attack. Middle rank reformers deplore the destabilizing effects of the gambling table, in particular its arbitrary and "hyperactive" (Kavanagh's word) redistribution of wealth. These moralists do understand that gambling is performance, but they argue that it is the wrong kind of performance. As a result of its appeal to a broad range of society, gambling allows people to pass themselves off as what they are not. In *A Dissertation on the Pernicious Effects of Gaming*, Richard Hey maintains that under gaming "Property is in constant Circulation; but then, like the Sea, what it loses on one Shore it gains on another: and if some few can be mentioned whom *Play* hath reduced to Beggary, it would engage (if it would not offend their Modesty) to name many more whom it hath *taken out of the Mire to set them with the Princess*."[9] Thus for Hey, gambling is a disruptive form of economic activity, one that moves money around in unpredictable ways.

Similarly, in Jeremy Collier's *An Essay Upon Gaming, in a Dialogue Between Callimachus and Dolomedes*, gambling is faulted for its ability to upset traditional hierarchies and for its tendency to redistribute, willy nilly, wealth among those believed not suited to its possession. As Callimachus argues, through gambling, "a *Manor* has been lost in an Afternoon, *Suit* and *Service* follows the *Cast*, and the Right is transfer'ed sooner than the Lawyer can draw the Conveyance. A Box and Dice are terrible Artillery, and a Battery of Cannon scarcely plays with more execution." Or, he explains, at the gaming table, "by accidental Events, Poverty and Riches are transplanted, and shift their Seat; and a Blast of Wind, than which nothing is more uncertain, drives good Fortune from one Hand to another"[10] In Collier's satire, Dolomedes enunciates a radical defense of this kind of economic instability. Speaking the "leveller's" viewpoint, he professes his tolerance for the vagaries brought on by the loose flow of property:

> This Misfortune (of loss) is nothing but shifting of Property, and putting the Prize into a new Hand: And is not this both a Common and reasonable Remove? Why should Wealth always be lodged in the same Family? Why should not the Generality of Mankind come in for their Turn of Plenty and Figure? Why should not all the Sons of *Noah* have a share in their Ancestor's Patrimony? To reply, that

> the common Right has been lost long since by Division, and that Property is now confin'd to Birth and legal Settlement: To say this, is in effect to confess the Partiality of the *Constitution,* and to tell me a few People are born to make Beggars of the rest.[11]

However, though Collier's satiric dialogue allows for such a radical viewpoint to be articulated, the author in no way endorses this dangerous idea. Eventually Callimachus' reasoned voice is meant to prevail, while Dolemedes' viewpoints are simply too radical to be seriously entertained.

By the end of the century, we find Christopher Anstey satirically attacking the ignorance of those, like Dolomedes, who simply fail to understand that the hyperactive circulation of wealth can never benefit a national ethos. In *The New Bath Guide*, Anstey's near-sighted narrator, who is enthralled by all forms of fashionable activity at Bath, sings the praises of a gaming table that puts money into wide-spread circulation,

> "Circulation—I say—circulation it is,
> "Gives life to commercial countries like this:"
> What thanks to the city of *Bath* then are due:
> From all who this patriot maxim pursue;
> For in no place whatever that national good
> Is practis'd so well, and so well understood![12]

According to this narrator, the gaming table allows successfully gaming wives to purchase vast quantities of consumer goods, thereby stimulating the economy: "Our trade is encourag'd as much, if not more,/ By the tender soft sex I shall ever adore..." In a comparison that is clearly meant to be absurd, the narrator compares the gaming wife to the woman praised in the Bible. He claims that Solomon says that

> .... "if you find out a virtuous wife,
> She will do a man better all the days of her life
> She deals like a merchant, she sitteth up late."
> And you'll find it written in verse twenty-eight
> "Her husband is sure to be known at the gate.
> He never hath need or occasion for spoil,
> When his wife is much better employ'd all the while;
> She seeketh fine wool and fine linen she buys,
> And is clothed in purple and scarlet likewise."

From his perspective, the gaming wife is similarly productive, in that her gambling can also be seen as a form of economic activity:

> And follow th' advice of that worthy old king?
> Do they spare for expenses themselves in adorning?
> Don't they go about buying fine things all in the morning?
> And at cards all the night take the trouble to play
> To get back the money they spent in the day? [13]

That the narrator seems oblivious to the apparent absurdity of his comparison between the wife gainfully employed in legitimate business transactions and the wife busy at the card table only heightens the joke. While leaving unsaid the fact that women had few, if any, legitimate opportunities to engage in business, Anstey uses the comparison to mock the notion that card playing could contribute in a meaningful way to domestic economy. He focuses on the disruptive behavior of gaming wives, but the issue cuts deeper: he uses his satire to distinguish illegitimate from legitimate forms of economic activity, even while his satire suggests that husbands need to regain control of their wives' economic activities. Thus, Anstey's satire is important for its explicit link between the hyperactive circulation of wealth and out-of-control wives. While Anstey's narrator celebrates the potential of women's gambling, the poem ultimately discredits his naive optimism: the same speaker fails to notice when he is being cheated out of his fortune.[14] Only a fool, then, would allow himself to be taken in by the logic of gaming, and only a fool would endorse the idea of wives at the gambling table.

By setting up his naive gamester for a fall, Anstey implicitly positions himself alongside those who promote the idea that the principles of increase should be ultimately rational and subject to human—if not providential—control. In "Epistle to Bathurst," Pope best expresses the philosophy of those determined to believe that the circulation of wealth proceeds according to a plan: for Pope, the wide swing between profligacy and parsimoniousness testifies not to the irrationality of the market, but to divine control over the flow of capital: "Hear then the truth: ''Tis Heav'n each Passion sends,/ And diff'rent men directs to diff'rent ends./ Extremes in Nature equal good produce,/ Extremes in Man concur to gen'ral use." Thus what looks like an arbitrary effect—the fluctuating possession of a fortune—is in fact the sign of God's plan: "Ask we what makes one keep, and one bestow?/ That POW'R who bids the Ocean ebb and flow." [15] Yet, despite Pope's insistence that all economic increase and loss is "rational," it becomes difficult to recognize the guiding principle of the gambling table, where some men are arbitrarily enriched beyond measure, while others are precipitated into ruin. At the gambling table, money simply does not behave as it should. Moreover, as a form of speculation, gambling casts a shadow of illegitimacy over related forms of chance taking. The more that capitalistic increase depends upon luck, the more aggressive the insistence that gambling and other forms of speculation are different from each other.[16]

To summarize, then, gambling becomes an important topic for moralists and reformers in England at the turn of the eighteenth century for several reasons. First, as an extravagant type of performance, high stakes gambling had been tied to aristocratic self-display. Gambling had allowed for the presentation of rank, where rank was now to be redefined as a series of interior effects, as behaviors and manners visible only to the most discerning eye.[17] Second, in a world where anyone could—and did—gamble, gambling was identified with deception, with the mere show of rank where none in fact existed. Third, the attack on the illogic of the gambling table emerged simultaneously with an argument about the necessary logic behind the practices of nascent mercantile capitalism. In an attempt to argue for the "rational" behavior of money under capitalism, reformers distinguish legitimate from illegitimate forms of risk and investment, and they argue that the circulation of wealth must be controlled. At stake was the integrity of the social fabric itself: in a world where fortunes accrued "irrationally," traditional hierarchies appeared undermined and threatened by those—like the under classes or women—who stood to gain power and independence through recirculated wealth.

When we turn to the eighteenth-century stage, we find that the aristocratic male gambler who participates in an extravagant, yet potentially meaningful, display of rank has often been transformed into the powerful upper rank female character who must be controlled and recuperated within a family structure. In this way, the issue of gambling is both feminized and domesticated. In *The Basset-Table, The Lady's Last Stake*, and *The Provoked Husband*, gambling is associated with excessive and out of control feminine behaviors, behaviors which sorely need the guiding hand of a reasonable patriarch to rein them in. What can be lost at the gaming table in these plays is not aristocratic honor, but female sexual virtue. Representing the gambler as a woman allows these playwrights to suggest a solution to the problem of the hyperactive and irrational circulation of wealth: these plays demonstrate that controlling the flow of one's capital is as easy (or difficult) as controlling one's wife. Yet the issue is larger than familial solvency: the husband who controls his wife's expenditure also controls how and in what ways his wealth signifies. Nonetheless as we will see, as players of yet another sort, female actresses impersonating lady gamblers ultimately resist male containment, much as Georgiana seems to have resisted her husband's efforts to contain her.

In Centlivre's *The Basset-Table*, Lady Reveller is a widow possessing the troublesome freedom to act as she chooses. Or, in the words, of Lady Reveller's maid Alpiew, "Widdows are accountable to none for their Actions" (Act I, p. 5). The opening scene of the play suggests that in Lady Reveller's house, night and day have been reversed. Sleepy footmen, forced to stand on duty in the middle of the night, curse their lot while waiting for Lady Reveller's guests to quit her gaming table. Lady Reveller is criticized for crossing "the purpose of the Day and Night," (Act I, p. 6), further suggesting that she replaces light with dark, order, clarity, and reason with disorder, obfuscation, and illogic. This disruption manifests itself on the social level in her resistance to distinguishing among social ranks and her willingness to admit one Mrs. Sago, wife of a drugster, into her most intimate life. Lady Reveller's apartment is, in the words of her sharpest critic, Sir Richard, "a Parade for Men of all Ranks, from the Duke to the Fidler" (Act I, p. 3). For all these reasons, though Lord Worthy initially conveys his "despair of fixing her" (Act I, p. 10), Lady Reveller must be corrected.

In contrast, in *The Provoked Husband*, gambling is simply the most egregious way that Lady Townley thwarts her husband's authority. She catalogues a list of freedoms a married woman ought to enjoy, including the liberty to engage with men equally and without ceremony. These behaviors not only guarantee that she will be the center of attention, but also give her considerable power—including the power not to pay the very debts she incurs.[18] Lady Townley thwarts her husband's best efforts to place her under his regime, claiming for herself the freedom not only to gamble, but also to act as she pleases:

> To begin then, in the morning; a married woman may have men at her toilet, invite them to dinner, appoint them to a party in a stage box at the play, engross the conversation there, call 'em by their Christian names, talk louder than the players; from thence jaunt into the City, take a frolicsome supper at an India-House, perhaps (in her *gaité de coeur*) toast a pretty fellow, then clatter again to this end of town, break with the morning into an assembly, crowd to the hazard table, throw a familiar levant upon some sharp lurching man of quality, and if he demands his money, turn it off with a loud laugh, and cry—you'll owe it him, to vex him. (I, i, p. 16-17)

Cibber and Vanbrugh give Lady Townley comically hyperbolic lines to denigrate and make risible the licentious pleasures she enjoys. Lady Townley "dotes upon assemblies, [her] heart bounds at a ball, and at an opera [she] expires." She loves to play "to distraction," "Cards enchant [her] and dice put [her[out of her wits." Her lines give the impression of a giddy, breathless spendthrift, someone scarcely in control of herself or her circumstances.

Lady Townley's readiness to engage in dissipation, her ardent enthusiasm for nighttime pleasures in particular, indicates here, as in *The Basset -Table,* that she needs a well-ordered and disciplined life, one with less emphasis on giddy "performance" and with more emphasis on a deep and true domestic sentiment. Though the purpose of the staging is clearly to discredit her point of view, Lady Townley rightly identifies a mode of behavior that once served to mark aristocratic privilege from middle rank duty. What she imagines—certain freedoms in her bedroom, an easy familiarity with men, a liberated lifestyle giving her access to a full range of urban pleasures—is not quite a feminist agenda, but it is a long way from middle-rank, domestic subservience. She asks her husband: "which gives us the best figure in the eyes of the polite world—my active, spirited three in the morning, or your dull, drowsy eleven at night? Now I think *one* has the air of a woman of quality, and *t'other* of a plodding mechanic, that goes to bed betimes that he may rise early to open his shop—faught!" (III, lines 311-316, p. 82). What she defends—and what Cibber and Vanbrugh consistently undermine, presumable to the delight of their middle rank audience members—is a mode of self-presentation in which identity is manifest through ostentatious behaviors: the world knows who she is because she can afford to show up at the best parties in the middle of the night. Yet Vanbrugh and Cibber make their point: while Lady Townley (like Lady Reveller) exists out of harmony with the day, Lord Townley is in synch with nature's rhythms.

Unlike his wife, Lord Townley operates independently of social judgment. He appears to have internalized newer, class-bound notions about the proper dimensions of manhood. In this version, rank is made manifest through indirection, through a modest display, which nonetheless paradoxically expresses itself as superiority. In the pages of *The Spectator,* this new version of masculinity is described this way:

> It is below him to catch the Sight with any Care of Dress; his outward Garb is but the Emblem of his Mind, it is genteel, plain, and unaffected; he knows that Gold and Embroidery can add nothing to the Opinion which all have of his Merit, and that he gives a Lustre to the plainest Dress, whilst 'tis impossible the richest should communicate any to him. He is still the principal Figure in the Room...[19]

Though belonging to a class higher than the "middle ranks" targeted by the writers of *The Spectator*, Lord Townley apparently identifies with their newer understanding of gender as a "natural" effect, since he prefers to signal his power through indirection.

In their protracted verbal battle, husband and wife struggle over what gambling means. He attacks the company she keeps; she defends her behavior as an innocent diversion. Casting aspersions on the crowd surrounding the gaming table, Lord Townley believes they are an "unavoidable mixture with known rakes, concealed thieves, and sharpers in embroidery—or what to me is still more shocking, that herd of familiar chattering crop-eared coxcombs, who are so often like monkeys there would be no knowing them asunder but that their tails hang from their head, and the monkey's grows where it should do" (III, lines 326-332, p. 82). Echoing the moralists, Lord Townley condemns the gaming scene for its tendency to obscure social rank, throwing unequals into close company. Certain kinds of women, beaus (who are identified here by their preference for the queue-wig) and fops are lumped together, leaving "real" men immune to the pleasures of the table. This scene transpires as a domestic dispute, but I suggest that the action is more ideologically freighted. Here Cibber and Vanbrugh pit emerging ideas about "authentic" manhood against performative displays of gender, the "rational," patriarchal control of expenditure and public presentation against subversive, feminocentric practices of self-promotion. Later in the scene, Lord Townley claims he has a reputation to guard, but he misses a vital point: it is not that Lady Townley lacks reputation, but that she invests in an alternative definition of how reputation is best conveyed.

Lady Townley must, of course, be reformed. In Act V, she is finally turned out of doors by her husband and forced to confront the images of her own folly in a masquerade. Ironically masked as their true selves, a dissipated society of aristocrats and gentility parades before her eyes. Identified are "Lord Bite-Lord Arch-wag-young Brazen -Wit—Lord Timberdown—Lord Joint-life—and Lord Mortgage. Then, for your pretty fellows only, there's Sir Powder Peacock—Lord Lapwing—Billy Magpie—Beau Frightful—Sir Paul Plaster-Crown, and the Marquess of Monkey Man" (V, iii, p. 147). In this list, aristocratic identity rapidly deteriorates. First aligned with excessive social behavior (an arch tongue or a brazen wit), then with profligate fiscal habit (timberdown and mortgages), these masked aristocrats are quickly revealed as a series of "pretty fellows" and effeminates. By the end, they lose all claim to legitimacy, as in the simian marquess of monkey man. That Lady Townley now comes to perceive the true nature of her gaming associates suggests not only the ascendancy of her husband's viewpoint, but also how dangerous her gambling truly was. Here the mask unmasks social pretension, revealing also the "tradesmen's wives, Inns-of-Court beaus, Jews, and kept mistresses" attired in their tawdry, hired habits (Viii, p.147), in other words, a dangerous array of people on the make. No longer a glittering surface, or a showy world of performative potential, the gaming world is now revealed as depressing scene of human excess. Thus, the alternative perspective that has operated throughout the comedy, giving shape to the dramatic tension between Lady Townley and her husband, now vanishes. Seeing her own follies reflected back to her in the masquers, Lady Townley quickly repents, and soon delivers the closing lines of the play:

> In you, methinks, as in a glass. I see
> The happiness that once advanced to me.
> So visible the bliss, so plain the way,
> How was it possible my sense could stray?
> But now, a convert, to this truth I come—
> That married happiness is never found from home. (V, iv,p. 159)

Here Cibber uses metaphors of perception to insist polemically that there really is only one way to see the gaming table and the fashionable society that inhabits it. The correct view has always been available to Lady Townley; she only failed to see it properly.

In contrast to Lady Townley's gentle correction, Lady Reveller and Lady Gentle are tested by the threat of rape. Both of these plays deploy an often circulated idea that the gaming table was an especially dangerous place for women, who might find themselves forced to repay their debts with sexual favors. Richard Hey explains the scenario likely to occur when a woman "loses money beyond what she is able to pay":

> If a man to whom she has lost her money happens to be somewhat libertine in his principles, he will be apt to consider her as capable of discharging the obligation though she has not a shilling to advance. Should she settle the account in the method which he may suggest, he can threaten to expose her conduct to a set of persons whose good opinion she probably values far too highly: those with whom she is connected in parties of Gaming. Wherefore, not withstanding his proposal, if complied with, will in reality render her more truly infamous, she may yet be tempted to add vice to vice, in hopes that the whole may remain a secret....[20]

Hey's account only repeats the somewhat clichéd assumption that women gamblers necessarily compromised their virtue in the process of making themselves financially indebted to men of less than honorable character.

In *The Basset-Table*, Centlivre exploits this cliché by having Sir James Courtley hatch a plot to send Lady Reveller into the arms of Lord Worthy. In the middle of a heated game of basset,[21] he slips a purse of gold into Lady Reveller's apron, allowing her to play when her resources are depleted. But Lady Reveller soon discovers that this unrequested loan must be repaid. Locking her in a room, Sir James taunts her with the consequences of her indiscretion: he suggests that her playing at the table is tantamount to sexual play. Far from simply being a type of performance, her gambling is a serious and dangerous activity:

> "Can a Lady that loves Play so passionately as you do—that takes as much Pains to draw Men in to lose their Money, as a Town Miss to their Destruction—that Caresses all Sorts of People for your Interest, that divides your time between your Toylet and the *Basset-Table*; can you, I say, boast of Innate Virtue?— Fie, fie, I am sure you must have guess'd for what I Played so Deep—we never part with our Money without Design—or writing Fool upon our Foreheads;—therefore no more of this Resistance, except you would have more Money." (Act V, p. 56)

In this way, he reminds her that women play according to a patriarchal script no matter what: men never allow women access to money without demanding something in return. However, at this moment, taking his cue, Lord Worthy rushes in and saves Lady Reveller from harm. This rescue precipitates her change of heart. She yields both to her love for Lord Worthy and the supervision he offers her.

Writing about this scene in another context, Andreas Henderson writes "a woman who loves to play 'passionately' should not be surprised to find herself threatened with rape," since "the perceived link between financial and sexual economies gave rise to an analogy between the uncontrolled losses of gaming and rapacious and even violent sexuality."[22] However, this perspective overlooks the various levels of theatricality present in the scene. It should be clear to the audience that Sir James feels no real desire for Lady Reveller; he has already indicated to the audience that he only intends to correct her, and he is willing to take the fall in the process. Thus, the issue is not desire or even the sexuality unleashed by gaming, but *who controls Lady Reveller's behavior:* can she play by rules of her own making? Can she do what she wants, without concern for how others interpret or read her actions or is she subject to the controlling gaze of others? Can she actually perform publicly as she wishes, or will others—men in particular—decide what her performance—whether as a gamester or otherwise—signifies?

Centlivre's conservative comedy quickly sacrifices female self-determination to male control. When she discovers she has been "tricked into a marriage" (her words, Act V, p. 63), Lady Reveller yields gracefully nonetheless. No more basset-table means no more night for day, no more parade of social poseurs, no more association with the likes of Mrs. Sago. Similar to Mrs. Townley, then, Lady Reveller is punished for her participation in one kind of rash and especially egregious economic display. As a widow who spends and circulates money as she wishes, Lady Reveller must be reined in and put under patriarchal control. Once married to Lord Worthy, she will manage her household economically, according to her husband's wishes. Thus, in both *The Provoked Husband* and *The Basset-Table,* the struggle to control the scene of female expenditure is the struggle to assure an audience that wealth and rank—here embodied in the leading female role—can be disciplined and subjugated to domestic duty.

In *The Lady's Last Stake*, Cibber sets up a plot to correct the gaming Lady Gentle that is reminiscent of Centlivre's. Here, Lord George Brilliant, played by Cibber himself in one of his signature roles, similarly ensures that the gaming Lady Gentle will find herself indebted to him, only to demand sexual payment when she finds herself without money. However, this time the rape plot is thwarted by one Mrs. Conquest, cross-dressed and in disguise as her own brother. Her acting not only saves Mrs. Gentle from rape, but also redirects Lord George's affection towards herself, through a complicated series of events that will have her saving him as well in the next scene. In this play, as in *The Basset Table*, patriarchal protection is offered to women who give up their "playing." Lady Gentle internalizes and reflects upon this message:

> How strict a Guard should Virtue keep upon its innocence? How dangerous, how faithless are its lawful pleasures, when habitual! This Vice of Play, that has, I fear undone me, appeared at first an harmless, safe Amusement; but stealing into habit, its greatest Hazards grew so familiar, that ev'n the Face of Ruine lost its Terror to me. (V, ii, p. 87)

Once again, the pleasures of the gaming table are defined as excess. What appeared to be an innocent pleasure was actually a pernicious evil that drew Lady Gentle away from domestic duty. Her speech alludes to the long-standing assumption that women gamesters necessarily lost interest in familial matters and that they turned their heads from children and domesticity toward more illicit pleasures.[23] Yet Lady Gentle's reformation assures the audience that women can be recuperated and rescued from the seductive pull of the tables.

Thus, all three comedies attack the performative and apparently effeminate nature of gambling. All three undermine an ideology of display. All three promote husband over wife, day over night, moderation over excess, predictability over volatility. Yet unlike the other two plays, *The Lady's Last Stake* also suggests how deliciously paradoxical this theatrical message could be, as we can see from a closer examination of Mrs. Conquest. As a foil to the lady gamblers in all three comedies, Mrs. Conquest is an especially interesting female character: although she is represented as lacking financial resources, she nonetheless demonstrates another kind of worth. Where Lady Reveller finds herself in a plot not of her own making and simply surrenders, Mrs. Conquest seizes the initiative. Act Five finds her cross-dressed and on her way to duel Sir George. When she finds him set upon by robbers in the park, she fires a pistol and saves him from harm instead. This is a wonderful part, then, one with great dramatic and feminist potential. I read in Mrs. Conquest some indication of what the playwright Cibber knows —and what his character Lord George comes to know: that women's "playing" is always potentially powerful, even subversive. It always has the potential to thwart male expectation and even to subvert male control.

As is often acknowledged, the minute a female actor plays, she opens up semiotically in ways that male actors do not. Most often this semiotic surplus works to her disadvantage—signaling she is sexually available, even if she is not, for example. Yet historically the presence of live actresses on the stage also thwarted patriarchal assumptions about feminine sexuality, as Kristina Straub has argued: " As women whose profession was undeniably public, [eighteenth-century] actresses resisted the assumption that feminine sexuality was the private (and passive) opposite of masculinity.... the actress figures discursively as the site of excessive sexuality that must be—but never fully is—contained or repressed."[24] Live female performance can also confound male expectation in other ways, especially where a strong physical presence coincides with an otherwise controlling representation. Filmmaker Sally Potter gives the example of the ballerina who communicates her physical strength despite the scenario. Or, as Catherine Elwes points out, opera arias "demonstrate the virtuosity of the singer, the power and range of her voice as well as her ability to project the emotional intensity of the music," no matter how much the plot may suggest her weakness, vulnerability, or lack of power.[25]

Thus the work of feminist theater historians suggests that the semiotic power of a live, breathing actress is something we have consistently underestimated. While the text may work to construct one kind of female subject, it is equally possible that live female performance contests the very terms of that construct. An actress may demonstrate active strength, even when her role requires passivity, and she may similarly demonstrate power, even when the script suggests she has none. For all these reasons, it seems prudent to take performance history into account and to imagine the innumerable ways in which an actress's actual, physical presence may have enhanced the scene.[26] In the case of *The Provoked Husband* for instance, it is not difficult to imagine that we are meant to receive a double message: women's "playing" (in both senses of the word) is subject to male control, yet a woman *player* is a powerful agent, who is just as likely to direct the action herself. Audiences at live performances, unlike readers of a dramatic text, very likely internalize this double message. They internalize a moral, in other words, which may very well be at cross-purposes with their experience of the play's themes.

And Cibber himself seems to have considered just this possibility in his introductory comments "To the Reader," which were added to the published text of *The Provoked Husband* in 1728.[27] Praising the performance of all the stellar cast members of the original production, he takes special notice of Mrs. Oldfield, who had played Lady Townley, our dissipated lady gambler (and who had also played Mrs. Conquest in a production of *The Lady's Last Stake*). In an especially prescient comment, he suggests how Oldfield's performance ought to provide the grounds for a historical memory of his play: "perhaps my saying a little more of so memorable an actress may give this play a chance to be read, when the people of this age shall be ancestors." He then catalogues Mrs. Oldfield's physical characteristics—her graceful stature, her lively aspect, and "a command of a mien that, like the principal figure in the finest paintings, first seizes and longest delights the eye of the spectator." He praises her voice (strong, piercing, and melodious) her pronunciation (voluble, distinct, and musical), her phrasing. He memorializes her as genteel and elegant in air and dress—in other words, she was so utterly convincing in the role of the aristocratic lady that, in real life, aristocratic ladies met her as their equal. But he also isolates her ability to control expression: "The spectator was always as much informed by her eyes as her elocution: for the look is the only proof that an actor rightly conceives what he utters, there being scarce an instance where the eyes do their part, that the elocution is known to be faulty." [28]

What is surprising is that Cibber does not mention the nature of Mrs. Oldfield's role in this play—dissipated female gamester—only that she played it extraordinarily well. Earlier I suggested that Lady Townley's contests with her husband over the meaning of gambling were ideologically freighted, but Cibber's remarks indicate that the fight was fixed. Lord Townley was given powerful straight lines to cut his wife down to size, but Lady Townley was given a powerfully convincing actress to express her opinions. Thus, it is not difficult to imagine that the performative power of the actress Mrs. Oldfield was in fact larger than any message or moral written into the play about the evils of gambling.[29]

In the end, then, when presented with the spectacle of a powerful woman "playing," we are inevitably drawn to her position. In these three comedies, we are being told that wealth—like women—can be made to behave as powerful men would like it to behave. We are being assured that patriarchal economy will reassert itself over unruly feminine display, and that gaming women will ultimately be prevented from dissipating— or "hyperactively recirculating"—wealth. In the process, we receive the message that rank must never be egregiously performed, but internalized and indirectly asserted, and that effeminate display must be controlled. However, in performance, the female actress, even as she simulates discipline, potentially undercuts these messages. Though the lead female character speaks contrition, and though she agrees to place herself under make control, her powerful physical presence belies these claims: she inevitably appears to act according to her own volition.

And this is where Georgiana reenters the picture. Like Lady Townley being played by Mrs. Oldfield, the gaming Georgiana appears to have been a consummate player, a woman acutely aware of the power of performance. Early on, negative experiences in the public eye taught her that it would be a struggle to control the semiotics of her own public appearances. I would speculate that her gaming was also a performance of an especially dramatic kind. In Foreman's biography, the duchess's most excessive gambling bouts do seem to have occurred at moments when she was under greatest pressure to perform publicly as an aristocrat. Though her behavior now appears to have been pathological, mental illness provides only the thinnest rationale for why a woman would spend so much of her adult life extravagantly dissipating what she possessed too easily. [30]

Rather, following Kavanagh, I would suggest that Georgiana was a consummate "player": what better way to assert to an avid audience the superiority of birth than by demonstrating immunity to great financial loss? What better way to demonstrate rank than by risking it all? Although Foreman herself does not attempt to explain the intricacies of Georgiana's marriage, Kavanagh's account also explains why the Duke so readily tolerated his wife's behavior and often assumed responsibility for what she owed: "Gambling debts were, more than anything else, an occasion to affirm a superiority to the rule of money."[31] In the face of our utterly bourgeois insistence that money should behave—that it ought to accrue rationally and accountably—and in the face of our expressed investment in the idea of patriarchal economic control, our ongoing fascination with Georgiana's gambling suggests something else. We may commit to the idea that a "true" identity is never performed and that "authentic" subjectivity is far more than a series of exaggerated behaviors. However, the narrative pull of Georgiana's colorful dissipation intimates that we remain unconsciously fascinated by the possibility that "acting out" may still be the best indicator of true character. An aristocratic performance like the Duchess' retains the power to signal that, though we refuse to play, unlike Georgiana, we will never be the real thing.

NOTES

1. Amanda Foreman, *Georgiana: Duchess of Devonshire* (London: Harper Collins, 1998). Following its phenomenal success in the UK, *Georgiana* has recently been published in the United States by Random House (2000).

2. Foreman p. 183.

3. This is not to suggest that her husband was in any way happy with Georgiana's gambling, for this certainly was not the case. However her husband only sent her into exile when Georgiana became pregnant by Charles Grey.

4. Susanna Centlivre, "The Basset Table" in *The Plays of Susanna Centlivre*, edited by Richard C. Frusell, 3 vol. (New York: Garland Publishing, 1982). Volume I (no pages); Colley Cibber, "The Lady's Last Stake, or The Wife's Resentment " in *Plays Written by Colley Cibber*, 2 vol. (London: Tonson, 1721; Rpt. 1980 New York: Garland Publishing Inc., edited by Rodney L. Hayley), II: 1-97. Sir John Vanbrugh and Colley Cibber, *The Provoked Husband*, edited by Peter Dixon (Lincoln: University of Nebraska Press, 1973). In the Preface to *The Provoked Husband* Dixon explains the problematic relationship between the play that Vanbrugh started before his death and the dramatic text that Cibber completed and brought to the stage.

5. In several ways, my argument about fictional characters resembles that made by Gillian Russell in her recent essay on "Faro Ladies," that is, real life female gamblers at the end of the eighteenth century. Russell argues, for instance, that "the Faro ladies represented an older, more entrenched form of [Linda Colley's] 'womanpower'—the sexual, financial, and class power of the aristocratic woman, traditionally seen as threatening by both aristocratic men and middle-class opinion" ("Faro's Daughters": Female Gamesters, Politics, and the

Discourse of Finance, in 1790s Britain" in *Eighteenth-Century Studies* 33 (2000), p. 482.

6. Thomas M. Kavanagh, *Enlightenment and the Shadows of Chance: The Novel and the Culture of Gambling in Eighteenth-Century France* (Baltimore: Johns Hopkins University Press, 1993), p. 50.

7. Kavanagh, p. 50.

8. Kavanagh, p. 46. On the concept of the "gift," see: Marcel Mauss *The Gift :Forms and Functions of Exchange in Archaic Societies*, trans. Ian Cunnison (New York: W.W. Norton, 1967); Lewis Hyde, *The Gift: Imagination and the Erotic Life of Property* (New York: Random House, 1979); and James G. Carrier, *Gifts and Commodities: Exchange and Western Capitalism since 1700* (New York: Routledge, 1995), p. 20. Bataille expands upon Mauss in his essay "The Notion of Expenditure" in *Visions of Excess: Selected Writings 1927-1939* edited and translated by Allan Stoekl (Minneapolis: The University of Minnesota Press, 1985), pp.116-129. Derrida also discusses the gift in *Given Time: 1: Counterfeit Money*, trans. Peggy Kamuf (Chicago: The University of Chicago Press, 1992).

9. Richard Hey, *A Dissertation on the Pernicious Effects of Gaming* (Cambridge: T. Cadell, 1782), pp. 17-18.

10. Jeremy Collier, *An Essay Upon Gaming, in a Dialogue Between Callimachus and Dolomedes* (London: J. Morphew, 1713), p. 30.

11. Collier, p. 30.

12. Christopher Anstey, *The New Bath Guide* (London: Vernor, Hood, and Sharpe, 1807), Letter VIII, p. 57.

13. Anstey, pp. 57-59.

14. In Letter XV, the narrator announces he has been ruined by a card shark.

15. Alexander Pope, "Epistle III: To Bathurst" in *Poetry and Prose of Alexander Pope*, edited by Aubrey Williams (Boston: Houghton Mifflin, 1969), p. 182, lines 161-166. See also John Barrell and Harriet Guest "On the Use of Contradiction" in this poem in *The New Eighteenth-Century* edited by Felicity Nussbaum and Laura Brown (New York: Methuen, 1987), pp. 121-135.

16. Hey, for example, explains at length how risk taken in business differs from risk taken at the gambling table. The merchant who sends a ship out to sea may be said to take a chance, and yet, "it is the study of the Merchant to avoid every risque that is not necessary to the end he has in view; and wherever he can diminish his risque, he does it by Insurances and others methods of Caution which he can devise:—where he exposes himself to any hazard, it is as to a necessary Evil, for the sake of a greater Good connected with it.... But the Gamester has the appearance of seeking Risque for its own sake. With regard to so much as the Balance has been shewn to be against him, he acts like the man who should for mere amusement trust a share of his property to the mercy of the Waves or Pirates, without hoping for any return" (17). Hey obscures, of course, the historical connection between insurance and gambling, a connection that has been explored by a number of modern scholars, among them, Reuven Brenner (*Gambling and Speculation: A Theory, A History, and a Future of Some Human Decisions* [Cambridge: Cambridge University Press, 1990], especially Chapter Four on "Gambling, speculation,

insurance," pp. 90-106.

17. Or, as Erin Mackie writes in *Market à la Mode: Fashion, Commodity, and Gender in 'The Tatler' and 'The Spectator',* "From the bourgeois point of view, which is that of *The Tatler* and *The Spectator*, good taste emphasizes modesty, restraint, practicality, and decorum in distinction to bad (aristocratic) taste corrupted by ideologically retrogressive qualities of personal ostentation, irrational excess, arbitrary election, and libertine abandon" (Baltimore: Johns Hopkins University Press, 1997, p. 20).

18. Apparently, Vanbrugh's draft included a scene, later excised by Cibber, in which Lady Townley taunts her mercer by refusing to pay what she owes. (See Dixon's introduction, p. xxi.) This scene would have further emphasized the notion of Lady Townley as an irrational dissipater. To pay the mercer is at least to keep money in circulation by allowing it to "trickle down" (a fact that both Bernard Mandeville and Alexander Pope acknowledge). To refuse to pay one's debts, especially when those debts are owed to tradesmen, is to thwart any sort of "rational" flow of capital.

19. The Spectator, No. 467, Tuesday, August 26, 1712, rpt. in *The Commerce of Everyday Life: Selections from The Tatler and The Spectator,* edited by Erin Mackie (Boston: Bedford St. Martin's, 1998), p. 544. On the construction of masculinity, see also *Proposing Men: Dialectics of Gender and Class in the Eighteenth-century English Periodical* by Shawn Lisa Maurer (Stanford: Stanford University Press), 1998.

20. Hey, pp. 62-63.

21. Why basset? According to *The Compleat Gamester*, basset was, on the one hand, said to be "the most Courtly"of the French card games, "because properly, by the understanders of it, thought only for Kings and Queens, great Princes, Noble-Men, & etc. to play at by reason of such great Losses, or Advantages as may possibly be on one side or the other, during the time of Play." On the other hand, "this Game...is so tempting and decoying a Nature by reason of several specious Multiplications and Advantages which seemingly it offers to the unwary *Punter,* [player] that a great many like it so well, that they will in some Coffee-Houses, and other public places, play at small Game rather than give out, and rather not play at all, will Punt at a Groar..." In other words, a player was not very likely to win this game, yet it was very tempting because of its illusory promises of high-stakes winnings (*The Compleat Gamester: or, Instructions How to Play all manner of usual and most Gentile Games...to which is added The Game at Basset, never before Printed in English* [London: Charles Brome, 1709], p.177).

22. Andrea Henderson, "Commerce and Masochistic Desire in the 1790s: Frances Burney's *Camilla*" *Eighteenth-Century Studies* 31(1997): 69-86, p. 73.

23. In *Adam and Eve Stript of their Furbelows: Or, the Fashionable Virtues and Vices of Both Sexes expos'd to publick view* [London: A. Bettesworth, n.d.], a woman is said to be so bewitched by Gaming, that "she loves a Pack of Cards much better than her Children; for she will quit the satisfaction of toying with the one, for the avaricious Pleasure of playing with the other; and thinks every

Knave in the Pack, a better Companion than her Husband " (p. 53).

24. Kristina Straub, *Sexual Suspects: Eighteenth-Century Players and Sexual Ideology (*Princeton: Princeton University Press, 1992), p. 89.

25. Catherine Elwes cites Sally Potter from a catalog for a show entitled *About Time* (London: ICA, 1980). Elwes's essay is entitled "Floating Femininity: A Look at Performance Art by Women" in *Women's Image of Men*, edited by Sarah Kent and Jacqueline Moreau (London: Pandora, 1985), p.171.

26. For one example of a reading that takes into account the history of an actress' physical presence, see Ellen Donkin, "Mrs. Siddons Looks Back in Anger: Feminist Historiography for Eighteenth-Century British Theater" in *Critical Theory and Performance* edited Janelle G. Reinelt and Joseph R. Roach (Ann Arbor: University of Michigan Press, 1992), pp. 276-290).

27. Pope, among others, famously mocked and derided this preface for its several infelicitous uses of the English language. (See Dixon xv-xvi.)

28. Colley Cibber, "To The Reader" in *The Careless Husband*, edited by Peter Dixon, pp. 7-8.

29. Indeed, this point would seem to be confirmed by Frances Burney's use of *The Provoked Husband* in *The Wanderer* (1814). There Burney's heroine "Incognita" (Ellis) is coerced, against her better judgment, into playing the Lady Townley role in an amateur production. What her superlative performance reveals is not the evils of gambling (about which Burney says nothing) but the true nature of the Incognita's hidden, genteel identity. (See *The Wanderer*, edited by Margaret Anne Doody, Robert L. Mack, and Peter Sabor [New York: Penguin, 1991], pp. 90-97 and Appendix VI, pp. 900-905).

30. Thomas Kavanagh also moved in this direction in the introductory comments to his keynote address at WSECS. Without explicitly suggesting that Georgiana's gambling was performative in nature, Kavanagh expressed similar skepticism about Foreman's assumption that the duchess's gambling was merely aberrant or pathological. Thomas Kavanagh, "Cards and Culture in Eighteenth-century France," keynote lecture WSECS, Las Vegas, February 25, 2000.

31. Kavanagh, p. 47.

"Spare from Your Luxuries": Women, Charity, and Spending in the Eighteenth Century

CATHERINE KEOHANE

The eighteenth century was proud of its charitableness: across a range of texts, including novels, sermons, conduct books, and periodical essays, writers identify their time as an age of charity or benevolence. Common is Henry Fielding's mid-century assertion that "Charity is in fact the very Characteristic of this Nation at this Time.——I believe we may challenge the whole World to parallel the Examples which we have of late given of this sensible, this noble, this Christian virtue."[1] Yet, giving was also worrisome, and such congratulatory characterizations of the period coexist with equally common depictions of the age as misdirected in its charity. The reported consequences of misdirected charity were quite serious and included the impoverishment of the country and the perpetuation of poverty.[2] Given such worries, it is not surprising that many contemporary didactic tracts and sermons attempt to regulate giving. In one 1773 example, the sermonist Beilby Porteus alleges the presence of a "spirit of universal philanthropy," but also observes that the benevolent need direction: "The chief thing necessary is not so much to urge them to do good, as to show them, how they may do the most good; in what way they can bestow their alms to the greatest advantage."[3]

That this "greatest advantage" could benefit more than the poor is suggested by two methods that proposed how polite women were to fund their charity: the economy argument and its apparent inverse, consumer charity, attempt to regulate polite women's outlays of money not just in charity, but also in their consumption of so-called luxuries. As a result, these methods have larger significance for understanding eighteenth-century concerns about women's spending more generally. On the one hand, the economy argument (the model to which we will devote the most attention here) posits consumption and charity as mutually exclusive forms of spending, urging women to "sacrifice" luxuries in the interest of having money for charity; on the other hand, the model of consumer charity combines charity and consumption by identifying forms of consumption that can serve charitable ends. Focusing on the construction of charity allows us to see that, as Ken Jackson reminds us, charity "does not just involve charitable practices or good works, but a whole cultural belief system which helps determine and explain those practices."[4] Looking at these two models of women's charity will allow us to see the concerns about women's money handling that "determine and explain" them and, in doing so, will open up our understanding of the opportunities available for eighteenth-century polite women's participation in the public arena.

Charity is a significant component of this participation, being a site of the intersection of both developing notions of feminine propriety and women's agency. Speaking to notions of propriety, conduct books and didactic literature assign women an innate charitableness and allege that its cultivation will develop polite women's character and fill up their time with appropriate activities. On the one hand, assigning women charitable duties allows them a degree of agency, by giving them some work to do. Yet, on the other hand, the models proposed by the economy argument and consumer charity seek to harness women's so-called natural charitableness in order to restrict their activity in the area of consumer spending. While conduct literature recommends charity as an activity that develops women's character, a byproduct of the inculcation of habitual charity, as we will see, is making them less self-interested in a more basic, economic sense. Although apparently contradictory models, the economy argument and the model of consumer charity both mask, as they also respond to, a more general fear of women's distribution of money that is fueled by the growing array of consumer products and increasing opportunities to spend money. While my emphasis here will be on conduct books' and charitable treatises' construction of these two models of charity, brief considerations of the fictional representations of women givers in Frances Burney's *Cecilia* (1782) and Sarah Scott's *Millenium Hall* (1762) will confirm that conduct-book prescriptions about charity in part reflect a fear of women's spending and will allow us to raise questions about these models of charity. Using this combination of didactic and literary materials, I will argue that the attempt to redirect women's spending into charity serves eighteenth-century society's larger efforts to control women's expenditure of money, efforts that are indicative not just of limits but of opportunities. In addition, although my intention is not to provide in-depth interpretations of the novels, this method will allow insight into some of the problematic aspects of each.

*

Turning first to the context of these two models of charity—the discussion of how individuals were to fund their charitable expenditures—we find that eighteenth-century conduct writers often emphasize careful household budgeting. In *Letters on the Improvement of the Mind, Addressed to a Young Lady* (1773), Hester Chapone contends, "The prudent distribution of your charitable gifts may not improperly be considered as a branch of Economy, since the great duty of almsgiving cannot be truly fulfilled without a diligent attention so to manage the sums you can spare as to produce the most real good to your fellow-creatures." Budgeting for charity is similarly recommended in Mary Wollstonecraft's 1788 conduct book, *Original Stories from Real Life: with Conversations, Calculated to Regulate the Affections, and Form the Mind to Truth and Goodness*, a series of short narratives in which a governess instructs two girls in key concepts. Although the governess Mrs. Mason's understanding of charity is grounded in Christian piety, it does not neglect practical concerns. When one of her charges finds herself unable to assist a poor family because she has spent all her money on "paltry ornaments," Mrs. Mason reprimands her, reminding her that "Oeconomy and self-denial are necessary [in every station], to enable us to be generous, and [to] act conformably to the rules of justice."[5]

The emphasis on economy is particularly relevant for eighteenth-century polite women since "Oeconomy, or the Art of House-Keeping," was being identified as "the most immediate Female business." Emphasizing economy ostensibly makes it easier for women to have the means to participate in charitable giving, suggesting this model is empowering. Yet, as is highlighted in Thomas Gisborne's discussion of the claims on married women in his 1797 *Enquiry into the Duties of the Female Sex*, the focus on budgeting has a strong regulatory undercurrent. The conduct writer there advises the married woman to reorder her expenses so that she does not "squander[], in extravagance and parade, that property which ought partly to have been reserved in store for the future benefit of [her] offspring, and partly to have been liberally bestowed for the present advantage of those whom relationship or personal merit, or the general claim which distress has upon such as are capable of granting relief, entitles to [her] bounty."[6] According to arguments that emphasize economy, careful budgeting permits giving.

*

A refinement of this reasoning, the economy argument takes direction and regulation a step further by suggesting specific categories of spending that can be modified to raise money for charity. In the economy argument, charity is positioned as a form of spending that is at odds with the consumption of luxuries. In short, the economy argument proposes a form of comparative budgeting that involves retrenching, sacrificing, or suppressing "unnecessary" expenses in order to create a ready fund for charity. For instance, Frances Burney concludes her little-known charity solicitation by arguing that women can have money to donate if they "[s]pare from [their] luxuries, [and] diminish from [their] pleasures." Notably, this model intersects with conceptions of women's alleged compassion: the virtuous woman as depicted by the conduct writer Wetenhall Wilkes in 1740 "prefers the Necessities of others to her own superfluous Delicacies; she moderates her own Enjoyments, to be the better enabled to relieve them." The advice to suppress luxuries, while at times directed to men, has a prominent place in period arguments about women's charitableness; as Wilkes's version indicates, the economy argument reasons that women could have money for charitable donations through economizing and, in particular, through substituting others' needs for their own.[7]

In the presentation of Sarah Trimmer, a well-known advocate of women's involvement in the Sunday-School movement, economizing is an easy, painless way to be charitable: "the occasional sacrifice of a superfluous ornament would enable many in middling ranks to be charitable, who cannot afford to be so while they covet all the varieties and extravagancies of fashion. . ."[8] While part of Trimmer's larger strategy to present charity as both worthwhile and doable, this advice emphasizes charity's connection to economy, especially in terms of that household management which was being assigned to women. As Trimmer's passage illustrates, the suppressed purchase is often figured as something that is unnecessary: the exchange of a self-interested luxury—here "a superfluous ornament"—for charitable activity. The connection between charity and consumption, or, rather, between charity and restrained consumption, is made clear in Hannah More's plea on behalf of the French emigrant clergy, where, like Trimmer, she argues that charity can be given by "the suppression of one luxury for a charitable purpose."[9]

Proceeding to define such suppression, More, as is common in deployments of the economy argument, suggests that the money in question will be made through singular, minor sacrifices. As she advises, "Let her who indulges such habits, and pleads such excuses in consequence, reflect, that by retrenching *one* costly dish from her abundant table, the superfluities of *one* expensive dessert, *one* evening's public amusement, she may furnish at least a week's subsistence to more than one person[.]" Significantly, More implies that, through economy, women can give without added expense and without needing to ask their husbands for any money. Already in control of the household budget, they simply need to reallocate funds. Cutting back on one gourmet item or one entertainment will allow them, almost magically, to make money: "For the suppression of one luxury for a charitable purpose, is the exercise of two virtues, and this without any pecuniary expense." More's argument that such a reallocation of funds exercises both charity and self-restraint indicates a way in which the discourse of charity is drawn into debates over commerce and consumption, and has as its byproduct an attempt to regulate women's consumer spending. Notably, however, the economy argument erases the actual expense involved, suggesting that money *is* created from nothing, from the substitution of a charitable gift for one self-interested purchase. This, of course, is a question of accounting since money that would otherwise be spent on luxury is still spent, just differently. In other words, because charity often does involve a pecuniary expense of some kind, the exchange of charity for luxury is not the equivalent of saving money; yet, while spent money is spent money, in the economy argument the virtue apparently lies in how it is spent.

Yet, this is also more than a question of accounting, of more than merely comparing one instance of consumption against one opportunity for charitable giving, something our discussion of *Cecilia* in the next section will make clear. Rather, the habituation of women to charity, the creation in them of an indoctrinated desire to give and to have funds ready to do so, is proposed as a method of instilling preemptive budgeting that weighs possible future giving over current and future luxury expenses. It is here that the camouflaged element of attempted control becomes visible: this more general saving for future charity implicitly serves to entice saving itself. As the conduct writer Gisborne's comparison of the habits of fashion and charity confirms, women's habituation to charity is proposed in part to counter self-indulgent consumption and, by implication, to reduce its expense:

> The fact is, that an unguarded fondness for ornament has been known, in a multitude of examples, to overpower the native tenderness of the female mind . . . . If the purse be generally kept low by the demands of milliners, of mantua-makers, of jewellers, and dealers in trinkets, and of others who bear their part in adorning the person; little can be allotted to the applications of charity. But charity requires, in common with other virtues, the fostering influence of habit. If the custom of devoting an adequate portion of the income to the relief of distress be long intermitted, the desire of giving relief will gradually be impaired. The heart forgets, by disuse, the emotions in which it once delighted.

While championing the inculcation of charity as a habit, Gisborne's text highlights for us the oppositional relationship between women's consumerism and their charitableness that is at the heart of the economy argument: by potentially leaving no funds for charity, women's alleged delight in ornament impinges upon their ability to be charitable. To preempt such self-directed expenditures, the "fostering influence of habit" must be combined with economy argument rationale to rein in consumer desires. In the words of Wollstonecraft's Mrs. Mason, "when we squander money idly, we defraud the poor, and deprive our own souls of their most exalted food. If you wish to be useful, govern your desires . . . . "[10]

The economy argument governs desires by offering them an alternative focus in charity. Having suggested women indulge their concern for dress and ornament at the expense of their charitable offerings, Gisborne proposes the preventative conditioning that is central to this model:

> Before the world has repressed, by its interested lessons, the warmth of youthful benevolence; let experience establish a conviction, that the greatest of all pleasures is to do good. She who has accustomed herself to this delight, will not easily be induced to forego it. She will feel, that whatever she is able, without penuriousness or improper singularity, to withdraw from the expense of personal ornament, is not only reserved for much higher purposes, but for purposes productive of exquisite and permanent gratification.

Gisborne's language—suggesting that funds are "withdrawn" from the account of personal ornament and reallocated to charitable giving—spotlights the accounting mind-set that lies behind the economy argument itself. This is also evident in More's later didactic novel *Coelebs in Search of a Wife* (1808) which seeks to prove the economy argument's validity through the negative example of the Miss Ranbys. Representing incorrectly educated young ladies who have not been trained to reallocate funds from personal ornament to charity, the Miss Ranbys' desires are not governed. Contrary to Gisborne's recommendations, "the exercise of benevolence . . . [*was*] left to depend on the accidental state of the purse": "If no new trinket happened to be wanted," as More writes, "these young ladies were liberal to any application. . . . But if there was a competition between a sick family and a new brooch, the brooch was sure to carry the day."[11] Accordingly, if suppressing one luxury is proposed as a method of freeing money for one particular instance of charitable giving, habituation to charity on the level of general economy is proposed as a check on luxury and self-indulgence, a way to ensure that the brooch fails "to carry the day" every day. The economy argument, then, makes consumption and charity appear incompatible by advocating the redirection of money away from self-interested things to benevolence. In this way, charity—or, rather, cultivated charitableness—does "make" money through reallocating spending and prompting saving for a ready fund which may (or may not) be distributed in charity.

Notably, however, the method proposed by the economy argument differed from contemporary practice: as the historian Donna Andrew reports, "benevolence, like prodigality, did not usually come from revenue—people did not cut back on their personal expenses so that they could give alms or pay the poor rates—but from capital."[12] In other words, eighteenth-century charity was not generally funded through reductions in personal expenses—or quite the opposite of what the economy argument proposes. The apparent split between rhetoric and practice indicates the coupling of attempts to inspire giving with those to regulate consumption. Significantly, if the economy argument is not evidence of charitable practice, it is indicative of charity's being enlisted to address other concerns. In other words, because the exchange of charity for luxury is not necessarily the equivalent of saving money, this type of advice intersects with the larger issues of women's control of money and stereotypes about their consumption. For our purposes, it is not important whether redirecting women's spending into charity was an effective means of controlling their consumption: what is important is the construction's implicit acknowledgment that, whatever limits might be placed on women's control of money by law or custom, eighteenth-century genteel women did indeed have some control over money, control this argument finds significant enough to seek to restrict.

As is reinforced by the economy argument's figuring of the suppressed purchase as a self-interested luxury—a lavish table, an item of fancy dress, or a social pleasure—, an area in which women had some control was the growing consumer economy. Women's participation in what some have labeled the new "consumer revolution" of the eighteenth century was quite complex. Although scholars have debunked the claim that women's participation in the consumer economy was proportionally greater than men's, what is clear and important is that this was the contemporary perception. In keeping with their responsibility for managing the family budget, polite women were assigned "the daily *management* of consumption . . . and with it control of routine decision-making," an assignment that exacerbates fears about women's spending.[13]

For, while eighteenth-century women's legal possession of property was relatively limited (as was married women's in particular), consumption does not depend on proprietorship; a wife's responsibility for the household budget would not require ownership of the family's property. Given this gap between ownership and consumption, it is not surprising that, as Susan Staves has noted, "[a]nxiety over ruin at the hands of a spendthrift wife is a common eighteenth-century theme," one that Margot Finn observes was quite entrenched.[14] These perceptions allow concerns over women and luxury to seep into understandings of charity. The impulse to harness spending—and to use charity as a means to do so—, then, is significant in itself. In one manifestation, the economy argument is mustered in an attempt to regulate women's consumption by offering charity as a habit to replace their fondness for dress.

*

Because conduct books assert a model rather than document a way of life, the gaps between the life projected and the life lived are vital evidence of eighteenth-century culture. Burney's second novel, *Cecilia*, allows us to see beyond such gaps and to grasp the unstated next step in economy argument rationale. *Cecilia* provides an interesting test case because its heroine appears to follow economy argument rationale in organizing her charitable expenditures. Despite this, she still faces significant criticism, something suggestive of the larger implications of the economics of charity. *Cecilia* is a novel rich in detail: its complicated love plot, turning on the name provision attached to the heroine's landed estate, has received a significant amount of critical attention as have Cecilia's apparently problematic distributions of money to her bankrupt but high-living guardian Harrel. My interest in *Cecilia* in our context, however, rests in the heiress's understanding of her economic responsibility with respect to charity. In chronicling her heroine's charity and the reaction to it, Burney exposes the competition between models of women's charitableness and conceptions of their ability to handle money, and, in doing so, permits questions about the shapes women's agency could take in the eighteenth century. In addition, the novelist's acknowledgment of the economic context that is often ignored or downplayed in didactic material makes *Cecilia* especially valuable in our effort to comprehend the import of the gap between didactic prescriptions and the reality of polite women's charity. In place of a conventional reading of the text, a focus on Cecilia's notions of personal economy and charity will allow us to mine the implications of the economy argument.

Cecilia, having inherited two substantial fortunes, sees her wealth as bringing with it a responsibility to share with the less fortunate. Disgusted with the fashionable life of dissipation practiced by the guardian with whom she lives, she decides to "project[] and adopt[] some plan of conduct, better suited to her taste and feelings than the frivolous insipidity of her present life, to make at once a more spirited and more worthy use of the affluence, freedom and power which she possessed."[15] In so doing, she develops a "scheme of happiness" in which charity is a central component. What is particularly important for us about Cecilia's notion of social obligation—an understanding that reflects traditional models of Christian stewardship and aristocratic hospitality—is the heiress's understanding of her wealth as the producer of her obligation. As Cecilia reflects on her approaching majority:

> not without trembling did she then look forward to the claims which the splendid income she was soon to possess would call upon her to discharge. A strong sense of DUTY, a fervent desire to ACT RIGHT, were the ruling characteristics of her mind: her affluence she therefore considered as a debt contracted with the poor, and her independence, as a tie upon her liberality to pay it with interest. (55)

The conduct writer Chapone's advice that "[t]he larger are your funds, the stronger is the call upon you to exert your industry and care in disposing of them properly" highlights for us the terms of the contract: it is a binding one in which the "splendidness" of Cecilia's fortune impels the debt. Moreover, the compelling force inherent in the very possession of wealth is further increased by her independence.[16]

In accepting this solemn social obligation, Cecilia takes steps to govern her economy so that the needs of others are not dependent on her desires. Even though she is introduced as an heiress to a landed estate worth £3000 a year from her uncle and an additional £10,000 cash from her father, Cecilia restrains her own expenses, living instead as if her income were

£500 a year (792). Her wealth would seem to excuse Cecilia from such strict requirements of economy: she obviously does not need to suppress a luxury to be able to contribute money to someone's relief. Nevertheless, as Cecilia reasons:

> Her income was very large, and she was wholly without family or connection; to spend it merely upon herself would be something still worse than extravagance, it must result from wilfulness the most inexcusable, as her disposition was naturally averse to luxury and expence. She might save indeed, but for whom? not a creature had such a claim upon her; and with regard to herself, she was so provided for it would be unnecessary. She would never, she declared, run in debt even for a week, but while her estate was wholly clear, she would spend it without restriction. (795)

By proposing such a balance, an overall weighing of others over self in the division of expenses, Cecilia's economic philosophy is aligned with the economy argument, even though the latter's specific language is absent from Burney's novel. On the one hand, this absence is unremarkable given that Cecilia's resources make it unnecessary for her to compare one purchase against one charitable case. On the other hand, the absence is remarkable because, although Cecilia could afford both luxury and charity, consumption does not tempt her. This particular passage marks her as someone who has imbibed the spirit of preemptive budgeting; modifying the conduct writer Gisborne's phrasing, "an unguarded fondness for ornament" has not "overpower[ed] the native tenderness of [Cecilia's] mind." In other words, this is not a case in which the brooch comes close to "carrying the day," unlike that of *Coelebs*' two Miss Ranbys. Consequently, because dissipation and luxury do not form part of Cecilia's happiness, her happiness and her social duties are not incompatible; on the contrary, sacrificing fashionable diversions appears to secure others' and her own happiness. In this way, she proves herself to be someone who follows the conduct advice that greater personal economy enables one to have more to devote to charity.

Yet, although Cecilia's economic philosophy is thus in line with conduct-book prescriptions, many in the novel view her charitable donations negatively. They do so because Cecilia adheres to her plan of spending "without restriction." Even disregarding the heroine's problematic loans to her guardian Harrel which, though beyond our scope here, appear to be perverted forms of charity, "[t]he bounties of Cecilia, extensive, magnificent, unlimited, were the theme of every tongue, and though sometimes censured and sometimes admired, they were wondered at universally" (794). It is significant that Cecilia's distribution of money in charity is marked not just for praise but for censure: this is not a case of a woman indulging a taste for personal ornament, but for charity, for what is so often presented by conduct literature as an appropriate outlet for polite women's spending. This criticism leads us to question the economy argument itself. What exactly is Cecilia doing wrong by deciding to spend her wealth on others and not on herself? Her treacherous adviser Monckton, who wishes to marry her for her money (once his first rich wife dies), provides the answer: it is her very expenditure of money at all that is troubling. Her charity sickens him: "to see money thus sported away, which he had long considered as his own, to behold those sums which he had destined for his pleasures, thus lavishly bestowed upon beggars, excited a rage he could with difficulty conceal, and an uneasiness he could hardly endure; and he languished, he sickened for the time, when he might put a period to such romantic proceedings" (771). While stemming from selfishness, Monckton's reaction is not unique, but merely an extreme version of that of others in the novel.

While for Cecilia her wealth produces solemn social obligations to be met through charitable donations, for fashionable society, Cecilia's wealth marks her as a commodity in the marriage market, an eligible match. Accordingly, Cecilia arrives in London already assigned a place in the social order. Gossip confirms Cecilia's place; as Lady Honoria Pemberton remarks, "Every body one meets . . . disposes of Miss Beverley to some new person" (354-55). A key word in the text, "dispose" is usually associated with Cecilia's fortune; its use here positions Cecilia herself as a disposable and controllable object, underlining the common equation of her and her fortune. Thus, when she reflects on news of another's marriage prospects which are dependent on financial considerations, Cecilia is wrong in "rejoic[ing] that [her] independent situation exempts [her] from being disposed of for life, by thus being set up to sale!" (468). Even her uncle positions Cecilia as marriageable—and as needing to marry—naming a default heir "in his will as the successor of Cecilia, in case she died unmarried or changed her name, as a mark that he approved of her doing neither, [rather] than as a matter he thought probable, if even possible, to turn out in [the heir's] favour" (861).

This understanding of Cecilia colors opinions of her right to dispose of money and suggests why Cecilia's charity appears so troubling: to those who consider Cecilia's fortune something she holds in trust for a future husband, Cecilia appears to distribute in charity what really should be her husband's—and notably without his sanction. For, while society shares Cecilia's belief that her wealth binds her to give it to someone else, they differ over who that someone else should be: the poor or her husband. This difference in assumed recipients exposes the true issue as not simply the disposal of Cecilia's riches, but who gets to direct that disposal. As the guardian in charge of Cecilia's money bluntly puts it when turning down her request for funds, "Keep it for your husband" (180). Briggs's syntax is important. The miser's characteristic compression of words functions both as a command—"You keep it for your husband"—and a claim: he has swallowed the true subject "I"—in "I'll keep it for your husband." The narrator's later paraphrasing of the conversation makes clear that Briggs subscribes to the view that women need men to keep their money for them: Briggs "sa[id] that her uncle had left her a noble estate, and he would take care to see it put in proper hands, by getting her a good and careful husband" (181). Believing "that girls knew nothing of the value of money, and ought not to be trusted with it" (180), Briggs never considers the possibility that Cecilia's may be "proper hands," an oversight that reflects the lingering view that "[t]he only acceptable role for the singlewoman [in early modern England] was as a household dependent, not as an independent female head of household, outside the control of a father or master."[17] While, as the historian Amy Froide notes, this view was modified over the early modern period, Burney's fictional depiction of Cecilia reflects its core's continuation, something exemplified by both the heiress's having three guardians and also the negative response to her adherence to economy argument rationale. While the great significance placed on Cecilia's charity implicitly marks charity as one way women participate in the public world, it also suggests that their participation appears unproblematic only when restrained through methods like the economy argument or, better yet, when controlled by a male figure.

Cecilia's charity, then, is emblematic of the discomfort she causes as a young woman who not only accepts the social obligations of wealth but also does not let herself be directed in the marriage market. The difference in opinion over Cecilia's ability and right to distribute her money recalls Lynne Vallone's argument that didactic material for girls in the eighteenth and nineteenth centuries promotes a limited definition of charity. She contends that charity sermons

> do not consider the biblical ideal of Charity as one of the duties particular to women. . . , and the disposal of property is generally not considered a female right. . . . Conduct manual writers, however, call "charity"—that narrowed aspect of philanthropy which involves the giving of the self and/or minor financial support, a feminine imperative —"the great duty of almsgiving" that is essential to the social and moral development of the Christian girl.[18]

By not giving the impression that she is the temporary custodian or intermediate holder of social obligations, Cecilia's "scheme of happiness" does not mirror this distinction. Rather, although she does conform to the conventional idea that her husband will take over the management of her fortune after marriage, she casts this as a future event that will not impede her current plans, making the obligation now clearly and definitely hers. By distributing her money in charity before marriage, then, Cecilia assumes the responsibility society wants to assign to another, her husband. By causing discomfort to observers who view it as a waste of a man's money, Cecilia's charity illuminates the final, unstated step in the economy argument's comparative budgeting: while charitable expenditure is preferable to the consumption of luxuries, women's spending nothing at all trumps even charitable expenditures.

*

The negative response to Cecilia's subscribing to an economic philosophy reflective of economy argument rationale reveals for us the contradictory regulatory impulse of the economy argument itself: spending on charity is better than spending on luxury provided that the charity itself is not "extravagant." While certain of Cecilia's other financial outlays are criticized, it is critical, if often overlooked, that so too is her charity—or that which conduct literature suggested would be an appropriate use of money. This unexpected reaction to the thorough implementation of preemptive comparative budgeting suggests that the problem lies in the economy argument's failure, in Cecilia's case, to restrain women's overall expenditure sufficiently, making it worthwhile to look quickly at a coexisting model of charity which attempts to wed, rather than divorce, consumption and charity. In short, if the economy argument makes consumption and charity appear incompatible, the model of consumer charity suggests they are quite compatible. According to this model, luxury can take the place of charity through carefully directed purchases that help poor tradespeople stave off the need for charity. In arguments that build upon notions that the poor contributed to society through their work and the rich contributed through their support of commerce, consumption was proposed as a genuine method to be charitable.[19] Moreover, in eighteenth-century charitable discourse, properly directed consumption was another method that had the potential benefit of controlling consumption. Consequently, while period conduct writers try to harness women's spending by promoting saving for charity through the economy argument, they also attempt to utilize notions of women's tendency to spend in a different way, suggesting the inverse that spending can be giving. While an advocate of the economy argument, the conduct writer Gisborne also encourages giving through spending that is rightly and appropriately directed toward supporting the industry of women. Urging polite women to be "[m]indful of the scarcity of modes of employment in which persons of the female sex can properly engage for a subsistence," Gisborne contends that by "encourag[ing] women in all such occupations by steady and active preference . . . . [ladies] can scarcely render to [their] own sex a more important benefit."[20]

Period charities also take advantage of the connection between charity and discriminating, properly directed consumption. In one example, Joseph Massie's 1758 *Plan for the Establishment of Charity-Houses for Exposed or Deserted Women and Girls, and for Penitent Prostitutes* combines charity with consumption. In line with contemporary arguments that promote helping charitable recipients become self-sufficient and productive members of society, one element of Massie's plan calls for the spinning and manufacture of yarn and textiles. Contending that the home would become cost effective—even profitable—over time, Massie envisions "CHARITY, HUMANITY, PATRIOTISM, and OECONOMY, be[ing] made to go Hand-in-Hand; and the Ways to form this most pleasing quadruple Alliance [being] so obviously proper and so easily practicable, that one can scarcely help wondering how so much Good can be obtained by such simple Means." For Massie, women as consumers are key to ensuring this "most pleasing" alliance, leading him to assign the home's governesses the tasks of choosing the colors and setting the prices for the goods to be manufactured: as women, they in theory will know what will appeal to potential buyers. Looking forward to Gisborne's advocacy of the patronage of tradeswomen, Massie argues that women should buy English products so that "suitable Employment [will be] found for the most ingenious of their distressed Countrywomen": buying English goods will provide for poor Englishwomen, both by helping the proposed Charity House become self-supporting and also implicitly by erasing the need for charity.[21]

In contrast to the economy argument, the model of consumer charity implies that luxuries need not be suppressed if their suppliers are chosen carefully; yet, the potential for outside misreadings of this consumption as self-indulgent rather than charitable is illustrated by the striking conflation of the economy and spending threads in Sarah Scott's *Millenium Hall.* Scott's 1762 novel about a group of women who found a utopian, charitable community exposes the complexities involved in the consumer charity model, complexities again tied to women's expenditure of money. The ladies' combining a religious, providential understanding of stewardship with works like a carpet manufacture intended to become profitable; their acknowledgment of the pleasures of benevolence; their understanding of the special pressures of gratitude and dependence borne by recipients; their combining the work of a Lady Bountiful caring for the neighborhood poor with that of associated charities devoted to specific problems; and their exhibition of the compassion and sensibility "natural" to women all mark *Millenium Hall* as a text cognizant of and participating in the contemporary discourse of charity. While, as with *Cecilia*, there is not time here to provide an in-depth reading of the text, what is significant for our purposes is the Hall ladies' charitable philosophy and the outside reaction to it.

The ladies' charitable philosophy is rooted in a desire to exercise control over their own lives. The series of interpolated histories which detail the ladies' lives prior to the founding of the Hall dominates the text and provides the unstated answer to the narrator's curiosity "to know by what steps women thus qualified both by nature and fortune to have the world almost at command, were brought thus to seclude themselves from it, and make as it were a new one for themselves."[22] In this "new world," they are free from the oppressive obligations of patriarchal society, such as lecherous guardians, loveless marriages, or financial dependence, that threatened them in their pre-Hall lives. It is telling, however, that the new world they choose to create reflects principles of contemporary charitable discourse. As many conduct writers and divines advise, the initial co-founders of the Hall, Mrs. Morgan and Miss Mancel, arrange their expenses so that they can enhance their power to help others: "As they ordered every thing in their own family with great oeconomy, and thought themselves entitled only to a part of their fortunes, their large incomes allowed them full power to assist many, whose situations differed very essentially from theirs" (159).

Like Cecilia, the Hall ladies follow conduct-book prescriptions relative to their budgeting and still find that their charity becomes a source of concern. This is highlighted by the ladies' own particular anxiety to be able to defend their expenditures, to position their charity as not excessive. An accounting of their assets and expenses is provided to demonstrate to the narrator (and readers) that their charity, while extensive, is also discreet, careful, and within the bounds of their income. In addition, in keeping with consumer charity, the ladies' employment of servants parallels the recommended patronage of women's businesses because most of the servants are disabled in some way. Yet, as Scott's narrator observes, this attempt makes the ladies objects of his curiosity and admiration: "There was something so whimsically good in the conduct of the ladies in these particulars, as at first made me smile; but when I considered it more thoroughly, I perceived herein a refinement of charity, which, though extremely uncommon, was entirely rational" (169).

The narrator's reflection acknowledges the two-faced appearance of the ladies' charity: it is either "whimsical" or "rational," hidden or extensive, depending on the observer's point of view. This potential confusion stems from their unlikely combination of the seemingly opposite models of the economy argument and consumer charity evident in their casting all expenses as charity. As the narrator continues,

> I found, that not contented with meerly bestowing on the indigent as large a part of their fortunes as they can possibly spare, they carry the notion of their duty to the poor so far as to give continual attention to it, and endeavour so to apply all they spend, as to make almost every shilling contribute towards the support of some person in real necessity; by this means every expence bears the merit of a donation, in the sight of him who knows their motives; and their constant application is directed towards the relief of others, while to superficial observers they seem only providing for their own convenience. (169-70)

Significantly, this description suggests that the ladies' charity is so very refined that it is visible only to the most careful and knowledgeable of observers. The magical transformation of expense into donation serves to erase the taint of spending on one's self—but only to those aware of what the ladies are doing; to others they may appear to fit stereotypes of consuming women. The ladies' perfect charity, an object of wonder to the narrator, highlights the difficulty the women face. Having removed themselves from the world, the ladies must be extra careful to be able to justify each expense, even for such "basics" as household help. Their charity appears easy, but it is a deceptive easiness: since their control of money, like the later Cecilia's, seems inherently unnatural, they must appear to be not simply sacrificing minor luxuries, but rather suppressing all luxuries for charity or, at most, accepting luxuries only in the interest of charity. The notion that all expenses are charity—and seemingly must be charity—provides the most striking evidence that concerns about women's distribution of money intervene in eighteenth-century constructions of charity.

The intersection of the economy argument and consumer charity in the *Millenium Hall* ladies' combination donation-expenses epitomizes charity's complicated place in eighteenth-century culture, in particular when extended by women. A source of pride and anxiety, a naturally appropriate activity for polite women harnessed as a manager of their time and money, charity and the period discourse about it respond to the contemporary fear of women's control of money, allowing us to see some of the disguised forms this fear could take. As we have seen, the economy argument, while asserting that women can magically make money from nothing by suppressing luxury or self-interested purchases, and the consumer charity model, which seeks to combine charity and consumption, are potentially problematic. At the core, each strand of advice responds to a continuing uneasiness with women's control of money, even when this money is apparently directed appropriately toward charity and away from the self. By urging economy either in terms of preemptive budgeting or carefully-aimed consumption, then, charitable discourse participates in society's attempts to address its anxiety over women's participation in the growing consumer culture. *Cecilia* and *Millenium Hall,* however, suggest we should focus not merely on the presence of these regulatory attempts, but on the significance of the attempts' very existence. Their existence directs us to continue to rethink the rigidity of domestic ideology in the eighteenth century, the economy argument's and consumer charity's proposed regulations being evidence not necessarily of restriction but of the presence of significant opportunities for public action.

NOTES

1. Henry Fielding, *The Covent-Garden Journal and A Plan of the Universal Register-Office*, ed. Bertrand A. Goldgar (Middletown, Conn.: Wesleyan University Press, 1988), 247. Other examples include: Thomas Francklin, *A Sermon Preached in the Chapel of the Asylum for Female Orphans, at the Anniversary Meeting of the Guardians, On Monday the Sixteenth of May, 1768* (London, 1768), 5; and Hannah More, *Estimate of the Religion of the Fashionable World,* in vol. 5 of *The Works of Hannah More* (New York: Harper & Bros., 1835), 220.

2. In the *Covent-Garden Journal* issue cited above, Fielding expresses concern about the ways charity is expressed (see 247). See also Lady Sara Pennington, *A Mother's Advice to her Absent Daughters* (1817; reprint, New York: Garland Publishing, 1986), 88.

3. Beilby Porteus, *A Sermon Preached in the Chapel of the Asylum for Female Orphans, at the Anniversary Meeting of the Guardians of that Charity, May 19, 1773* (London, [1773]), 3.

4. Ken Jackson, "Bedlam, *The Changeling, The Pilgrim* and the Protestant Critique of Catholic Good Works," *Philological Quarterly* 74 (1995): 378.

5. Hester Chapone, *Letters on the Improvement of the Mind, Addressed to a Young Lady* (a new edition; London, 1793), 160-61; and Mary Wollstonecraft, *Original Stories from Real Life: with Conversations Calculated to Regulate the Affections and Form the Mind to Truth and Goodness,* in vol. 4 of *The Works of Mary Wollstonecraft*, ed. Janet Todd and Marilyn Butler (London: William Pickering, 1989), 445, Todd and Butler's emendations.

6. Wetenhall Wilkes, *A Letter of Genteel and Moral Advice to a Young Lady* (6th ed.; London, 1753), 179; Thomas Gisborne, *An Enquiry into the Duties of the Female Sex* (1st American ed.; New York, 1820), 187. For more on the assignment of household economy to women, see Amanda Vickery, *The Gentleman's Daughter: Women's Lives in Georgian England* (New Haven: Yale Univ. Press, 1998), 127-60 passim.

7. Frances Burney, *Brief Reflections Relative to the Emigrant French Clergy* (reprinted with *Considerations on Religious and Public Education* by Hannah More, ed. Claudia Johnson [Los Angeles: Augustan Reprint Society, 1990]), 26; Wilkes, 89. Suppression is at times recommended to men: for example, the sermonist Francklin pleads for the imprisoned debtor by reminding his listeners of their freedom and asking, "shall we not willingly abridge ourselves of any little superfluous sensual gratification to promote a fellow-creature's freedom, to communicate that pleasure which we possess, to impart that happiness which we ourselves enjoy[?]" (*A Sermon Preached at the Chapel in Great Queen-Street, Lincoln's-Inn-Fields, On Sunday, March 20, 1774, for the Benefit of Unfortunate Persons confined for Small Debts* [London, 1774], 11; see also Richard Allestree, *The Whole Duty of Man: Necessary for all Families* [London, 1687], 357). Notably, Francklin leaves the type of "superfluous sensual gratification" unspecified—something markedly different from what is presented to women.

8. Sarah Trimmer, *The Oeconomy of Charity; Or, an Address to Ladies Concerning Sunday-Schools; the Establishment of Schools of Industry under Female Inspection; and the Distribution of Voluntary Benefactions* (Dublin, 1787), 124-25.

9. Hannah More, "Prefatory Address to the Ladies, &c. of Great Britain and Ireland, in behalf of the French Emigrant Clergy," in *Considerations on Religious and Public Education* (reprinted with Frances Burney's *Brief Reflections Relative to the Emigrant French Clergy*, ed. Claudia Johnson [Los Angeles: Augustan Reprint Society, 1990]), 4. The More quotations in the following paragraph are also from this page.

10. Gisborne, 87-88; Wollstonecraft, 445.

11. Gisborne, 88; Hannah More, *Coelebs in Search of a Wife* (1808-09;

reprint, introd. Mary Waldron, Bristol: Thoemmes Press, 1995), 29-30.

12. Donna T. Andrew, *Philanthropy and Police: London Charity in the Eighteenth Century* (Princeton: Princeton Univ. Press, 1989), 144.

13. Amanda Vickery, "Women and the World of Goods: A Lancashire Consumer and Her Possessions, 1751-81," in *Consumption and the World of Goods*, ed. John Brewer and Roy Porter (New York: Routledge, 1993), 274, 279, original italics. While Vickery and other scholars have criticized elements of his argument, Neil McKendrick remains the leading advocate of the eighteenth century's having had a "consumer revolution" (Neil McKendrick, John Brewer and J.H. Plumb, *The Birth of a Consumer Society: The Commercialization of Eighteenth-Century England* [Bloomington: Indiana Univ. Press, 1982]).

14. Susan Staves, *Married Women's Separate Property in England, 1660-1833* (Cambridge: Harvard Univ. Press, 1990), 169-70; Margot Finn, "Women, Consumption and Coverture in England, *c.* 1760-1860," *The Historical Journal* 39 (1996): 703.

15. Frances Burney, *Cecilia, or Memoirs of an Heiress* (1782; reprint, ed. Peter Sabor and Margaret Anne Doody, New York: Oxford Univ. Press, 1988), 54-55. Subsequent citations to this text will be given parenthetically.

16. Chapone, 161.

17. Amy Froide, "Marital Status as a Category of Difference: Singlewomen and Widows in Early Modern England," in *Singlewomen in the European Past, 1250-1800*, ed. Judith M. Bennett and Amy M. Froide (Philadelphia: Univ. of Pennsylvania Press, 1999), 237.

18. Lynne Vallone, *Disciplines of Virtue: Girls' Culture in the Eighteenth and Nineteenth Centuries* (New Haven: Yale Univ. Press, 1995), 22.

19. For one example of this argument, see Henry Fielding, *A Proposal for Making an Effectual Provision for the Poor*, in vol. 13 of *The Complete Works of Henry Fielding, Esq.* (New York: Barnes and Noble, 1967), 138.

20. Gisborne, 212-13.

21. Joseph Massie, *A Plan for the Establishment of Charity-Houses for Exposed or Deserted Women and Girls, and for Penitent Prostitutes* (London, 1758), 9, 12.

22. Sarah Scott, *Millenium Hall* (1762; reprint, ed. Gary Kelly, Peterborough, Ontario: Broadview Press, 1994), 76. Subsequent citations to this text will be given parenthetically.

"One Soul, tho' not one Soyl"? International Protestantism and Ecumenism at the Beginning of the Eighteenth Century*

BRIJRAJ SINGH

The recent decision of the Lutheran Church in the United States to enter into communion with the Episcopalians, which is being regarded, rightly, as a great success of the ecumenical movement among Protestant churches, may be a good reason for narrating the little remembered story of the close collaboration that developed in the early years of the eighteenth century between the Pietist wing of the Lutherans in Germany and the Church of England in Britain, and involved certain members of the American Puritan movement and missionaries in India as well. Indeed, what happened between roughly 1707 and 1717 was not only ecumenical in nature but also international in scope; and when the difficulties of maintaining international contacts nearly three hundred years ago are taken into account, as is the fact that the personages involved in the events were as unlikely and, in some cases, prickly a group of individuals as ever collaborated in a common cause, the events that my paper tries to narrate may well appear to have been no less momentous than the recent communion of churches.

*An earlier and shorter version of this essay appeared in *Topic 51 - A Journal of the Liberal Arts,* Washington and Jefferson College, Washington, PA. 2001

There are four protagonists in the story, the Rev. Cotton Mather (1663-1728), Anton Wilhelm Boehm (1673-1722), August Hermann Francke (1663-1727), and Bartholomaeus Ziegenbalg (1683 ?-1719). Each has been the subject of several studies. But because these studies have focused on individuals, the wide scope and international aims of an ecumenical Protestantism appear only in a glimmering, fitful fashion: each study throws certain details into heightened relief, but a sense of the whole remains shadowy. Perhaps the only scholar to address the relationship of the four figures and their collaborative endeavors towards the establishment of an ecumenical Protestantism is Ernst Benz. But his essay "Pietist and Puritan Sources of Early Protestant World Missions," though erudite and compendious, is also disorganized, and some of the bibliographical details are unhelpful.[1] It is my hope that my paper will present the story more clearly and cogently than has yet been done and also incorporate the latest findings.

My story starts in Boston, where Cotton Mather, the Puritan leader, was minister of the Second Congregational Church. Hot headed, polemical, immoderate and dictatorial, he had scant use for the Church of England. He thought that with its bishops and archbishops it was little better than Papist, and abhorred its attitude towards Dissenters.[2] If he did not write the whole of *A Brief Discourse Concerning the Unlawfulness of Common Prayer Worship* (1686)—and his bibliographer Thomas James Holmes thinks he might have[3]—he certainly penned the introduction and helped to print it, albeit anonymously. The work castigated Anglican practices such as the use of the Book of Common Prayer in church services and kissing the Bible while taking oaths. *A Brief Discourse* caused a warrant to be issued against him, which he saw as further proof of persecution by the Church of England.[4] His antipathy extended to the newly-founded (1701) Society for the Propagation of the Gospel (hereafter SPG), not only because its leadership consisted largely of the British Episcopate, but also because he suspected it of trying to wean Harvard men away from Congregationalism to Anglicanism, and in 1716 he derisively labeled it the Society for the Molestation of the Gospel in Foreign Parts.[5] Richard F. Lovelace, a recent scholar of Mather's religious thought, believes that this hostility extended to another Anglican society in Britain, the Society for Promoting Christian Knowledge or SPCK, which was founded in 1699.[6] However, though both the SPG and SPCK were firmly within the Anglican fold, they were different in several important respects. The SPCK had fewer bishops as members and was more lay-controlled. It was also, thanks in large part to the influence of Boehm, one of its important members, more tolerant of Dissent and more international in outlook.[7] Mather seems to have sensed this difference, for he was willing to maintain an intermittent correspondence with its secretary, the New England-born Henry Newman, who in turn introduced him to Boehm.[8]

Boehm, German by birth and Lutheran by persuasion, was educated at the University of Halle before coming to England in 1701 as a schoolteacher. According to the *Dictionary of National Biography*, he became proficient in English and the following year was appointed as assistant chaplain in the Royal Chapel of Prince George of Denmark, the Lutheran Consort of Queen Anne. The reason given is that George wanted to incorporate the Book of Common Prayer in his chapel services, but the Lutheran chaplain he had brought along with him from Denmark when he moved to England after marriage with Anne was not well versed in English. It was this chaplain, J.W. Mecken, who suggested that Boehm be appointed his assistant. After the Prince's death in 1708 the arrangement was continued, and no alteration was made on the accession of George I.

However, recently Daniel Brunner has provided further details and some corrections to this account. According to him, Mecken fell out with George when the latter twice took communion in the Church of England. George did so in order to qualify himself to execute the functions he had as Royal Consort. But Mecken found himself unable to give communion to him after he had received it at the hands of Anglicans. So he quit, and Boehm was tapped as his successor. Boehm asked George whether he wanted a Lutheran or Anglican preacher, and George answered that he wanted a Lutheran who would, however, allow him to commune "extraordinarily" in the Church of England. Boehm did not know quite how to react, but a solution was soon reached: he was retained as the preacher in the Royal Chapel, and a second Lutheran position was created just for the administration of the Sacraments.[9]

In 1705 Boehm published *Pietas Hallensis*, which was an English translation of a German work published in 1701, *Die Fussstapfen des noch lebenden und waltenden liebreichen und getreuen Gottes* by August Hermann Francke. Francke, a professor of theology at Halle where he had been one of Boehm's teachers, was one of the most important religious figures of his age and an acknowledged leader of German Pietism. Pietism was misunderstood in England at the time and regarded warily. It was seen as being little more than Quakerism and as preaching enthusiasm and schisms, both of which notions were anathema to a country that had recently undergone religious upheavals and was trying to establish religion on an even keel. Boehm hoped that his translation, and especially the preface, which gave the history of Pietism in Germany, would help to correct these misunderstandings and make Francke's work better known in England. In 1707 the preface was expanded and given its own title page when it was appended to the second edition of *Pietas Hallensis*.[10]

Boehm started his account with Johannes Arndt (1555-1621), author of four volumes of *Wahre Christentum*, or *True Christianity,* which he (Boehm) was to translate into English in 1712. In his time Arndt was known for earnest and simple sermons, and his followers made much of his idea that man could not be said to be saved simply because Christ had died on the Cross. True salvation required repentance, renewal, and faith, for all of which constant prayer and spiritual conversion were needed. Only then could the individual hope to be united with God in a one-to-one relationship. Arndt may have had a mystical element to his thinking; however, he saw the outcome of this union in intensely practical terms as being a life lived on a higher moral plane and issuing in acts of love and charity.[11]

The Arndtian insistence on practical piety was further developed by Philipp Jacob Spener (1635-1705). Spener's thinking is Arndtian and emphasizes that the essence of Christianity is a life of personal relationship with God lived according to His will. Indeed, his most famous book *Pia Desideria (Pious Desires*), published in 1675, was originally written as a preface to Arndt's *Postil*. It is not, then, for the originality of his thought that he is distinguished. His distinction lies partly in his practical genius, for he was responsible for setting up conventicles or little prayer groups which were to have great impact on a later generation of Pietists like Francke. But perhaps his greatest contribution to Pietiesm came through the power and patronage he was able to exercise after 1691 in behalf of his followers, for in that year he moved to Berlin as the court preacher at the invitation of Friedrich III, the Elector of Brandenburg who later became Emperor Friedrich I of Prussia, and was able to make his will prevail in all matters related to religious affairs.[12] One of his earliest acts of patronage also proved to be one of the most significant: at his behest August Hermann Francke, who had recently been barred from lecturing on theology at Leipzig and banished from Erfurt on account of his religious beliefs, was appointed as professor of Oriental Languages at the newly founded university in Halle.[13]

Francke became the most important German Pietist of the eighteenth century, and Boehm rightly focused on him. Born in a well-to-do family, Francke knew from his earliest years that he wanted a career in the church. He received a conventional education, and all seemed to be going well till he was asked to preach one Sunday in 1687 in the town of Luneburg. The feeling came to him that he did not really believe in anything that he was going to preach about. Overwhelmed, he began to pray, and suddenly he was filled with God's grace and experienced a spiritual conversion.[14] From this time forth he often talked and wrote of his experience and took to propounding the view that a Christian needed to have a personal and powerful sense of his own sinfulness and then, following a period of prayer and repentance, the experience of being flooded with the Holy Spirit before he could be saved. But once saved, he could not but engage in social work and make a commitment to the welfare of humanity.

These views form the foundation of his Pietist thought. He elaborated on them in various sermons and other writings throughout his career, but never changed them. In a sermon entitled "On Saving Faith" he insists, as Luther did, that justification is possible only through faith, not works. However, the individual who is so justified never lets go an opportunity of doing good. Thus justification through faith inevitably results in the performance of deeds which are acceptable to God.[15] In *Scriptural Rules of Life*, originally composed as part of his private devotions in 1689 around the same time that he spent two months with Spener in Leipzig, and *Scriptural and Basic Instruction to True Christianity*, Francke not only defines what he considers to be proper Christian conduct (being ever mindful of God, avoiding lies, etc.), but also social conduct appropriate to a Pietist (e.g. not interrupting others, avoiding improper facial gestures).[16] The emphasis is throughout upon self-examination and self-knowledge. Elsewhere he defines a Pietist as a person who "take[s] to heart the word of God, acknowledge[s] the saving grace of God…[denies] ungodliness and worldly lusts, and live[s] soberly, righteously and godly in the present world."[17]

Summarized thus, Francke's Pietism cannot be said to be in any way opposed to the tenets of the orthodox Lutheran Church. But it angered many orthodox divines. Orthodox faith at this time had come to mean assent to certain rationally ordered statements about Christianity made in acceptable words and phrases. Any deviation from this phraseology was viewed with suspicion. Moreover, it was characterized by a social insensitivity. The doctrine of justification by faith was held to the exclusion of belief in justification by works since such justification was seen as characteristic of Roman Catholic belief.[18] Therefore Francke's insistence upon individual conversion, upon emotion and upon the experience of grace, which perforce required each individual to find his own words for describing it, and upon a Christian life issuing in action, was viewed with suspicion by the orthodox and his teachings regarded as schismatic. Francke himself rejected the charge of being schismatic and told his accusers, "I desire no new religion, but a new heart."[19] He shared the basic tenets of Lutheran orthodoxy, though he did not see the Christian life as the orthodox did. Religion no longer meant a passive assent to doctrine. The individual's spiritual conversion, which not only brought him into a new, living relationship with God, but also made him take responsibility for his actions and direct them towards a social good, became central to his thought. F. Ernest Stoeffler, a historian of eighteenth-century German Pietiesm, has summarized this aspect well: "Lives changed, a church renewed, a nation reformed, a world evangelized—these were the great objectives" that Francke set for himself and the Pietists.[20] And again, Francke marks a shift from "'true' doctrine to right action, from theological speculation to devotional earnestness...from an intellectualized to an experiential approach to the Christian faith, from systematic theology to biblical exposition, from that which God has done in history to that which he wants to do in every human being now, from passive reliance on God's initiative to human responsibility."[21]

The Pietists who gathered at Halle under Francke's tutelage often used words like "illumination," "spiritual growth," and "living faith" instead of the Latinized, abstract and philosophical language of orthodox divines, and maintained that to be a Christian means to become a new man and develop a new pattern of life. Insistence was placed upon a close association between theology and the leading of a moral life, one of whose qualities was seen as the furtherance of social action.[22] However, it was not for these theological positions that Pietism gained an international reputation as for the practical and charitable works that Francke undertook. No city needed them more than Halle and the neighboring Glaucha, where he served as pastor of St. George's Church. To the ravages of the Thirty Years' War had been added the devastation of the plague in 1682 and the fires of 1683 and 84. Drunkenness was rife, illiteracy rampant, social hierarchies extremely rigid. It was taken for granted that the only way in which the poor could survive was by begging and robbing, and of the approximately 200 houses in Glaucha, 37 were brothels.[23] On discovering how totally ignorant of the Scriptures the poor were, Francke decided to open a school for indigent children in his house. Subscriptions poured in, and his venture grew till new buildings were needed, and he erected an orphanage as well. The success was not entirely unrelated to the support he had from Spener and the latter's influence over Friedrich of Prussia. But there is no denying that in running his establishments Francke showed himself as a man of great organizational genius and vision. While in the rest of Europe orphanages were regarded as little more than a source for cheap child labor, and the inhabitants lived with vagabonds and criminals, Francke's orphanage catered to the child's whole being, the physical, mental, and spiritual. He provided separate beds for his charges, a luxury unheard of in eighteenth-century orphanages, fed them *gratis*, taught girls as well as boys German poetry, letter writing, history, geography, mathematics, speech and declamation, gave regular instruction in the Bible, catechized them, and apprenticed them all to a trade, whether printing or book binding or pharmacy work. If a child proved talented, he was taught Latin, Greek, theology, and prepared for the university. In return, each beneficiary had to contribute to the establishment, whether by teaching, or taking care of others, or working in the trade he had been taught. In addition, Francke also encouraged students from other countries to come to Halle for studies. As his reputation spread, students began to come from Russia, Sweden, Czechoslovakia, Hungary, Poland, Slovenia and Britain, and on returning to their countries, usually with a degree in theology, propagated his Pietist thought and tried to carry on his social reforms. At his death his institutions had 134 orphan children looked after by ten male and female overseers, 2207 scholars in various schools taught by 175 teachers, free dinner was provided to 148 and free supper to 212 poor students, and an additional 255 students were fed from funds of the orphan house.[24] No other charitable venture had hitherto functioned on such a vast scale.

Another significant practical achievement of Francke was in the area of making cheap copies of the Bible available to the masses. Under his inspiration Carl Hildebrand von Canstein set up the Canstein Bible House in Halle in 1710. By using a new innovation in printing, that of not breaking up type after an edition was printed, the establishment was able to make available at very affordable prices two million Bibles and one million New Testaments.[25] Never before had the average German been able to keep the Bible in his home for regular study.

His successes convinced Francke that a new era had dawned in which God's providence would act more powerfully than ever before. As he told his auditors in a lecture, "[t]he Almighty cannot be sufficiently magnified for the great mercy he has manifested during the last few years. Many thousand souls have been awakened to repentance. Nay, even many thousand preachers have been roused to manifest more earnestness in their office than they previously evinced."[26] This is the message motivating a detailed account of his activities that he published as *Fussstapfen* in 1701 and which Boehm translated under the title *Pietas Hallensis* in 1705.

In publishing his translation Boehm hoped that Francke's work would become better known in England and the Anglican Church would shed its prejudice against Pietism. This hope came to pass. So well was the translation received that the SPCK asked Boehm to bring out an abridged version, which appeared in 1706 under the title *An Abstract of the Marvellous Footsteps of Divine Providence*. A second edition of this abridgement appeared in 1707 with the title of *Pietas Hallensis*. Part II of *Pietas* was published in 1710 and Part III in 1716. In each new edition the progress of the work at Halle was updated. The 1716 edition also contained Boehm's English translation of Francke's letter to Cotton Mather, about which we shall have more to say presently.[27] The SPCK purchased 500 copies of this edition for distribution among its correspondents. One consequence of the success of Boehm's translation was that British munificence to Halle increased. Prince George gifted Halle a thousand pounds in 1706; later, Queen Anne settled sixty pounds per annum to support an "English" table at Halle so that twelve English scholars could learn German and help Francke with the translation of English texts into German. The 1716 edition of *Pietas Hallensis* carries Francke's reference to the English House or Institute which British financial aid made possible.[28]

Boehm was gratified by the success of his translation; and since he had recently started correspondence with Cotton Mather, he sent the latter a copy of *Pietas Hallensis* shortly after it appeared in 1705.[29]

The effect on Mather was electric. He had thought that American Protestantism, and especially Puritanism, represented the fulfillment of the Reformation and the establishment of a pure religion, movement towards which had stopped in Europe shortly after Luther. In Francke he was discovering that not only did the spirit of the Reformation continue to prevail at Halle but also that there were significant similarities between the Puritanism he represented and the Pietism of Germany. Though they had different roots, both were attempts to create a new piety, a practical Christian lifestyle on Lutheran foundations. Richard F. Lovelace, who has studied connections between the two movements, points out that in both a spiritual re-birth was important because it was seen to mark the beginning of Christ's grace in the individual. This insistence on conversion distinguished Puritanism as well as Pietism from the orthodox Lutheran view that it was the sacrament of Baptism that vouchsafed salvation to the baptized through the imputation of Christ's righteousness. Both Pietism and Puritanism stressed frequent and spontaneous prayer as a way of nourishing the spirit and strengthening a sense of personal communion with God. Both were more emotional and experiential than established churches, whether the Church of England or the Reformed Lutheran Church. Both, in emphasizing the need for the individual to attain what Francke called "the closest communion with God," stressed abstinence from the pleasures of this world and frowned on fashionable dress, good food, dancing, alcohol and tobacco. Both were millenarian in the sense that they felt the spirit of God operating powerfully through them and in their midst, and leading to a better future. Indeed, Mather expected the millennium to be realized shortly, though he hedged about the exact date. Francke, too, saw the present as marking a new beginning when the church was starting to grow and the Gospel to spread, though unlike Mather he did not think that the thousand years of peace were imminent.[30]

Above all, both were ecumenical. Boehm was only echoing a Franckean sentiment when he said, in his translation of Arndt, that "[t]here will be a Time, when the Church of Christ will come up from the Wilderness of various Sects, Parties, Nations, Languages, Forms, and Ways of Worship…leaning upon her Beloved."[31] Francke's message linked Germany together with like-minded people in Scandinavia, Poland, Czechoslovakia, Russia, Britain, and India. Mather, too, for all his intemperateness, preached church unity. In several writings, notably *Malachi*, he tried to reduce the complexities of Christianity to three simple principles to which all rational men, wherever they lived or whatever denomination they belonged to, could give assent, and which, if followed, would lead to lives of piety: obedience to one God who subsists in the Trinity, Christ being the only redeemer, and the "Golden Rule" to love our neighbor and do to others that which we would have them do to us.[32] Indeed, he prided himself that church unity had progressed further in America than anywhere in Europe, and told Francke, more idealistically than realistically, that in New England churches whoever was united in Christ was admitted to communion in other churches without restriction, so that Calvinists could take communion with Lutherans, Presbyterians with Episcopalians.[33] Of course, this ecumenism did not extend to the Roman Catholics.

Pietas Hallensis brought another revelation to Mather. Always practical, and valuing practical action, he decided, around 1710, consciously to cultivate the Christian virtue of doing good as an antidote to his sharp tongue and quick temper. Boehm's 1705 translation of Francke showed him that the cultivation of this virtue had progressed far in Germany, and the 1712 translation of Arndt further confirmed this view. Mather developed an admiration for the Pietists' down-to-earth social and educational program, particularly as it related to the running of charity schools, relieving the suffering of the poor, and training for the priesthood. In *Bonifacius* he praised these aspects of Francke's work, especially the fact that the seminary at Halle not only offered "a most polite education" but also ensured that those who trained there would have their "souls … fired with the *fear* of God, and the *love* of Christ, and a *zeal* to do good, and a *resolution* to bear poverty, and obloquy, and all sorts of temptations, in the service of our holy religion."[34] And he suggested that rich New Englanders should direct their charity to similar ends and help Francke's work in Germany.[35]

From around this date glowing references to Francke and to the work of the Halle orphanage become common in his diaries. Kuno Francke's essay entitled "Cotton Mather and August Hermann Francke" offers a detailed study of these diary references from the first one dated 9 December, 1709, to the last one of 25 June, 1724.[36] Reading the essay it becomes obvious that Mather sensed a spiritual affinity with Francke from the very beginning. As he put it in his first entry, "My intention was, to lodge these Treatises [*The Heavenly Conversation* and *Dust and Ashes*] in ye Hands of many Ministers, throughout ye Country. I represented ye Methods of *piety* proposed in these Essayes, as being the true American *pietism*. I shall also endeavour to send these things unto Dr. Franckius, in Saxony."[37] By 1711 he is noting his desire to send gold to support the Halle orphanage. On 7 March, 1716 he says that his correspondence with Glaucha has been one of the blessings of his life and has brought him a measure of fame and greatness. On 2 August, 1716 he calls Francke "incomparable" and declares that in his work in Germany Christ Himself has preached a living sermon. Twice in October 1716, on the 9th and again on the 16th, he announces his decision to read accounts of the Halle orphanage out aloud to his family. On 15 May, 1718, and again on 13 July of that year, he sends more money to Halle. His last entry is about his decision to write to Francke later that week.[38]

As we read through these diary entries, it becomes clear that when Mather first encountered Francke's work through Boehm's translation, he thought that since his own works preached more or less the same course of conduct as was being taught by Francke, were his works to be translated into German, they would help strengthen Pietism there. It was in that spirit that he decided to send his writings to Francke. But after he read Boehm's 1712 translation of Johannes Arndt's *True Christianity* as well as other works of Francke, also translated by Boehm, he came to see that American Puritanism had some catching up to do with German Pietism. The American Puritan may have been a redeemed individual who had entered into true communion with God and led a virtuous and simple life. But there was nothing that he had been able to create in America that equaled Francke's work. It was, therefore, in a spirit of some humility that Mather addressed his first letter to Francke on 28 May, 1711; and when he said in it that reports of the wonder that is the orphanage in Halle have reached the remotest of the West Indies (i.e. America) like a fragrant odor across the oceans and have excited religious fervor there, the floweriness of the language must not lead us to treat the sentiment as insincere.

The letter never reached its destination, as Francke informed Mather in his first and only letter to him of 19 December, 1714. However, when Mather wrote to Francke for the second time, on 10 January, 1712, he enclosed a copy of his first letter, and that copy is preserved in the Franckesche Stiftungen in Halle. It was published in Kuno Francke's essay entitled "The Beginning of Cotton Mather's Correspondence with August Hermann Francke."[39] Mather's letter is written in Latin since Francke knew no English and Mather no German, and is short. The style is florid, the salutation exaggerated. Francke is called a man celebrated for learning throughout the world, and Mather tells him that the "wonder" ("Mirabilis") of Francke's orphanage is not unknown in America. He encloses money for Francke's charitable works and hopes that the notion of America as an ignorant land will be dispelled in Europe.

Besides the letters of 28 May, 1711, and 10 January, 1712, Mather addressed a third letter to Francke sometime in 1717. Although it is preserved in the Franckesche Stiftungen, it has never been published, though extracts have appeared in Ernst Benz's two essays entitled "Pietist and Puritan Sources of Early Protestant World Missions (Cotton Mather and A.H. Francke)," and "Ecumenical Relations between Boston Puritanism and German Pietism Cotton Mather and August Hermann Francke." In it Mather first takes issue with those who see America as the "outer darkness" of Matthew into which the worthless servant is cast. For, he says, not only is the spirit of "true and original Christianity" more prevalent there, but a more inclusive ecumenical spirit prevails than can be found in Europe.[40] He then goes on to talk about the mission work that is going on among the native population, and finally moves on to discourse about what he calls the fourteen principles of the Eternal Gospel or *Evangelium Aeternum*. Benz maintains that the concept of the *Evangelium Aeternum* is at least as old as the thirteenth century and may be traced to Joachim of Fiore. Certainly it seems to have appealed to John Eliot, the first missionary to work with native Americans and whom Mather mentions to Francke. Mather reduces these fourteen principles to what he regards as the one cardinal principle of all Christianity: the so-called Golden Rule of doing unto others as you would have them do unto you.[41] This precept enables true piety to be put into the practice of daily life.

In corresponding with Halle, Mather used Boehm as the intermediary since there was no direct shipping between Boston and Germany in the early decades of the eighteenth century and all correspondence had to be routed through London. Thomas James Holmes's bibliography of Mather contains only one reference to Boehm, when Mather, writing to Henry Newman, the Secretary of the SPCK on 7 September, 1717 (actually 1719) speaks of "dear Mr. Boehm" (Holmes II, 554).[42] But there seems to have been frequent contact between Mather and Boehm. Boehm was instructed to read all of Mather's letters to foreign correspondents and make copies before forwarding them to their addressees. Similarly, all foreign correspondents writing to Mather directed their letters through Boehm, and he was instructed to read and make copies of them as well. It was through Boehm that Mather received the only letter that Francke ever addressed to him, and on 2 October, 1715 Mather thanked Boehm and also sent him several religious tracts for his as well as Francke's use.[43]

Francke's letter to Mather of 19 December, 1714, is more a pamphlet than a letter. In Part III of *Pietis Hallensis*, where Boehm published a translation from German, the work runs into sixty duodecimo pages.[44] For all its length, it has but one personal note. Francke says that he has, in his possession, a copy of a letter written on 12 July 1682 by one "Crescentius" Mather to John Leusden of Utrecht about the work that John Eliot had done among the Algonquin, and surmises that this "Crescentius" was a relative of Cotton Mather.[45] (Actually, Crescentius is Francke's Latin translation of Increase, the name of Cotton Mather's father). For the rest, the letter is a detailed account of Francke's work in Halle and of the missionaries Heinrich Plutschau and Bartholomaeus Ziegenbalg in Tranquebar in south India. We shall consider the Tranquebar mission in more detail later in this paper. In his account of his schools and orphanage, Francke takes some pains to establish his British connections. Thus he says that twelve students are maintained in his school on money allotted by Queen Anne. They teach English, learn German, and translate English books into German, so that they are referred to as the English Table. They lodge together in rooms in a new building, with the result that those rooms are known as the English house. There are six hundred children and eighty six teachers in the German school, over three hundred pupils in the Latin school, and several foreign students from Holland, Switzerland, Hungary, Sweden and Poland. In addition, there is a theological seminary for students training to be teachers and priests. Most of the scholars receive a free education, and those who cannot afford meals are fed free of cost. There are common dining facilities for all males; the females eat separately.

Francke mentions other educational institutions with which he is associated: the *Paedagogium Regium*, which teaches languages, geometry, natural philosophy, metaphysics, ethics, genealogy, botany, anatomy, astronomy, and other useful sciences, and the *Gynaeceum*, where girls are educated at their parents' expense in handwriting, French, arithmetic, and other subjects appropriate to their sex. He refers to his work with Carl Hildebrand von Canstein in making cheap Bibles available, and says that by typesetting whole pages and not breaking up type after an edition has been pulled off the press, they have been able to ensure great accuracy and speed. In thirty months 38,000 copies of the New Testament have been printed, and each unbound copy is sold for four pence, which is one-sixty third of a British pound. Twenty British shillings may buy thirteen copies of the larger sized or twenty of the smaller sized copies of the entire Bible.

Francke takes pride in describing the political support his work has won in the highest circles. He describes a visit that emperor Friedrich William of Prussia paid to Halle. He had been prejudiced against Francke by some of his advisors, but after inspecting the institutions that Francke was running, expressed himself satisfied and even increased the financial support that his father Friedrich had settled upon Francke's projects.[46]

Mather received the letter early in 1715 and was truly pleased that Francke had "admitted us Obscure *Americans* into correspondencies."[47] Believing that news of Francke's work would "very much" enlarge the Americans' "*Opportunities to do Good in the world*," he lost no time in publishing a translation or summary of large portions, together with his own commentary, under the title *Nuncia Bona e Terra Longinqua. A Brief Account of Some Good and Great Things Adoing for the Kingdom of God in the Midst of Europe Communicated to——from Cotton Mather, D.D. & F.R.S.*[48] Not the least of his motives in publishing this work was his hope that it would further an ecumenical spirit. As he put it, "something of the *Communion of Saints* may be this way expressed in *this Country*, and at so vast a Distance from those Dear Servants of God."[49]

The full title of *Nuncia Bona* suggests that the good news from Europe is being communicated *by* rather than *to* Mather. Perhaps this is what led Kuno Francke to say that Mather "wanted to appear as the first to spread [the news of Francke's work]...and he wanted to draw a reflection of the glory...upon himself," and again, that there "is no doubt that a certain vanity is one of the reasons why Cotton Mather substituted his own name [in place of Francke's] as the sender."[50] But the work itself makes it clear that Mather is only the translator, though obviously worthy enough to be the recipient of "very Copious Letters from that Admirable and Illustrious Person, Professor Franckius." More intriguing is the fact that though he includes the smallest detail in connection with Francke's orphanage in Halle, he leaves out altogether the large section in Francke's letter dealing with the Tranquebar mission.

Partly to make up for this lack, and partly also perhaps in order to correct any wrong impression about authorship that a reader might receive from merely looking at the title of Mather's work, Boehm published, the following year, a translation of Francke's entire letter as a prefix to Part III of *Pietas Hallensis*.[51] Kuno Francke throws doubt on the accuracy of Boehm's text, claiming that it is a "rather free and not very correct… translation."[52] He offers his own version as the more authentic. But amazingly, he leaves out from Francke's letter large chunks that deal with Ziegenbalg's work, and includes only those portions that deal with things American and Francke's own activities. For this reason Boehm's text remains the best available version we have.

The text in its entirety as presented by Boehm reveals, more clearly than Mather's or Kuno Francke's extracts, August Hermann Francke's international vision. He is fully cognizant of the connections between himself, Britain and America, and can see better perhaps than any other man at the time how similar activities within the Protestant churches are being undertaken in Scandinavia, Poland, Hungary, and various other countries. And his account of Ziegenbalg and the Tranquebar mission and of the cooperation that began to develop between the SPCK in England, the missionaries in Tranquebar, and their headquarters in Halle in the second decade of the eighteenth century, is a significant record of internationalism and ecumenism.

The honor of being the first Protestant missionary anywhere in the world must perhaps go to John Eliot (1604-1690) who worked with the Algonquin and published his translation of the Bible into the Natick language in 1663. However, he did not have to travel abroad to fulfill his mission, nor did he spend his entire life among the native Americans. Insofar as we understand a missionary to be a person who not only works with people of another race or culture but also travels abroad to reach them, and lives all his (or her) life in their midst, it is Heinrich Plutschau (1677-1746) and Bartholomaeus Ziegenbalg (1683?-1719), both students of Francke at Halle, who must be regarded as the first Protestant missionaries. Sent to the small Danish possession of Tranquebar on India's south-east coast, about 200 miles south of Madras, they arrived there on July 9, 1706. Plutschau returned to Europe in 1711, but Ziegenbalg, who was only 23 when he arrived in India, spent his entire life there except for one year when he visited Europe. With the exception of medical work, he did all those things which have, since his time, become the hallmarks of missionary endeavor. He preached, converted, built churches, raised money, carried on a voluminous correspondence, learned the local language Tamil, produced the first Tamil dictionary, produced the first Tamil translation of the Bible, set up the first Tamil printing press and printed several works, opened schools, including what was perhaps the first school for girls in India, and wrote accounts of local religious and social customs which are of tremendous anthropological and historical significance today. Another very significant achievement was the fact that he carried on an inter-faith dialogue for many years. At his request several Hindus wrote to him about Hinduism, about India, and about how they viewed the presence of Europeans in their midst. Though some of these views must have been anathema to him, Ziegenbalg faithfully translated these letters into German and published them, and they remain the first as well as the most sustained and articulate expression of non-White, non-Christian, non-European people's views on the subject of European civilization and religion at the very moment when Europe was beginning to found an empire in the east.[53]

However, the account that Francke sent to Mather of Ziegenbalg's activities did not highlight these aspects. Rather, motivated by the ecumenical spirit, he describes in detail the cooperation that has developed between Ziegenbalg and the SPCK in London. What he does not say, though it must have been obvious to Mather, is that this development was, in large part, the result of Boehm's good offices. In 1709 Boehm, who acted as the intermediary and clearing house between the Tranquebar missionaries and their German mentors in Halle, in the same way that he fulfilled this role between Mather and Francke, published an English translation of Ziegenbalg's letters to Germany under the title *Propagation of the Gospel in the East; Being an Account of the Success of Two Danish Missionaries sent to the East Indies for the Conversion of the Heathen in Malabar*. A second volume followed in 1710, and the third in 1711. Boehm dedicated his translation to the Archbishop of Canterbury and the SPG in the hope that that Society would become one of Ziegenbalg's sponsors. But though the SPG sent Ziegenbalg £20, it was unable to provide him with further assistance since its Charter confined its activities to the colonies. Thereupon Boehm approached the SPCK for help. So successful was he that the SPCK not only sent money to Ziegenbalg but also elected him as one of its corresponding members, though he and his church at Tranquebar were Lutheran, not Anglican. Three years later, in 1712, the SPCK bought a printing press and type and shipped it out, at its cost, to Tranquebar together with a printer and 1250 copies of the New Testament in Portuguese specially printed for use in India. In December 1712, when Tamil type was cast in Halle, the SPCK provided hospitality to the three printers from Germany who were to carry it to India, and also secured them passage on a British ship to Madras free of cost.[54] It is the growth of this Tranquebar-London-Halle connection that Francke is at pains to describe in his letter to Mather as an example of the success international ecumenism is enjoying in the Reformed churches.

Mather was familiar with the work of the Tranquebar mission even before he received Francke's letter. Boehm had sent him a copy of his translation of *Propagation of the Gospel in the East* and also of Ziegenbalg's *A Letter to the Rev. Mr. Geo. Lewis*, and a letter exists dated June 6, 1716, acknowledging receipt.[55] But Francke's letter also carried a request. Acknowledging the work that people like Eliot and Increase Mather had done with native Americans, Francke asked Mather to write to Ziegenbalg about proselytizing activities in the American Colonies. Ziegenbalg would be cheered, he believed, if news reached him that people in America were doing the kind of work that he had undertaken in India.

Ziegenbalg did not know English, and therefore Mather's letter of 31 December 1717 is in Latin. It was sent to Boehm for onward transmission to Tranquebar, but unfortunately, by the time it reached its final destination, Ziegenbalg was dead, and therefore the reply was sent by his successor John Ernst Gruendler on 10 December 1719. Mather published his letter in the original Latin as well as in an English translation, Gruendler's reply, extracts from Francke's letter of 1714, and various observations on the spread of the Protestant faith throughout the world, in 1721 under the title *India Christiana. A Discourse Delivered unto the Commissioners for the Propagation of the Gospel among the American Indians which is Accompanied with several Instruments relating to the Glorious Design of Propagating our Holy Religion in the Eastern as well as the Western Indies*.[56] It is obvious from the title that the purpose of the work is to underline the commonality of proselytizing efforts in both India and America by Protestant churches of different denominations. Internationalism as well as ecumenism are the themes.

Much of Mather's letter to Ziegenbalg is taken up by praise of Christianity and laments that Protestants have been much slower than Roman Catholics in proselytizing. But he also commends Ziegenbalg's work and, echoing *Proverbs* 25:25, says that news of his success has been to America like "cool waters to thirsty throats." Finally, he tells Ziegenbalg that he and the Tranquebar mission are "Joined in our Minds, tho' parted by the Waters; One Soul, tho' not One Soyl," and advises him that in India they should underplay doctrinal and denominational differences between Christians that prevail in Europe but should rather teach those elements which bind all Christians. There are three such principles: first, that we must obey the one God who subsists in the Trinity, second, that Christ is the only redeemer and will return to judge us, and finally, that we must love one another and practice piety and sobriety in our lives.[57] These three principles are the same as those which, as was noted earlier, Mather propounded in *Malachi*.

Ziegenbalg would have agreed that it was not for missionaries to teach their new converts about sects and schisms. As he told Boehm, his converts were not taught about any of the doctrinal differences that plagued European churches; indeed, they scarcely ever heard of Luther or Calvin, only of Christ.[58] But it was not he but Gruendler who replied to Mather. Gruendler described Ziegenbalg's death and talked about the work of the mission, the charity schools that were being run, the catechists who were being trained, the books that were being printed. He talked about exhorters, who were specially trained converts responsible for visiting other converts from house to house and praying with and teaching them, and expressed the hope that from this group would emerge Indians who could be ordained and carry on mission work among their own people. He said that one possible candidate had already been identified and put in charge of a church in a village. Clearly the Tranquebar mission showed an interest from the outset in creating an indigenous leadership and rooting the church in native traditions. Then he moved to religious and theological matters. He did not harp on differences between Mather and the Tranquebar mission, insisting that what the mission taught was exactly what Mather had recommended. But it becomes obvious as we read his letter that that was not so, for whereas what Mather wanted the missionaries to preach was not only Christ but also living a moral life, what the Tranquebar missionaries preached was perseverance in Christ. As Gruendler put it, the three principles the missionaries taught were, first, that there is only one true God who has manifested Himself in the Trinity; second, that man was made in God's image which he lost through sin, but God sent his Son to bring us out of sin by repentance, and that through Christ God's image in man can be restored; and third, that only they who accept Christ and, having experienced a spiritual conversion, persevere in their faith, can be saved.[59]

There is clearly a difference between Gruendler's three principles and Mather's. Gruendler does not lay too much emphasis on the ethical aspects of Christianity, which were so central to Mather. Instead, he insists on the need for spiritual conversion, as all Franckean Pietists did, and the need to persevere in the faith. This need grew out of the peculiar situation in India where many people claimed that they were drawn to the teachings of Christianity, but few persevered in their interest to the point of accepting baptism and conversion. Or, if they converted, many would eventually revert to their original religions under social pressure. Ziegenbalg had had this experience with Kanabadi Wattiar, his most promising and talented pupil.[60]

On the other hand, Mather's three principles were developed not only on the basis of his understanding of Christianity but also in part as a result of his American experience, for the emphasis that he put on the ethical precepts of

Christianity grew to an extent out of his dealings with native Americans. Though his acquaintance with them was relatively slight, he felt a repugnance towards them and regarded them as "ravenous howling wolves" who had not only to be Christianized but also "civilized" because they were addicted to drink.[61] In 1689 he exhorted troops not to turn back till they had killed the "lazy drones" and "impudent liars."[62] Preaching to converted native Americans in Martha's Vineyard in 1713, he advised them to recognize their dependence upon the British Crown and accept the white man as a benevolent father figure.[63] And he thought that just as American Indians needed to be instructed in morality, Indians in India needed to be taught how to live decent lives.

But in India the situation was very different. The Tamils had a very highly evolved and complex moral code; indeed, as Francke made it plain to Mather in his letter, the main reason why they refused to convert was because they saw Europeans leading immoral lives and asked why they should exchange their superior moral condition for the inferior one exhibited by Christians. Ziegenbalg recognized this fact fully, and indeed praised the Indians' "quiet, honest and virtuous life."[64] Moreover, he was not a racist, nor did he look down upon Tamil culture. He had no desire to replace it with a European culture or interfere in any way with the traditions and customs of the land. For him, to be Christian did not mean to be any less Indian, and he made every effort to see that Tamil Protestant Christianity remained indigenous.[65] Therefore it was not morality or Western culture and values that he preached. Rather, he had to argue that a moral life, no matter how perfect, was not enough to win salvation; to be saved it was necessary to accept Christ.[66]

The correspondence between Boston and Tranquebar points to the fact that though, in their desire to cooperate, the various churches occasionally underplayed their differences, these differences were real. American Puritanism prided itself on being ecumenical, but it could be fierce in controversy. On the other hand, German Pietists were more irenical, more desirous of avoiding controversy, but they adhered to their theological positions with a tenacity that must have sometimes tried the patience of their partners such as the more accommodating SPCK. It is significant that though Francke referred to British support for his ventures in Halle, and the SPCK's help to Ziegenbalg, in glowing terms, he never corresponded with the SPCK though he was the first foreigner to be elected a corresponding member. This example of aloofness drew a surprised remonstrance from Boehm.[67] But Francke knew that the Anglicans viewed certain key tenets of Pietism, such as its stress on conversion and its experiential and emotional quality, warily. As Brunner says, while for the Church of England the formal, prescriptive ordinances of the Church sanctioned by law and tradition, that is, the Liturgy and the Sacraments, were the primary and only necessary means of expressing devotion, and the Book of Common Prayer central in the act of devotion, the Pietists went in for private devotions and spontaneous and frequent prayer. Pietists saw the insistence on forms as opening the door to a fake or hypocritical piety.[68] Besides, the Lutherans believed in the doctrine of consubstantiation and ubiquity, which, though different from the Roman Catholic doctrine of transubstantiation, appeared to the Anglicans to be one and the same thing. Consubstantiation meant that Christ was seen as being bodily present in the Sacraments. This the Anglicans did not believe. On the other hand, the Anglicans believed in the episcopacy and that only those who were ordained by a bishop in the Apostolic Succession were validly ordained, but the Pietists pooh-poohed this notion.[69]

Boehm, as the intermediary through whom the different churches maintained contact with one another, was intensely aware of these differences. That his vision was characterized by tolerance, ecumenism and internationalism is abundantly clear. Brunner quotes from an unpublished letter to Henry Newman in which Boehm recommends George Lewis, the Anglican chaplain at Madras. The greatest praise that Boehm can give is that Lewis is not of "so narrow a Spirit, as to confine himself to one Nation onely or to one Party in Acts of Love and Charity, but to do Good in a manner most ample and universal, without regarding such petty Ends as use to contract a Man's kindness into that narrow Compass, which in these Days so visibly appears among ye several Denominations of Christians." And he adds: "I believe that a Spirit of universal Love & Benignity is one of the chief and constitutive Characters of a Member of a Society concerned about the Propagation of Christian knowledge: Nay, I can hardly believe a Man to be fit for so large a Design as the Propagation of the Knowledge of CHRIST is, except he be endued with a Mind proportioned to the Thing he enters upon. For how can a narrow Soul but tolerably answer so vast and extensive a Design as the knowledge of Christ is…? May the Lord give us that Wisdom which is without Partiality."[70]

However, for all his unwillingness to confine himself to one nation only or to one denomination or party, Boehm recognized the existence of real barriers. He did not advocate tearing them down, but was at pains to suggest, rather, ways of circumventing them. His strategy is best seen in his handling of two situations that developed in Tranquebar's relations with the SPCK in England: Archbishop Tennison's complaint in 1713 regarding the Catechism printed in Tranquebar, and Gruendler's request, after Ziegenbalg's death, that he

(Gruendler) be recognized as a missionary of the SPCK.

One of the first works that Ziegenbalg printed on his press, which, as we have seen, was a gift of the SPCK, was Luther's Shorter Catechism. He sent copies over to England, and one came to the attention of Tennison, who noticed that there was an omission from the second Commandment of the injunction against false images. It appears in Anglican and Reformed but not Lutheran or Roman Catholic catechisms; and the Archbishop saw this as a continuation of Popish elements in Ziegenbalg's (and Halle's) theology. He brought the matter to the attention of the SPCK, which had no alternative but to ask Ziegenbalg to revise the catechism, though it also sent £ 70 with this request, presumably to signal its own lack of hostility towards the work of the Tranquebar mission. When, a year later, no change had been made to the catechism, Tennison brought up the matter again. Now Boehm had to write to Ziegenbalg and Gruendler. This letter of 8 January, 1714, shows his attempt to steer a middle course between the demands of the Anglican church and the Lutheran creed. Boehm tells the missionaries in India that he has always furthered their interests in England, and it would not be prudent for them to offend the Archbishop of Canterbury. Therefore they should include the injunction against false images in the second Commandment in their next edition of the catechism, but it need not be numbered as such. Instead, all Commandments can be printed as in *Exodus* xx with no numbers, much as he has himself done in the prayer book used in the Royal Chapel. He also urges that the name "Luther" be dropped from the title of their work *Luther's Catechism*, and the missionaries should refrain in future from dealing with theological matters in detail in their correspondence with London, but confine themselves to generalities. At the same time, he insists that they should remain staunchly Lutheran in their own beliefs and practices.[71] In short, Boehm's advice boils down to this: remain Lutheran, but abjure that label. That is, respect inter-denominational barriers, but learn to function around them.

Shortly after Ziegenbalg's death Gruendler, recognizing that though the British valued missionary work in India, they were not likely to send their own missionaries in the foreseeable future, asked Boehm if the SPCK would recognize him as its representative. If it did so, he could extend his mission to Madras which was in British possession. However, Boehm vetoed the suggestion immediately. He knew that for Gruendler to be designated as a missionary working on behalf of the SPCK, he would have to come to England in order that he could be ordained in the Anglican church by a bishop. But if he did so, he would lose Halle's support. Boehm did not want that to happen. Indeed, he did not want Gruendler to move away from the Lutheran faith. He himself, for all his close contacts with the Anglicans, never gave up his Lutheranism or took communion with the Anglicans. Therefore he advised Gruendler to abandon the idea of extending his work to British territories in India, though doing so would mean that the conversion of large numbers of Indians would be delayed.[72]

But though Halle might have withdrawn support from Gruendler had he become Anglican, the SPCK was more liberal and therefore willing to look the other way when questions were raised regarding Anglican support of Lutheran missionaries. John Stevenson, George Lewis's replacement as the Anglican chaplain of Madras, raised questions in 1716 about the fact that Ziegenbalg and Gruendler were using SPCK funds to preach Lutheran doctrine in Tranquebar. Stevenson's letter was read out at a meeting of the SPCK in London. All present heard it in silence and no one responded, whereupon the matter was allowed to drop. The attitude of the SPCK is best summed up in a letter that Henry Newman addressed to John Chamberlayne on 19 December, 1713, concerning the Society's support for the Lutheran missionaries at Tranquebar: it was better "that the heathen should be Lutheran Christians rather than no Christians."[73]

Mather, half a world away from Ziegenbalg and with no hope of any contact save that through letters which could take over a year to reach, felt generous enough to claim that the two were "one Soul." The Anglicans and Lutherans, having far closer dealings, realized, on the other hand, just how strong the barriers were against two like-minded souls joining. They acted in concert to the extent possible, and the SPCK, in particular, went out of its way to be accommodating. But it was not till 1999, when the Lutherans and the Episcopalians entered into communion, that a claim of being "one Soul" could be realized.

NOTES

1. Ernst Benz, "Pietist and Puritan Sources of Early Protestant World Missions (Cotton Mather and A.H. Francke)," *Church History* 20, 2. June 1951: 28-55.

2. Kenneth Silverman, *The Life and Times of Cotton Mather* (New York: Harper and Row, 1984), 241; Richard F. Lovelace, *The American Pietism of Cotton Mather: Origins of American Evangelism* (Grand Rapids, MI: Christian UP, 1979), 271.

3. Thomas James Holmes, *Increase Mather A Bibliography of his Works I* (Cleveland, OH: privately printed at Harvard UP, /1931), 48-63.

4. Holmes, *Increase Mather* I, 54; Silverman, 68.

5. Silverman, 241.

6. Lovelace, 272.

7. Daniel L. Brunner, *Halle Pietists in England: Anthony William Boehm and the Society for Promoting Christian Knowledge* (Gottingen: Vandenhoek and Ruprecht, 1993), 24, 222.

8. William Reginald Ward, *The Protestant Evangelical Awakening* (Cambridge: Cambridge UP, 1992), 303; Brunner, 222.

9. Brunner, 51-52.

10. Ibid., 85.

11. F. Ernest Stoeffler, *The Rise of Evangelical Pietism* (Leiden: E.J. Brill, 1965), 204, 207, 209.

12. Stoeffler, *Rise*, 228, 235; Gary R. Sattler, *God's Glory, Neighbor's Good. A Brief Introduction to the Life and Writings of August Hermann Francke* (Chicago: Covenant Press, 1982), 13.

13. Henry Ernst Ferdinand Guericke, *The Life of August Hermann Francke*, trans. from German by Samuel Jackson (London: Henry Bohn, 1847), 30-36.

14. Ibid., 13-19.

15. Ibid., 39-48.

16. August Hermann Francke's *Scriptural Rules of Life* is included in Sattler, *God's Glory, Neighbor's Good*, 115-48, and *Scriptural and Basic Instruction* in ibid., 149-254.

17. Guericke, 30 n.

18. Stoeffler, *Rise*, 183-84.

19. Guericke, 31 n.

20. F. Ernest Stoeffler, *German Pietism during the Eighteenth Century* (Leiden: E.J. Brill, 1973), 7.

21. Ibid., 23.

22. Ibid., 45-55.

23. Ibid., 41-43.

24. August Hermann Francke, *Die Fussstapfen des noch lebenden und waltenden liebreichen und getreuen Gottes*, 1701. Translated into English by Wilhelm Anton Boehm as *Pietas Hallensis: Or, An Abstract of the Marvellous Footsteps of the Divine Providence Attending the Management and Improvement of the Orphan-House at Glaucha near Halle; and of other Charitable Foundations relating to it. Part III. To which is prefix'd A LETTER of the Author to a Divine in New-England* (London: J. Downing, 1716), 6-48. See also Guericke, *Life of August Hermann Francke*, 140-75; and Sattler, *God's Glory, Neighbor's Good,* 52-53, 63-64.

25. Stoeffler, *German Pietism*, 55-56.

26. Qtd. Guericke, 72.

27. See n. 24 above.

28. Information in this paragraph comes from Brunner, *Halle Pietists in England*,

85, 88, 39.

29. Ernst Benz, "Pietist and Puritan Sources," 54 n.

30. Richard F. Lovelace, *The American Peitism of Cotton Mather*, 73-74, 177, 64.

31. Qtd. Ibid. 254.

32. Cotton Mather, *Malachi, Or, The Everlasting Gospel* (Boston: T. C[rump] for Robert Starke, 1717), 6-8, 20-21, 22, and esp. 34-35.

33. Ernst Benz, "Ecumenical Relations between Boston Puritanism and German Pietism: Cotton Mather and August Hermann Francke," *Harvard Theological Review* 54. 1961: 173-74.

34. Cotton Mather, *Bonifacius. An Essay upon the Good.* Ed. David Levin (Cambridge: Harvard UP, 1966), 141.

35. Ibid. 115-16. See also Silverman, *Life and Times of Cotton Mather*, 230-33.

36. Kuno Francke, "Cotton Mather and August Hermann Francke," *Harvard Studies and Notes* 5, 1896: 57-67.

37. Qtd. Ibid. 58.

38. Ibid. *passim.*

39. Kuno Francke, "The Beginning of Cotton Mather's Correspondence with August Hermann Francke," *Philological Quarterly* 5. 3. 1926: 193-95.

40. Qtd. Benz, "Pietist," 32-33; "Ecumenical," 172.

41. Benz, "Ecumenical," 173-74.

42. Thomas James Holmes, *Cotton Mather A Bibliography of his Works II* (Cambridge: Harvard UP, 1940), 554.

43. Kuno Francke, "Cotton Mather and August Hermann Francke," *Harvard Studies and Notes*, 60, 62.

44. See n. 24 above.

45. *Pietas Hallensis* III, 57.

46. *Pietas Hallensis* III 6-48; Kuno Francke, "Cotton Mather and August Hermann Francke,"*Americana Germanica* I, 4. Reprint 12. 1897: 31-66.

47. Qtd. Kuno Francke, "Cotton Mather and August Hermann Francke," *Americana Germanica*, 55.

48. (Boston 1715). Rpt. Kuno Francke, "Cotton Mather and August Hermann Francke," *Americana Germanica,* 54-66.

49. Qtd. Kuno Francke, Ibid., 55, 64.

50. Ibid., 39.

51. See n. 24 above.

52. Kuno Francke, "Cotton Mather and August Hermann Francke," *Americana Germanica*, 31.

53. Brijraj Singh, *The First Protestant Missionary to India Bartholomaeus Ziegenbalg 1683-1719* (New Delhi: Oxford UP, 1999), 3.

54. Ibid., 30-34.

55. Kuno Francke, "Cotton Mather and August Hermann Francke," *Harvard Studies and Notes*, 63.

56. (Boston: W. Green, 1721).

57. Cotton Mather, *India Christiana*, 62-74.
58. Qtd. Daniel Brunner, *Halle Pietists in England*, 110-11.
59. Cotton Mather, *India Christiana,* 75-87.
60. Singh, *The First Protestant Missionary*, 17-18.
61. Qtd. Silverman, *The Life and Times of Cotton Mather*, 238.
62. Ibid., 239.
63. Ibid., 239.
64. Singh, *The First Protestant Missionary,* 23, 122-23.
65. Daniel Jeyaraj, *Inkulturation in Tranquebar: der Beitrag der Fruhen danische-hallesche Mission zum Werden einer indisch einheimischen Kirche, 1706-1730* (Erlagen: Ev-Luth. Mission, 1996), 249; 256, 260-61; Singh, *The First Protestant Missionary*, 96-97.
66. Singh, 126.
67. Brunner, *Halle Pietists in England*, 47.
68. Ibid., 203-05.
69. Ibid., 209.
70. Qtd. Ibid., 225.
71. Ibid., 107-11.
72. Ibid., 115-16.
73. Ibid., 120, 123-24.

Poetry and American Revolutionary Identity: The Case of Phillis Wheatley and John Paul Jones

DANIEL J. ENNIS

The impetus for this article is a letter the American Revolutionary War hero John Paul Jones wrote to his friend and fellow naval officer, Captain Hector McNeill, on October 31, 1777. Jones was on that day preparing to sail from Boston aboard his soon-to-be famous vessel, the *Ranger*. His letter to McNeill reads as follows:

> I am on the point of sailing, I have wrote to you, pray be so good as [to] put the Inclosed into the hands of the Celebrated Phillis, the African Favorite of the Nine and of Appollo—should She Reply, I hope you will be the bearer.[1]

"The Inclosed" to which Jones refers is a poem. As far as eighteenth-century poems go, it is a fairly pedestrian piece. The stanzas are written upon an unidentified black profile, and the speaker praises the subject of the silhouette in the established mode of the gentleman-devotee, as in this stanza, which declares that the woman's beauty is worthy of a full-color portrait:

> Pity so excellent a face,
> Should in a shade preserve thy name,
> Such beauty, harmony and grace,
> The painter's softest tints may claim![2]

Jones continues in this vein for some nine further metrically indifferent stanzas, the penultimate being,

> The loveliest form, the fairest face,
> The brightest eye, the gentlest mind,
> And every virtue, charm and grace,
> Should be to endless fame consigned.

As tempting as I find the mission, it is beyond me to rescue the literary reputation of John Paul Jones. Americans are fortunate that Jones kept his day job.

Jones' day job, of course, was to be the most dashing and quotable American Revolutionary war hero—the man who shouted "I have not yet begun to fight," and who gave the United States Navy an enduring slogan when he declared "I wish to have no connection with any ship that does not sail fast, for I intend to go in harm's way."[3] However, in October 1777, when Jones sent his poem to Wheatley, he was still one of many officers in the infant Continental Navy, and while he had just returned from a successful raid against British shipping off Newfoundland, he was perhaps a minor hero–not quite famous. The John Paul Jones of 1777, in fact, shows signs of being insecure about not only his reputation, but also about his very identity, and his sending of a poem to Wheatley illuminates the role of poetic discourse in the formation of eighteenth-century American identity.

For Jones, writing poetry was part of a larger project of gentrification that preoccupied the sailor his entire life. He was born in Scotland, the son of a gardener, and was christened simply John Paul. Lacking prospects ashore, he was sent off to sea at age thirteen. By age twenty-one he was a successful merchant captain, was half-owner of his ship, and had amassed a small fortune in the West Indian trade. Yet a mysterious murder charge in 1773 caused John Paul to flee the Carribean, apparently one step ahead of the law. The evidence against John Paul was such that he abandoned his ship, property and accounts. Upon arriving in North Carolina sometime in the intervening months, he changed his name first to Paul Jones, then later to the now-familiar John Paul Jones.[4]

The murder charges are best treated elsewhere; what interests me is the newly created John Paul Jones that surfaces in the colonies on the eve of the Revolution. The name change is the most obvious evidence that the sailor was trying to fashion an identity, but there are other suggestions that the fugitive Scottish sea-captain was actively creating a new image, and he was doing so just as more and more colonists were beginning to question their own national identities. For Jones (like many Defoe heroes), America was, ironically perhaps given our nation's putatively democratic origins, a place to become a gentleman. Samuel Eliot Morison describes the beginning of Jones' gentrification:

> [Jones] grasped every occasion to improve himself, socially and otherwise. He learned to avoid low company...and to associate, as far as he could, with gentlemen. He got rid of his Galloway brogue [and] taught himself English by good reading and practice in writing.[5]

Once in America, Jones attempted to enter society. His letters refer to an abortive attempt to court Dorothea Dandridge, daughter of a prominent Virginia plantation owner, and he became an active Mason. Jones' Masonic connections helped him secure, in 1775, a commission in the newly-formed Continental Navy.

Jones' commission contributed to his gentrification. It appears that the former John Paul saw in the traditional image of the naval officer a means of social mobility, and while the Continental Navy was in reality led by ex-merchantmen and privateers, for Jones it was a nursery for his own developing genteel persona. In 1776 Jones wrote a letter to a friend in the Continental Congress describing what an American naval officer should be:

> in my opinion a captain of the navy ought to be a man of strong and well connected sense with a tolerable education, a gentleman as well as a seaman both in theory and practice–for, want of learning and rude ungentle manners are by no means characteristic of an officer.[6]

This passage, incidentally, was for years required memorization for Annapolis midshipmen and appears to have been the origin of the 1872 phrase "an officer and a gentleman."[7] In a later letter Jones strengthens the connection between officers and gentlemen, and he does so by associating both those titles with writing ability:

> None other than a Gentleman...is qualified to support the character of a commission Officer in the Navy, nor is any man fit to command a ship of war, who is not also capable of communicating his ideas on paper in language that becomes his rank.[8]

It was in that same year, 1777, that Jones ordered a coat of arms to be cut. Morison describes it this way:

> The arms are a stag used by several Jones families of Wales, Quartered with those of a Paul family of Gloucestershire. The crest is the Jones stag; and the motto, the only original part, is Pro Republica.[9]

In the early 1770s the future naval hero took the name "Jones" in a attempt to protect "John Paul" from prosecution–he has no obvious blood connection to any eighteenth-century Joneses whatsoever. His mother's name was MacDuff. Jones' crest was ordered, however, at a time in his life when he had little reason to fear prosecution for the Carribean murder (had the British gotten their hands on Jones, piracy would have been first on their list of charges). The heraldry, incongruous as it may appear for a man who was serving the new and publically anti-aristocratic United States, formalized Jones' name change. In fact, the coat of arms inscribes his new name upon the chivalric tradition.

Jones'equation of writing with social status invests his 1777 correspondence with Phillis Wheatley with material importance. Jones and Wheatley were actually engaged in similar projects: They were both trying to overcome and/or erase given identities by fashioning new, specifically American identities. Somehow poetry and military heroism had a special connection for them. In fact, each had something the other needed. Jones–whose gentrification project required proficiency in both arts and arms—corresponded with Wheatley in the time-honored tradition of a gentleman using a poet for polish. For Wheatley, of course, Jones provided a link to the truly epic struggle, to the glorious military tradition-in-the-making that she saw in the Revolution–a tradition that would need laureates (or *griots*) for permanence.

Jones's poem to Wheatley is fairly representative of the poetry he wrote throughout his life, but, to paraphrase Johnson, while it is not done well, you are surprised to find it done at all. Clearly the approbation of Wheatley, perhaps a return letter from the "uncultivated barbarian" who became a "poetical genius" would have served Jones in his fashioning of identity.[10] John Paul Jones obsessively collected testimonials from his associates on everything from his seamanship to his ability as a diplomat, and by the end of his career he had accumulated massive documentary evidence of others' good opinions of him. A note from Wheatley expressing admiration for his poetry would have been filed by Jones alongside favorable letters he had saved from Adams, Jefferson and Franklin. Jones's self-fashioning was very much a matter of accumulating outward signs of social distinction–letters, medals, clothing, mistresses were all put into the service of advancement: Jones' motto is *Pro Republica*, but republics (as Addison's *Cato*, a play Jones knew, teaches) do not preclude gentlemen.

The Continental Navy, like the British Royal Navy of the period, was a means by which a man of ability could rise without family connections. That Jones took outward signs of his rise seriously can be seen in his later letters. Once Louis XVI named Jones Chevalier in 1781, Jones used the title even when he was corresponding with close American friends. The "Chevalier Paul-Jones" ceased to exist only when a more lofty designation became available in 1788, when Jones became Kontraadmiral Pavel Ivanovich Jones in the Imperial Russian Navy of Catherine the Great. Beyond an affinity for titles, it appears Jones cultivated an image of gentility to the point of near-effeminacy. Abigail Adams provides a famous portrait of Jones, and her description contains nothing of the swashbucker:

> I expected to have seen a rough, stout, warlike Roman–instead of that I should sooner think of wrapping him up in cotton wool, and putting him in my pocket, than sending him to contend with cannon-balls. He is small of stature, well-proportioned, soft in his speech, easy in his address, polite in his manners, vastly civil, understands all the etiquette of a lady's toilet as perfectly as he does the mast, sails and rigging of his ship.[11]

Not mentioned by Adams, but lurking in Jones' character, was an interest in that other gentle art–versifying.

Perhaps mercifully, only five poems by John Paul Jones survive. Nonetheless, it is the placement of his poetry that makes it significant. For example, one of Jones' most dramatic displays of sensible refinement was his handling of a raid on his native Scotland during the Revolutionary War. Jones took the *Ranger* to St. Mary's Isle in Solway Firth (the same body of water Jones had plied as a boy) and sent a raiding party ashore to take hostage the Earl of Selkirk. Finding the Lord away from his mansion, the sailors instead took the Selkirk family plate as Lady Selkirk looked on. Once the silver was secured aboard ship (and the countryside sufficiently alarmed) the *Ranger* put to sea again, defeated *H.M.S. Drake* in single combat, and reached the safety of a French harbor on May 8, 1778. Instead of reveling in plunder, however, Jones used the "Rape of the Plate" (as Morison calls it) as a opportunity for both gallantry and delicacy. He wrote to Lady Selkirk with an offer to return the plate (which he eventually did), and includes in his letter a fairly awful couplet of his own:

> ...When the Plate is sold, I shall become the purchaser, and will gratify my own feelings by restoring it to you...Had the Earl been on board the Ranger the following evening, he would have seen the awful pomp, and dreadful carnage, of a sea engagement; both, affording ample subject for the pencil, as well as Melancholy reflection for the contemplative Mind. Humanity starts back from such scenes of horror, and cannot but execrate the vile promoters of this detested war.
>
> For *they*[,] 'twas *they* unsheath'd the ruthless blade,
> And, Heaven shall ask the havock it has made.[12]

As difficult as it is to imagine John Paul Jones as a poet, it is even more surprising to see him indulging in nigh-Rousseauian sensibility. Yet this is 1778, when sensibility was still enobling (and not necessarily gendered female): John Paul Jones as Sir Charles Grandison. Unlike most heroes of sensibility, though, Jones is not satisfied with the mere display of his capacity for feeling and contemplation. He damns the "vile promoters of this detested war" with a couplet that faintly echoes Shakespeare's Antony: "Cry 'Havoc!' and let slip the dogs of war."

The Selkirk letter was circulated among Jones' friends (and enemies), so much so that copies appeared in newspapers on both sides of the Atlantic, thus contributing to Jones' public image as a dashing and courteous captain. A later document, his *Memoir of the American Revolution* (1786), gave Jones a further opportunity to use poetry to emphasize his worth as a gentleman. Jones includes in the *Memoir* verses of his own devising designed to praise Louis XVI (and lived long enough to see the irony in calling the Borbon the "Protector of fair Freedoms Rights").[13] In the supposedly private sphere, too, Jones turned to poetry in order to impress others. One of the most reliable weapons in the captain's romantic arsenal was a poem on parting that he sent to at least two different mistresses–Jones simply rewrote a key line and replaced the name of the lover in question.[14] For Jones, poetry was to be deployed strategically. It could abet his social climbing just as taking a British ship could advance his military career. Two hundred years before Bourdieu and Passeron coined the term, John Paul Jones understood cultural capital.

Let us consider, then, this relationship from the Wheatley side. As Helen M. Burke says in her 1991 article on Wheatley,

> to establish a literary identity, to earn the title"poet," one had to insert oneself into this [Western poetic] tradition, recognizing the tradition, even while asserting one's own right to speak. When, in the first poem

> of her 1773 volume of poetry, Wheatley discusses her own poetic talents in the context of Homer and Virgil, she implicitly makes this assertion.[15]

Scholars like Burke, Walt Nott and Merle Richmond see Wheatley as a pioneer–a black woman able to assert her identity through poetry–but a pioneer who had to construct an identity using a foreign discourse.[16] Indeed, most commentators on the poetic career of Phillis Wheatley make much of Wheatley's use of the tropes and ideologies of the Western (specifically British) tradition, some to damn her for compromise, others to praise her for resourcefulness. Most recently, Vincent Carretta has used the Mansfield decision of 1772 (which declared that slaves could not be exported from Britain against their will) to reemphasize the "transatlantic subtext" of Wheatley's poetry and to show how much role choice played in Wheatley's self-fashioned national identity.[17] Most critical commentary on Wheatley agrees that there is something constructed and/or artificial about who she is.

It is a pity that we have no record of Wheatley's reaction to Jones's letter. In fact, it may well be that Wheatley never got Jones's poem, or if she did receive it, that she did not respond–from everything we know of Jones's character he would have copied a response from Wheatley and sent it to a dozen of his closest friends. It is tempting to imagine they were personally acquainted while Jones was in Boston in 1777, but no documentary evidence of such contact has yet emerged.[18] Nonetheless, the attentions of a military figure of even small repute were probably welcome to Wheatley in 1777. She was, after all, in a difficult position. Her early attempts to have a collection of poetry published in Boston in 1772 had been rebuffed, so Phillis' mistress, Susanna Wheatley, made arrangements for the manuscript to be sent to London. As William Henry Robinson points out, Wheatley's shift to a London publisher reveals her acute sense of audience: "She dropped all of her anti-British selections, which were to have been published in the rejected American volume, and substituted several flatteringly pro-British pieces along with non-political, lyrical and reflective poems."[19] Wheatley's awareness of the rhetorical power of poetry extends beyond her attempts to appeal to her British audience in her *Poems on Various Subjects*. The corpus of her work is distinguished by her frequent panegyrics–first to politically powerful Britons (like the Earl of Dartmouth in 1773) and later militarily significant Americans (most prominently Washington, praised in a 1775 ode).

The connection between Wheatley and Jones is made all the more interesting by Wheatley's earlier exchange with a *British* naval officer in a few 1774 issues of the *Royal American Magazine.* In a series of three poems (Wheatley's initial "To a Gentleman of the Navy" from the October 30, 1774 issue, a response by the gentleman on December 2, 1774, and Wheatley's final response, "Phillis's Reply to the Answer" on December 5, 1774), the relationship between the warrior and the bard is clearly defined. In the first poem of the exchange, Wheatley declares that naval officers "deserve my lays / The sacred tribute of ingenious praise."[20] The poem then becomes a pseudo-Homeric celebration (mediated through eighteenth-century poetic diction) of two particular officers' virtues–the addressee (Carretta identifies the "Gentleman" as John Prime Iron Rochfort, a British officer who was promoted to Lieutenant in late 1774) and a fellow officer, "Greaves." Both men are "blooming sons of Neptune's royal race" who deserve "Celestial friendship and the muse's care."[21] But like Virgil lyrically immortalizing Augustus (or less sublimely, Robert Southey doing the same for George III), Wheatley recognizes that the success of a panegyric is actually a function or reception, not aesthetics: "Yours is the song, and your's the honest praise, / Lo, Rochfort smiles, and Greaves approves my lays."[22]

Rochfort's poetic response, "The Answer [By the Gentleman of the Navy]," hinges on two concepts. First, Rochfort sees Wheatley as an exotic ("daughter of the Affric shore") that is endowed with natural genius: "...nature taught, (tho' strange it is to tell,) / Her flowing pencil Europe to excell."[23] Second, he suggests that while Britain, once the home of Milton, is now militarily successful, it has lacked great poets in recent days, and thus Wheatley, despite her origins, is an important addition to the State:

> But now this blissful clime, this happy land,
> That all the neighboring nations did command;
> Whose royal navy neptunes waves did sweep,
> Reign'd Prince alone, and sov'reign of the deep:
> No more can boast, but of the power to kill,
> By force of Arms, or diabolic skill.
> For softer strains we quickly must repair
> To Wheatly's song, for Wheatly is the fair[.][24]

This praise touches on a process extant in much of Wheatley's later poetry. Wheatley is indeed an Other by birth, but poetry allows her to join a lineage that runs Homer-Virgil-Milton. All of these poets are national poets, and all took as their subject titantic struggle. Rochfort suggests Wheatley is essential to the British Empire because she can immortalize Britannia's "force of arms" with "softer strains." Yet this is a description of John Paul Jones' use of poetry, too: Not content with mere "diabolic skill," Jones knew that "softer strains" were an important part of the cultural equation; military success without accompanying poetic production is barbarism.

That Wheatley welcomes the role of poet-as-adjunct-to-victory can be seen in the final poem of the series, "Phillis's Reply to the Answer." While much of this poem is concerned with praising Rochfort's ability as a poet, Wheatley does accept a place in the British tradition: "Then fix the humble Afric muse's seat / At British Homer's and Sir Isaac's feet."[25] Lines like these, of course, along with the London publication of her book, suggest that calling Wheatley, as Sidney Kaplan does, "probably the first truly American poet in our literary history" runs the risk of minimizing the true liminality of her poetic production.[26] In 1774, then, Wheatley quite publicly embraces something like poetical *British* citizenship, and she does so by aligning herself with a martial tradition, first by trading verses with an officer of the Royal Navy, and more significantly by tacitly acknowledging that officer's proposition that Britain's eighteenth-century military success cries out for a poet worthy of immortalizing it.

Had the revolution not intervened, who knows what Wheatley would have become as a subject of the British Empire? Ann Yearsley at least, perhaps something far greater. However, by 1777, when Jones wrote to Wheatley, Afric's muse had indeed been humbled. The 1773 success of Wheatley's London edition was long past, Susannah Wheatley had died, and, in the words of Robinson, Phillis Wheatley's poetic career was "practically ended."[27] She published just six poems from 1774 until her death ten years later. Nonetheless, the poems Wheatley *did* write reveal a continued awareness of the connection between military glory and poetic success, and a keen sense of the shifting national consciousness. John Paul Jones saw poetry as *noblesse oblige*. Wheatley saw poetry as a means to citizenship. For example, in 1775 Wheatley sent a flattering poem to George Washington, parts of which suggest that, like Jones, Wheatley did not necessarily associate America with democracy, but instead with a sense of paternal monarchalism mediated though neoclassical poetic figures:

> Proceed, great chief, with virtue on thy side
> The every action let the goddess guide
> A crown, a mansion, and a throne that shine,
> With gold unfading, Washington, be thine![28]

Washington publicly acknowledged the tribute, and it suddenly becomes hard to imagine Wheatley as a British poet. Nonetheless, British or American,

Wheatley position vis-a-vis poetry and military glory is unchanged from her 1774 view. If poetry might make a gentleman out of a fugitive Scottish sailor, might it also make a laureate out of a former slave?

That next year Wheatley wrote "On the Capture of General Lee," a poem that mourns the seizure of Washington's respected second in command. Lee was actually captured, rather ingloriously, in his dressing gown, having neglected to post a proper guard around his temporary headquarters in a tavern.[29] Nonetheless, to Wheatley, Lee's capture meant that General Washington was even more essential to her new country, and after praising Lee she concludes the poem with these lines:

> Columbia too, beholds with streaming eyes
> Her heroes fall–tis freedom's sacrifice!
> So wills the Power who with convulsive storms
> Shakes impious realms, and nature's face deforms;
> Yet those brave troops innumerous as the sands
> One soul inspires, one General Chief commands
> Find in your train of boasted heroes, one
> To match the praise of Godlike Washington.[30]

A third poem on military matters, "On the Death of General Wooster," was part of a 1778 letter from Wheatley to Mary Wooster, wife of the late general. In the poems on Washington and Lee we see Wheatley using the rhetoric of panegyric to associate herself with revolutionary heroes. In the poem on General Wooster we see Wheatley attempting to contrast glory of military martyrdom with the indignity of chattel slavery. Wooster was shot in a 1777 skirmish, and Wheatley imagines the dying general's last prayer: a plea to the "great power" to "lead Columbia thro the toils of war" and to keep the new nation's citizens "Virtuous, brave and free."[31] Standard fare, perhaps, and similar sentiments are found in poems by Philip Freneau and Hugh Henry Brackenridge, but Wheatley then has Wooster connect America's fate with that of Wheatley's fellow African[-American]s:

> But how, presumptuous shall we hope to find
> Divine acceptance with th' Almighty mind–
> While yet (O deed ungenerous) they disgrace
> And hold in bondage Afric's blameless race?[32]

John C. Shields has argued, quite convincingly, that these lines "express the ironic contradiction between what Christianity professes (universal brotherhood of all men) and what Christians practice (the institution of slavery)."[33] They are, as well, as evidence that Wheatley was a canny student of poetic power. Like so many poets before and after her, Wheatley knew that poetry associated with popular political and/or military figures was read and appreciated. Of the four known Wheatley poems from the Revolutionary War era, three are associated with military heroes. What better way for a former slave to show her loyalty to the new nation than by celebrating that new nation's protectors? Furthermore, what better way to remind that nation's protectors that there were Americans that were still in bondage than to include in a panegyric not only references to abstract freedom but also mentions of the still-enslaved?

The creation of a new nation in North America was an opportunity for thousands to shed their pasts and take up new identities, yet the transformations of Phillis Wheatley and John Paul Jones are more dramatic, and certainly more lyrical, than most. The poetic career of John Paul Jones was process of remaking that was only possible in the context of the American Revolution. In America, the gentry was not necessarily predetermined by birth, so Jones was able to fashion a definition of a gentleman that fit his attributes. His correspondence with Wheatley, and his poetry in general, was a way to help forge his new identity as an American officer and gentleman. So successful was Jones in this regard that one tends to forget that he was born in Scotland, was on the run from the law, achieved his highest military rank in the service of Russia, and died in Paris–John Paul Jones, American Revolutionary War Hero, was at best a temporary American. For Wheatley, the Revolution was a similar opportunity–the former slave found a role as propagandist for the struggle, and having already used Britain–that is, the London publisher of her 1773 volume of poetry–to disprove so many racist assumptions, she used Columbia to prove her worthiness for citizenship. Jones, a Scot of dubious reputation, and Wheatley, a prodigy who was intensely aware of her racial otherness, both seek to legitimate themselves as "Americans" by occupying a public space where the military and poetic worlds collide.

Scholars and students often conceptualize American Revolutionary identity using a British paradigm. That is, Americans naturally looked to Britain for models–for ways to act, write, dress and live. In the cases of Wheatley and Jones, however, we must complicate this mechanism just a bit–the poet and the sailor both used the British tradition as a guide to their own self-fashioning, but they did so by looking back to the seventeenth century, not across to their contemporaries in the eighteenth. Critics like Albertha Sistrunk, Charles Scruggs and Carolivia Herron have established a formal, prosodic connection between Wheatley and Alexander Pope,[34] but I think Wheatley's sense of poetry's place in the public discourse during times of crisis is far more reminiscent of John Dryden–a man who knew much better than Pope the value of well-placed complements to those in high places. For a British model for John Paul Jones, we have to look back even further—past successful but unimaginative eighteenth century British admirals like Anson and Vernon, past even Cromwell's efficient but colorless captains, back to Sir Walter Raleigh, a man who could court a lady, swing a cutlass and mangle a meter with the best of them.

NOTES

1. John Paul Jones to Hector McNeill, 31 October 1777, The Pierpont Morgan Library. I would like to thank the library for allowing me access to the Jones papers. I would also like to thank my colleagues, Jill Sessoms, Maria Bachman and Steve Hamelman, for their assistance in the early drafting stages. My research assistant, Cindy Garris, went beyond the call of duty during revisions. In all quotations, I have retained original spelling and punctuation.

2. "[Pity so excellent a face]" in *The Papers of John Paul Jones,* ed. James C. Bradford (Cambridge, UK ; Alexandria, VA : Chadwyck-Healey, 1986), 1934, microform. Bradford suggests the connection between this poem and the October 1777 letter to McNeill. My personal examination of the October 1777 letter from Jones to McNeill in the Pierpont Morgan Library sheds no new light (the letter is now unaccompanied), but "[Pity so excellent a face]" is undated and makes sense in the context of the letter to Wheatley. In the end, though, it matters little which of Jones's poems was sent to Wheatley, as it is the act of *sending* such poems to Wheatley that is of interest. Most of the poetry Jones wrote throughout his career is addressed to women, and deploys utterly traditional eighteenth-century tropes and versification.

3. The famous "I have not yet begun to fight" first appears in print in John Henry Sherburne's 1825 *Life and Character of the Chevalier John Paul Jones.* Samuel Eliot Morison, in his *John Paul Jones: A Sailor's Biography* (New York: Atlantic Monthly Press, 1959) offers the most complete treatment of the battle off Flamborough Head (the engagement where Jones supposedly uttered the famous sentence) and concludes that Jones probably did speak those words. The "harm's way" line appears in a letter dated 16 Nov. 1778. I lean heavily on Morison for the biographical facts in this article. A newer Jones biography, James Mackay's *I Have Not Yet Begun to Fight: A Life of John Paul Jones*

(London: Mainstream Publishing, 1998) has been so tainted by allegations of plagiarism that its American publisher, Atlantic Monthly, has withdrawn it from the market. Plagiarized or not, it is a monument to sloppy scholarship and cannot be used with any degree of confidence. Morison remains the standard, and my debt for biographical details lies to him.

4. Morison provides the best explanation of these mysterious charges.

5. Morison, 12.

6. John Paul Jones to Joseph Hewes, 19 May, 1776. *The Papers of John Paul Jones,* ed. James C. Bradford (Cambridge, UK ; Alexandria, VA : Chadwyck-Healey, 1986), microform. This letter is also quoted *in toto* in Morison, 53-54.

7. See *The Articles of War*, annotated by Lee S. Tillotson (Harrisburg, Pa.: Military Service Publishing Company, 1946).

8. John Paul Jones to Robert Morris, 21 January, 1777.

9. Morison, 111.

10. The phrase "uncultivated Barbarian" appears in the "To the PUBLICK" notice in Wheatley's *Poems on Various Subjects* (London, 1773). "Poetical genius" was applied to Wheatley by George Washington in a 1776 letter (see William H. Robinson's *Critical Essays on Phillis Wheatley* [Boston: G. K. Hall & Co., 1982], 35).

11. Abigail Adams to Elizabeth Cranch, 3 December 1784. *The Adams Papers: The Adams Family Correspondence*, ed. Richard Alan Ryerson et.al. (Cambridge: Harvard University Press, 1993).

12. Jones, 91. Morison writes, "Nobody has been able to identify this couplet as a quotation, and I believe that Jones composed it himself" (148). Indexes and databases developed since Morison wrote *John Paul Jones: A Sailor's Biography* offer no new insight, and I see no reason not to attribute the couplet to Jones. Indeed, I have a hard time imagining anyone else who would *want* it.

13. John Paul Jones. *Memoir of the American Revolution*, Translated and Edited by Gerard W. Gawalt. (Washington: Library of Congress, 1979), 4.

14. See "When Jove from high Olympus goes" in *The Papers of John Paul Jones*.

15. Helen M. Burke, "The Rhetoric and Poetics of Marginality: The Subject of Phillis Wheatley," *Tulsa Studies in Women's Literature* 10 (Spring 1991): 34.

16. See Nott's "From 'Uncultivated Barbarian' to 'Poetical Genius': The Public Presence of Phillis Wheatley" (*MELUS* 18 [Fall 1993]) and Richmond's *Bid the Vassal Soar: Interpretive Essays on the Life and Poetry of Phillis Wheatley and George Moses Horton* (Washington: Howard University Press, 1974), 54-66.

17. Carretta, Vincent. "Phillis Wheatley, the Mansfield Decision of 1772, and the Choice of Identity."in *Early America Re-Explored: New Readings in Colonial, Early National, and Antebellum Culture*, ed. Klaus H. Schmidt and Fritz Fleischmann (New York: Peter Lang, 2001) 201-224. Carretta deploys the useful term "Afro-British" to describe writers like Wheatley.

18. Of course, new work by Wheatley continues to come to light; most recently, her heretofore unpublished poem "Ocean" appeared in print for the first time in June, 1998, the manuscript having been purchased at auction recently for $68,500. (This information is reported, and "Ocean" published, in a limited edition reprint of William Henry Robinson's *Phillis Wheatley and the Origins of African American Literature* [Boston: Old South Meeting House, 1999], 26). "Ocean" also appears in Wheatley's *Complete Writings*, ed. Vincent Carretta (New York: Penguin, 2001). All subsequent quotations of Wheately's poetry are taken from this latest edition of her works.

19. Robinson, 14.

20. Wheatley, 83.

21. Wheatley, 84.

22. Wheatley, 85.

23. Wheatley, 85.

24. Wheatley, 86. Of course, this poem is not by Wheatley, but "Rochfort."

25. Wheatley, 86.

26. Sidney Kaplan. *The Black Presence in the Era of the American Revolution 1770-1800* (Washington: Smithsonian Institution Press, 1973), 150.

27. Robinson, 21.

28. Wheatley, 88.

29. This incident is well-narrated in Benson Bobrick's *Angel in the Whirlwind: The Triumph of the American Revolution* (New York: Simon & Schuster, 1997), 225. Wheatley's poem on Lee takes on far more significance when the reader is reminded that during the early years of the Revolution Lee "was widely (if mistakenly) perceived as the most capable American commander" (225).

30. Wheatley, 90.

31. Wheatley, 92.

32. Wheatley, 92-93.

33. John C. Shields. "Phillis Wheatley's Struggle for Freedom" in Wheatley, *Collected Works* (New York: Oxford, 1988) 238. Sistrunk in "The Influence of Alexander Pope on the Writing Style of Phillis Wheatley" (in Robinson's *Critical Essays on Phillis Wheatley*); Scruggs in "Phillis Wheatley and the Poetical Legacy of Eighteenth-Century England," *Studies in Eighteenth-Century Culture* 10 (1981), 279-95; Herron in "Early African American Poetry," *The Columbia History of American Poetry* ed. Jay Parini (New York: MJF Books, 1993), 23-32.

Quelling the French Threat in Frances Burney's *Evelina*

LEANNE MAUNU

A "little character-monger," Dr. Johnson once called Frances Burney as she was leaving an evening party at Lady Galway's London home shortly after the publication of her first novel, 1778's *Evelina*. Pleased herself with the description, Burney recorded the incident in both her journals and in her preface to *The Wanderer*, essentially registering the appellation in the annals of literary history.[1] The import of Johnson's epithet, of course, is that it draws attention to Burney's writing style, which Johnson meant to celebrate as one that used common character types in order to amuse and delight. Dr. Johnson was, however, not the only reader to point out Burney's facility with drawing interesting characters. In his 1843 review of Burney's published letters and diaries, Macaulay backs up Johnson's claim, stating that "It was in the exhibition of human passions and whims that her strength lay; and in this department of art she had, we think, very distinguished skill."[2] According to Macaulay, Burney's skill as an author lies in her ability to show "human passions and whims," emotions and behaviors that are shared by all humans, and so which can also be recognized as general personality types. Writing even earlier in the century than Macaulay, William Hazlitt also noticed this tendency in Burney's work, remarking that Burney's "*forte* is in describing the absurdities and affectations of external behaviour, or the *manners of people in company*."[3] Hazlitt is quick to point out, however, that Burney's characters fall into general types and categories. While Burney is adept at recreating these "manners" of those in society, "Her characters, which are all caricatures, are no doubt distinctly marked, and perfectly kept up; but they are somewhat superficial, and exceedingly uniform."[4] Hazlitt recognized in Burney's early novels her tendency to make characters and actions appear simpler than they really are or could be, yet he failed to realize that this oversimplification resulted from Burney's own view of the world. The "superficial" and "exceedingly uniform" characters she created in her early works were the direct result of her own belief that society is relatively superficial, relatively easy to interpret. The representation of Burney as a "character-monger" thus developed from the idea that Burney peopled her early novels with exaggerated personalities. The frenchified fop, the naive country girl, the handsome lord: all of these are characterizations that were easily recognized by Burney's readers.[5]

While Burney's skill in drawing these character types has long been recognized by many critics, what has gone relatively unexamined is the darker side of Burney's characterizations as exemplified in that most puzzling and disturbing pair of characters in the novel: Captain Mirvan and Madame Duval. Burney's other relationships have received much critical attention over the past two hundred years, but few have stopped to question the function of these two particular characters and the nature of their relationship. Having slipped through most of the cracks, the Captain and Madame Duval usually receive only cursory treatment, for most readers of the novel do not quite know what to make of these two odd characters. When discussed at all, the Captain and Madame Duval are rarely paired together, usually receiving separate treatment instead.[6] Despite their neglect, however, this fascinating couple is an important indicator of nationalist sentiment in Britain during the mid to late eighteenth century. In creating these two ribald characters, Burney had to look no farther than the nationalist rhetoric and anti-French propaganda of the day for inspiration. The young Burney draws upon some of the more nationalistic attitudes and stereotypes of her society, reinforcing a vision of France that adhered to the negative portrayals already put into place by her fellow Britons. Here the work of historian Linda Colley elucidates our understanding of these portrayals. In her groundbreaking text *Britons: Forging the Nation 1707–1837*, Colley laid the foundation for a new understanding of how the idea of Britain developed. Drawing upon Benedict Anderson's idea of nations as imagined communities,[7] Colley demonstrates how a unified Great Britain emerged out of a period of intense warfare with France. Britain and France had been traditional enemies for centuries, yet competition between the two nations intensified during the eighteenth century as each country struggled to expand its imperialist empire and establish new trade routes. Heightened passions led to war, and war led to the cohesion of Britons, who, for the first time, began to envision themselves as members of a larger collectivity. Since Britons had a 'natural' enemy close at hand, this otherwise heterogeneous group therefore found commonality in a shared fear and hatred of their rival nation. Colley explains this model at greater length:

> . . . men and women decide who they are by reference to who and what they are not. Once confronted with an obviously alien 'Them,' an otherwise diverse community can become a reassuring or merely desperate 'Us.' This was how it was with the British after 1707. They came to define themselves as a single people not because of any political or cultural consensus at home, but rather in reaction to the Other beyond their shores.[8]

As a nation traditionally despised by Britain, France conveniently became this "Other" against which Britons could define themselves. The constant warfare between the two countries made mass allegiance to the British nation and the invention of 'Britishness' itself possible. In effect, Britons understood themselves relationally, as a group of people different from and superior to the French.

When examined through Colley's lens, the roles that Captain Mirvan and Madame Duval play suddenly become clearer, and we can now see that the antagonisms that exist between this British sea captain and this French woman are a direct result of the antagonisms that had long existed between their respective nations. The threat of France is embodied in the figure of Madame Duval, and the most frightening force in *Evelina*, in fact, wears the guise not of a heartless seducer, as it did in many of the period's novels, but rather that of this old, bawdy woman. Evelina's grandmother represents the threat of a dual national identity, of being both French and English, which is a prospect that Evelina finds horrifying. To develop this idea, Burney draws upon nationalist stereotypes and prejudices to portray Madame Duval as a foul, almost monstrous woman. Despised by those around her, Madame Duval still possesses, though, the ability to force Evelina to return to France with her. Evelina is essentially powerless in her grandmother's grasp, and has no choice but to try to appease her. Yet Burney does not let Madame Duval get away with uncontrolled power. To contain Madame Duval, Burney brings in Captain Mirvan, a character who is even cruder and more savage than Evelina's grandmother. The Captain, who has an inveterate hatred of anything having to do with the French, absolutely abhors Madame Duval, so he does everything he can to torment and humiliate her. Their verbal and physical exchanges make up the bulk of the comedic scenes of the novel, yet, as will be emphasized later on in this essay, these scenes also have a disturbing edge to them, one that reveals Burney's nascent sense of doubt about the nationalist rhetoric and imagery in which she engages.

*****

Throughout the novel, Evelina encounters characters whom she can easily and accurately read. Within the various social situations in which she is placed, Evelina may not know what to say or how to act, but she immediately knows how to evaluate the people to whom she is introduced. From the moment she first meets him, for instance, Evelina knows that her eventual tormentor Mr. Lovel is a conceited fop. As he tiptoes, simpering and preening, toward Evelina and Maria Mirvan at their first dance in London, Lovel, Evelina notes in a letter, "had a set smile on his face, and his dress was so foppish, that I really believe he even wished to be stared at; and yet he was very ugly."[9] This direct assessment of Mr. Lovel reveals Evelina's understanding of the place of this type of person in society; from the moment she first sees him, Evelina recognizes Mr. Lovel as a fool and a slave to society. Her first meeting with her cousins the Branghtons also produces similar results. Based on this initial encounter, Evelina pronounces the father to be "very contracted and prejudiced"; the son to be a "foolish, over-grown school-boy"; Miss Branghton to be "proud, ill-tempered, and conceited"; and Miss Polly to be "rather pretty, very foolish, very ignorant, very giddy, and, I believe, very good-natured" (68). Before this first visit is even over, the Branghtons prove themselves to be all that Evelina has imagined them to be. Another character, and this time a central one, that Evelina accurately reads is Lord Orville. When she meets him at the same ball where she meets Mr. Lovel, Evelina knows immediately what kind of person he is and the behavior that she can expect from him. Her understanding of Orville depends upon this same conception of the world and its members as relatively easy to fathom.[10] Far from discrediting Evelina's tendency to judge others based upon an initial encounter, then, Burney gives Evelina's assessments value and credibility. Although Evelina immediately judges the characters she meets, her evaluations are always accurate, always precise. Even the external appearances of the people she meets reveal for Evelina their true inner natures.

Burney's characterizations, however, reveal more than just a desire to create excessive figures in humorous situations. Being a "character-monger," as Dr. Johnson described her, was definitely one of Burney's strengths in

Evelina, and yet these characterizations serve more than just a stylistic purpose. In fact, they mirror Burney's own understanding of British society at this stage in her own life. Burney creates personalities in *Evelina* who exemplify specific traits, either good or bad, of human behavior because Burney herself saw the world as relatively easy to decipher. Burney's overall conception of the world is also reflected in the world of her heroine, and both Burney and Evelina view the world as a troublesome place, but one that is manageable since the people in it are easily decipherable. Evelina's entrance into the world is really an entrance into knowledge, into the rules according to which society functions and regulates its members. Although she has to learn how to navigate in the world around her, learning proper etiquette as she goes, Evelina still has the capacity to judge right from wrong, good characters from bad. In this respect, Evelina's world is a straightforward one, a world where appearances are, indeed, all they are made out to be. British society is relatively easy to understand: Evelina has to learn how to interact with the characters she meets, but she can do so because these characters are so completely obvious to her. While *Evelina* consistently delights its readers, its premise, that of a young woman making her entrance into fashionable British society, is light. Evelina must learn to regulate her behavior and to negotiate her place in the world, but she learns her lessons quickly and well. Her metaphorical journey to maturity is made easier by the fact that her world is a straightforward one, uncomplicated by characters that exhibit unusual or incomprehensible behavior. Although she does manage to get herself into a few dangerous situations (most notably at Vauxhall, in the Marybone-gardens, and with Sir Clement Willoughby), most of the time her mistakes are nothing more than *faux pas*, social embarrassments that she must live down afterwards.

This perspicuous understanding of the world also carries over from the realm of characters to the realm of nations, for even our heroine's view of what Britain and France are like is straightforward. In *Evelina*, France is undeniably the land of deceptive women and of women who are deceived, the land where bad things happen to good people because of the villainous characters who dwell there. Although Evelina has never been there herself, France is where things first went wrong for her. Mr. Evelyn, Evelina's grandfather, was the first of the family to "abandon his native land" (13) upon his unhappy marriage to the woman who would later remarry and metamorphose into Madame Duval. Ashamed of this marriage to Madame Duval, "then a waiting-girl at the tavern," and "contrary to the advice and entreaties of all his friends," Evelyn relocated to France, where he died just two years later from extreme unhappiness (13). Although the initial mistake, the marriage to Madame Duval, took place at home in Britain, Mr. Evelyn's mismanagement of the affair is what ultimately led to his residence in France. His friends' "advice and entreaties" favor him staying in Britain and making the best of his chosen path; overwhelmed by "shame and repentance," however, Mr. Evelyn chooses France as the most appropriate place to hide from the world (14). France thus became a site of self-enforced exile for Mr. Evelyn, a place where he will try to lose his shame, although gaining misery in return. Yet the Evelyn family's connection with France does not end here. Upon his death, Mr. Evelyn left his daughter Caroline Evelyn to Mr. Villars' guardianship back in Britain, knowing that his own wife would not care to raise their child. Mr. Villars provided for Evelina's mother until her own mother, recently married to Monsieur Duval, decided to send for her to come to France. Expecting to meet with maternal affection when she arrives in France, the young Caroline was instead faced with another episode of fraud. Madame Duval threatened her with a forced marriage, a marriage entirely abhorrent to Caroline.[11] When Madame Duval "found her power inadequate to her attempt, enraged at [Caroline's] non-compliance, she treated her with the grossest unkindness, and threatened her with poverty and ruin" (15). In the face of such disaster, Evelina's mother chose to privately marry Sir John Belmont, since he "promised to conduct her to England" (15). Caroline's homeland thus becomes the site of potential freedom from persecution. A return home to Britain would safeguard her from her mother's cruelty. Belmont, however "a very profligate young man," became enraged when he learned that Caroline's parents disapproved of their marriage: "Disappointed of the fortune he expected, by the inexorable rancour of the Duvals, he infamously burnt the certificate of their marriage, and denied that they had ever been united" (15). Without proof of her marriage, Caroline had no choice but to return home to her first protector, Mr. Villars, in whose arms she dies shortly after giving birth to Evelina. France also serves as the site of deception regarding Evelina's true identity as Evelina Belmont. That is, Mr. Villars and his friends have always believed that Sir Belmont has refused to acknowledge his marriage to Caroline Evelyn. By the end of the novel, however, they discover that Belmont *has*, in fact, acknowledged the girl whom he thinks is his daughter, although he has hid this daughter away in France for most of her life. Mr. Villars and his friends learn that within the year following Caroline's death, the nurse who had been with Caroline on her deathbed conceived the plan of substituting her own daughter for that of Caroline, bringing the false daughter to London to be raised by Belmont. This Dame Green's rationale was that Evelina's mother did not seem to care is her daughter received the fortune of Belmont, and "that, as *Miss* would never be the worse for it, she thought it pity *nobody* should be the better" (375). Belmont later validates the nurse's story: "unwilling . . . at that point in time to confirm the rumour of my being married, I sent the woman with the child to France; as soon as she was old enough, I put her in a convent, where she has been properly educated" (366). By sending the girl to France, Belmont assumed he was providing for her to the best of his ability. As Evelina explains in a letter to her guardian, "the child was instantly sent to France, where being brought up in as much retirement as myself, nothing but accident could discover the fraud" (375). Yet Belmont's hiding place for the girl is not merely coincidental, but rather symbolic. For not only is France the place where Belmont's initial deception took place, but it is also the place where he can perpetuate it, conveniently hiding the secret he wants to keep from the world. This decision to conceal the false daughter in France thus once more locates France as the novel's locus of deception.

The Evelyn lineage thus finds betrayal, cruelty, and regret, all while residing in France. Burney thus uses the image and idea of France in a nationalistic way, for she represents France, as so many other authors of this period also did, as a deceptive land. The family narrative has repeated itself from one generation to the next, as each member has invested the idea of France with feelings of peace and safety, only to find disappointment and disillusion. Just like her father, Caroline went to France to find refuge: while the father relocated to find peace from his own feelings of guilt and shame, the daughter relocated to find peace with her mother. Both father and daughter were deluded, however, in their choice of asylum. The father's unhappiness while in France led to his premature death, while the daughter's unhappiness while in France led to her marriage to "a very profligate young man," and thus indirectly to her own premature death as well.

The threat of France within Evelina's present world looms largest, of course, in the figure of Madame Duval. Returned to Britain to seek her granddaughter, Madame Duval represents Frances Burney's own early fears and anxieties about the French nation and her dislike of mixed, and so unstable, identities. Within the pages of the novel, Madame Duval poses very real and serious threats to Evelina's personhood, threats that are both physical and emotional. Physically, Madame Duval represents the possibility of taking Evelina back to France with her; emotionally, she represents the possibility of unsettling Evelina's sense of personal identity. The first of these dangers, the physical one, is the more obvious of the two, and surfaces during Evelina and Madame Duval's first private conversation. After she has slandered Mr. Villars, to Evelina's great dismay, Madame Duval reveals her true reasons for being in England. Evelina describes her own emotions as the subject turns from her guardian to herself: "grief and anger mutually gave way to terror, upon her avowing the intention of her visiting England was to make me return with her to France" (53). The emphasis here is not on Madame Duval's *asking* Evelina to go with her, but rather on *making* Evelina go with her, and, based upon her past treatment Evelina's mother, we know that Madame Duval typically relies upon force to get her way. Evelina's reaction to this threat is one of "terror," for she does not want to leave "that abode of tranquil happiness," Berry Hill (53). Her home is in Britain, and the idea of leaving it strikes terror into her.

Permanent removal from her homeland thus leaves Evelina in a state of panic, yet the more serious problem is the challenge to her sense of identity. From the moment of her first appearance in the novel, Madame Duval also represents the threat of a dual identity, an identity that challenges Evelina's way of seeing the world. If France is a dangerous land, then it is especially dangerous to encounter a woman from this country like Madame Duval, who is not quite French and yet not quite British, since this sort of woman is complex and difficult to decipher. Accustomed to easily assessing the people around her, Evelina is confounded when it comes to this strange amalgam of the both the French and British nations. Although in Great Britain and speaking English once again, the constant littering of her sentences with French exclamations and phrases marks Madame Duval as a Frenchwoman, although she is by birth British. This confusion as to Madame Duval's true national identity is present throughout the novel. Evelina's grandmother is first introduced to us in person, for instance, on what Evelina thinks will be her last night in London. Significantly, the Mirvan party has chosen to watch a Fantocini, a puppet show borrowing from both French and Italian traditions. On this night of dual nationalities, after the Fantocini has ended, the Mirvans are waiting outside for their carriage, when as Evelina will write to Mr. Villars, "a tall elderly woman brushed quickly past us," exclaiming "'*Ma fois, Monsieur*. . . . I have lost my company, and in this place I don't know nobody'" (49). Describing the woman, whom Evelina does not yet know to be her grandmother, Evelina observes that "There was something foreign in her accent, though it was difficult to discover whether she was an English or a French woman" (49). This difficulty is exactly what upsets Evelina's world view; confronted with an ambiguous national identity, Evelina can no longer trust her perceptions. This "supposed foreigner" (52), as Evelina will later refer to Madame Duval, throws Evelina's understanding of the world into question.

The fact that Madame Duval can pass as French although really English is a frightening prospect to Burney, and so to Evelina as well. Identities should be fixed, should be stable, and when a person has the ability to change an identity, whether national or other, the world is no longer as straightforward as it should be. Mutability thus represents a frightening prospect in this novel, one that undermines the basis of society and even the nation. One of the most telling passages in this respect is the one in which Madame Duval explains to her granddaughter how a French education would change Evelina for the better. A few days after she meets Madame Duval, Evelina calls upon her grandmother, who almost immediately begins a tirade against the British, concluding her harangue by once again threatening to take Evelina back to France with her. The physical threat of removal from Britain is severe, but even more severe is the national threat that this move would represent since it would mean that Evelina's identity would be disrupted. As Evelina explains in one of her letters to Mr. Villars:

> She talked very much of taking me to Paris, and said I greatly wanted the polish of a French education. She lamented that I had been brought up in the country, which, she observed, had given me a *very bumpkinish air*. However, she bid me not despair, for she had known many girls, much worse than me, who had become very fine ladies after a few years (sic) residence abroad; and she particularly instanced a Miss Polly Moore, daughter of a chandler's shop woman, who, by an accident not worth relating, happened to be sent to Paris, where, from an awkward, ill-bred girl, she so much improved, that she has since been taken for a woman of quality. (67)

This passage is significant for two main reasons: first, because it undermines the value of "a French education," and second, because it highlights Burney's ongoing critique of unstable identities. To address the first of these claims, Burney uses the tale of Miss Polly Moore to mock the Grand Tour, which, by the 1760's, had already come under attack in Britain as the formative part of an Englishman's education.[12] Coming where it does in the novel, only a few pages after a heated discussion between Madame Duval and Captain Mirvan about the Grand Tour, this passage offers a strongly nationalist claim. During this previous discussion of the Grand Tour, Madame Duval insists that travel to France would make "quite another person" of the Captain. His reply, however, is a sarcastic commentary on what that other person would be like: "What, I suppose you'd have me learn to cut capers?—and dress like a monkey?—and palaver in French gibberish? . . . And, powder, and daub, and make myself up" (61). Taken to their extremes, the merits of a French education are seen to consist of nothing other than learning to "cut capers," "dress like a monkey," "palaver in French gibberish," and "powder, and daub, and make [one]self up." The absurdities of what one learns abroad, the shine that comes from the "polish of a French education," are thus made obvious by the Captain's caricature, which is exaggerated, but held to be nonetheless true since the other characters laughingly seem to agree with the Captain's claims.[13] When Madame Duval learns during this same conversation that her other nemesis Sir Clement Willoughby has spent three years abroad, she scoffingly criticizes the use of his time: "I dare say you only kept company with the English" (60).[14] If her remarks on his behavior are accurate, though, then Sir Clement *has* made good use of his time, for associating with the French would have contaminated his manners. At the very worst, Sir Clement could have become like Sir Lovel, whose French mannerisms and expressions are ridiculed throughout the novel, beginning with Evelina and Maria Mirvan's mockery of him at the ball.

Besides offering commentary on education in this passage, Burney also shows the dangers of possessing an unstable identity. That is, in Madame Duval's words we can recognize not only Burney's doubts as to the value of a French education, but also once again her fears regarding individuals who are not really what they seem to be. This fear is best exemplified not in Madame Duval's comments on a French education, but rather in the tale that she relates of "a Miss Polly Moore, daughter of a chandler's-shop woman, who, by an accident not worth relating, happened to be sent to Paris, where, from an awkward, ill-bred girl, she so much improved, that she has since been taken for a woman of quality." Within the tale that Madame Duval weaves, Polly Moore comes to represent all individuals who smoothly glide their way across the strata of society, changing their identities in the process. In this respect, Madame Duval's, and hence Burney's, use of the indefinite article here is significant, for the fact that the young woman is not just "Miss Polly Moore," but rather "*a* Miss Polly Moore" emphasizes the commonness of her name and experience, as if there are more women who can tell the same story. Even the name "Polly" carries meaning with it, for it is a very general name, one shared by many women and one that also stands in for the actual full name of its possessor.[15] Polly Moore's transformation into "a woman of quality" is essentially a fraud, for society has been "taken" or fooled by this decoy, and, while Madame Duval approves of this deception, Evelina does not. If the "daughter of a chandler's-shop woman" can be "taken for a woman of quality," then there is no telling what frauds may be practiced upon society. Identities should be firm, should be stable, as we have already seen in Evelina's assessments of Lord Orville and Mr. Lovel, and in what critics have called her snobbery regarding the Branghtons' pretensions to gentility.[16]

Evelina's later 'adventure' with the prostitutes also underscores Burney's desire to view the world as straightforward, and analyzing this episode alongside Polly Moore's story provides further insight into Burney's conception of the world. In this later incident, Evelina goes to Marybone-gardens with the Branghtons and Madame Duval, but becomes separated from her party during a fireworks display. In her quest to find her friends, Evelina is repeatedly harassed by several young men who prey upon her distress, until one finally tries to grab her hand. Exceedingly frightened, Evelina runs away from the man and right into the arms of a pair of prostitutes, although she does not at first recognize them as such. She describes the episode to Mr. Villars in a revealing letter:

> I ran hastily up to two ladies, and cried, "For Heaven's sake, dear ladies, afford me some protection!"
>
> They heard me with a loud laugh, but very readily said, "Ay, let her walk between us;" and each of them took hold of an arm.
>
> . . . .
>
> But imagine, my dear Sir, how I must be confounded, when I observed, that every other word I spoke produced a loud laugh! However, I will not dwell upon a conversation, which soon, to my inexpressible horror, convinced me I had sought protection from insult, of those who were themselves most likely to offer it! You, my dearest Sir, I well know, will both feel for, and pity my terror, which I have no words to describe.
>
> Had I been at liberty, I should have instantly run away from them, when I made the shocking discovery; but, as they held me fast, that was utterly impossible: and such was my dread of their resentment or abuse, that I did not dare make any open attempt to escape. (233)

Initially deceived in both who and what these two women are, Evelina runs to them for protection, 'taking' them to be "dear ladies." Her mistake soon becomes apparent, however, as the realization hits her that these two woman are, in fact, prostitutes. Evelina's ability to read the world thus gives her the ability to figure out what kind of women they really are, but not before the initial fraud is practiced upon her. She is not, however, the only one deceived in the two women. Herself a practitioner of artifice, Madame Duval is still also fooled by the two new additions to their party: "As to Madame Duval, she was really for some time so strangely imposed upon, that she thought they were two real fine ladies" (236). This imposition, of course, has more disastrous results for Evelina than it does for Madame Duval since it compromises Evelina in front of Lord Orville, ultimately causing him to also question the true appearance of things. Pinioned as she is between the two women, Evelina must submit to being seen with them by Lord Orville. In hindsight, the episode occasions her to remark: "Whatever may be the construction that Lord Orville may put upon this affair, to me it cannot fail of being unfavourable; to be seen—gracious Heaven!—to be seen in company with two women of such character!" (237). Being seen in the company of prostitutes discredits Evelina's reputation since, as Mr. Villars has earlier reminded her, "nothing is so delicate as the reputation of a woman: it is, at once, the most beautiful and most brittle of all human things" (164). Proper decorum forbids her from offering an explanation, so Evelina must submit to Lord Orville's own interpretation.

The encounter with the two prostitutes thus serves as a striking parallel for the story of Polly Moore. In both instances, Evelina is confronted with women who are something other than that which they appear to be. Just as Polly Moore "has been taken for a woman of quality," so, too, are the prostitutes taken for "two real fine ladies," first by Evelina and then by her grandmother. Like Polly Moore, then, the two prostitutes take on identities not truly their own, identities that, within the views expressed in the novel, they do not actually possess. Appearing to be something other than they really are, the prostitutes are dangerous to Evelina because her association with them threatens her precarious position as a proper young woman in British society. Although the reader is not privy to the rest of Polly Moore's story, one can easily imagine that she might pose a similar threat to some other unsuspecting young man or woman. And Madame Duval, as the possessor of a dual national identity, also claims membership to their group. All four women thus represent the threat of the world turned upside down as a result of deceptive appearances. Over thirty years later, when writing *The Wanderer*, the much older Frances Burney would embrace the complexity of the world, with all of its shadows and nuances; for now, however, she rejects false appearances, favoring a world that continues to uphold all of its first promises.

*****

While Madame Duval therefore specifically threatens Evelina because of her unstable identity, striking at one of Evelina's biggest fears, that of an opaque society, she poses more of a *national* threat to the other characters in the novel and, indeed, to Burney's contemporary readers. For them, Madame Duval represents France and its people, and, since France has already figured as the site of danger and deceit in the novel, Burney's portrayal of Madame

Duval as a French woman would easily strike a chord with her more nationalistic and anti-French readers.[17] As a French woman, Madame Duval comes to embody the fears of a nation that had been at war with France at various intervals since 1689. France was Britain's greatest enemy. One of the dangers that Madame Duval represents by her 'Frenchness' is the importation of foreign customs into Britain, customs which could eventually undermine the basis of British national culture. The French phrases, habits, and dress of Evelina's grandmother could pollute, as it were, the British characters she encounters. To provide a cultural context for these interactions, it is useful to turn to another text so we can see how these same fears surfaced in other works from the period. Writing in 1783, only five years after the publication of *Evelina*, John Andrews set down some of these same nationalist observations in his *Remarks on the French and English Ladies, in a series of letters; interspersed with various anecdotes, and additional matter, arising from the subject.* In one of the letters from the *Remarks* on both the influence of French women and the dangers of travel to France, Andrews makes this point clear:

> Now, as neither the deportment of the men, nor the corresponding manners of the women in France, are desirable objects of importation, the less we are tempted to fetch them over, the better it most certainly is for a people, who with, for a variety of substantial reasons, to retain the plainness of their own manners, and to keep at a distance from these pretended refinements in the exterior habits of intercourse, and in the system of living, which always degenerate into expensiveness and effeminacy.
>
> The danger of following the examples we see in France is the greater, as the people take so much pains to impress foreigners with the highest notions of their superior judgment and propriety.
>
> In other countries, the travelers are much less liable to be inveigled into an adoption of the ideas and customs prevailing among the natives....[18]

According to Andrews, French manners insidiously work their way into British culture when foolish British travelers make these manners into "objects of importation" and are "tempted to fetch them over." What Andrews sees as "the danger of following the examples we see in France" results from the fact that these "pretended refinements" will ultimately "always degenerate into expensiveness and effeminacy." His fear, which was a common one of the period, was that French influence would create a nation of effeminate and self-indulgent men. The trade metaphor that Andrews employs to discuss this process of gradual degeneration becomes literal only a few pages later, however, when Andrews' fears about the French become even more obvious. Within this same letter, Andrews' tone becomes more paranoid and hostile as he goes on to assert that French influence not only destroys English morals and manners, but also that "our trade, our manufactures, our whole commercial interest suffers through them" and that English gentlemen "cannot be too much forewarned of the necessity, of not suffering themselves to be imposed upon by the specious pretences of a rival nation" (263). This Scotsman's fear of French customs thus gradually reveals itself to be a fear of "a rival nation." If the British let French manners slowly seep their way into British culture, the argument goes, the manners will eventually enable the French to overpower the British in political and economic matters as well.

Madame Duval thus represents economic and political threats, but she also represents the threat of actual physical assault. Although violence characterizes all of Madame Duval's relationships with the other characters in the novel, none of these relationships bear the same intensity as that between Madame Duval and Captain Mirvan. The relationship between these two aggressive individuals is one of the most underanalyzed aspects of the novel, and yet its role is central in understanding Burney's nationalist project. If Madame Duval represents a national threat to Burney's eighteenth-century audience, then that threat has to be controlled, and this is where the Captain comes in. Madame Duval is most marked as a French woman, and thus as a target of violence, through Captain Mirvan's interactions with her, and it is through the power of the Captain that Burney quells this French threat, rendering this obnoxious, vocal, and domineering old woman voiceless and so powerless.[19] The primary way in which Burney achieves this representation of Madame Duval via Captain Mirvan is by using war metaphors. Throughout the novel, Burney figures the relationship between Captain Mirvan and Madame Duval as an ongoing battle, one that is waged against the French nation in the name of the British. In his capacity as Madame Duval's aggressor, the Captain becomes the representative of the British state, which is defined by political theorist Ernest Gellner as "that agency within society which possesses the monopoly of legitimate violence. . . . [and] the specialization and concentration of order maintenance."[20] When the state initiates or condones violence, that violence is usually not even thought to be violent since it comes from a 'legitimate' power source. William Ian Miller provides additional insight on this point. He observes that violence that is condoned by the state is also sanctioned by society when it trickles its way down the social hierarchy:

> Of course, the state does not monopolize legitimacy, for it is intimately involved in all social hierarchy and is an issue in most all social action. Violence that works its way down the hierarchy is viewed as legitimate, order- effecting, and is often thus not even recognized as violence, or when recognized as violence is seen as less violent than the same amount of force opposing it. [21]

Miller's analysis applies especially well to our naval officer. A British seaman with a long history of aggressive behavior, Captain Mirvan's use of violence is most certainly "viewed as legitimate, [and] order-effecting" in Burney's novel. He comes to represent the force of Britain as it struggles to repel the French threat of inculturation and effeminization as personified in Madame Duval. His battles with her thus take on an importance that has far-reaching effects for Burney's British readers.

Before going on to look at some examples of how the Captain uses military jargon to justify his assaults on Madame Duval, it is important to stop for a moment to consider the larger significance of these assaults. Many critics, both from Burney's period and our own, have laughed at Captain Mirvan's antics, pleased that he has the ability to put Madame Duval in her place in these battles.[22] By sympathizing with the Captain at the expense of Madame Duval, however, these critics only buy into Burney's nationalist agenda, without stopping to question it. They implicitly agree that Madame Duval is a specifically French threat that needs to be stopped at whatever cost. When we recognize Burney's nationalist project and her emphasis on Madame Duval's *Frenchness* and Captain Mirvan's *Britishness*, however, we recognize the cultural and political significations of the character portrayals and the roles that they played within eighteenth-century British society. Burney's specific choice of governing metaphor in these encounters brings with it a nationalist overtone that would greatly influence her readers' positive reaction to Captain Mirvan's treatment of Madame Duval. As Mr. Lovel, one of several minor characters in *Evelina* and an egregious fop, will point out in a rare moment of insight, the Captain is "a fellow who has done nothing but fight all his life" (403). Although Mr. Lovel makes this statement in a condescending and rather off-hand manner, the statement is a significant key to understanding the exchanges between the Captain and Madame Duval. As modern readers of the novel, we have to remember that the Captain has good reason for hating the French: he had been at war with this country for many years, and France represented Britain's greatest enemy, because greatest rival. Linda Colley, of course, points this out, as does Walter Dorn. In his now-classic study on the competition between the French and British empires, Dorn maps the development of this antagonistic relationship, explaining how these two countries finally emerged from the eighteenth century as the two great colonial and imperialist Western European powers, ahead of Spain, Portugal, and Holland. Pitted against one another, Britain and France became fierce rivals in their quests for expansion.[23] The situation finds its modern analog in our own country, where the United States and the Soviet Union emerged as the two greatest super powers of the twentieth century, and, subsequently, the two greatest rivals in what would eventually become the Cold War. Burney's contemporary readers would have been greatly familiar with the hostilities between their own country and France, and would have recognized the Captain as the representative of Britain.[24] Battles won against Madame Duval thus symbolize battles won against France, even when those battles are read by a twenty-first-century audience. Not acknowledging this connection makes us complicit with Burney's nationalist agenda.

Returning to the novel, Captain Mirvan makes clear his antagonistic intentions towards Madame Duval by phrasing each of his plans in militaristic terms. Each time he confronts Madame Duval, he views the encounter as a battle. All of these attacks will ultimately cause Evelina to remark that Mrs. Mirvan's "principal study seems to be healing those wounds which her husband inflicts" (53). Leaving a series of wounds in his wake, the Captain engages in battle after battle with his sworn enemy. For example, when Sir Clement rejoins the Mirvan party as a guest at Howard Grove, Captain Mirvan begins to plan the elaborate scheme of pretending that Monsieur Du Bois is imprisoned, a scheme which will culminate in the false robbery episode. Declaring that "he was going to read his commission to his ship's company," the Captain warns Evelina and the others present that they must go along with his mission:

> I expect obedience and submission to orders; I am now upon a hazardous expedition, having undertaken to convoy a crazy vessel to the shore of Mortification; so, d'ye seem if any of you have any thing to propose, that will forward the enterprize,—why speak and welcome; but if any of you, that are of my chosen crew, capitulate, or enter into any treaty with the enemy,—I shall look upon you as mutinying, and turn you adrift. (139)

The "crazy vessel" that the Captain has "undertaken to convoy . . . to the shore of Mortification" is, of course, none other than "the enemy" Madame Duval. Captain Mirvan's use of the word *mortification* also brings up a crucial aspect of his relations with Madame Duval. Any process of mortification involves the process of making a person aware of his or her flesh, of the very physicality of the body, since its roots lie in the word *death*. Also wrapped up with this meaning, though, is the possibility of humiliation, and one definition that the *OED* gives for *to mortify* is "To cause a person to feel humiliated; to cause (a person) mortification." The Captain's war-like relations with Madame Duval are thus founded upon his ability to humiliate his enemy, to bring her low. Yet humiliating Madame Duval also involves making her aware of her own pretentiousness. The work of William Ian Miller is once again useful to elucidate this point. In his explanation of the differences between shame and humiliation, Miller carefully discriminates between these two states of being: "It is humiliation that disciplines those who pretend to positions they are unworthy of filling. . . . One of the most salient distinctions between shame and humiliation is that, at root, humiliation depends upon the deflation of pretension. . . . Being cool or looking cool is asking for humiliation, as much as it is a defense against what it is asking for. . . . *humiliation is the consequence of trying to live up to what we have no right to*."[25] Madame Duval's pretensions toward gentility and refinement, pretensions found in her self-representation as a French woman and hence superior to the British, is what particularly angers Captain Mirvan. He views her as an object in need of disciplining, an object in need of deflating, and he relies upon humiliation as his method of so doing.

A military strategist to the core, the Captain also carefully plans his battles and his line of attack. Each time he wages war against his enemy, the Captain sets his sights on Madame Duval's most prized possession: her voice. Since Madame Duval's two most dominant characteristics are her violence and her volubility, the Captain continually seeks to weaken her defenses, to humiliate her, by capturing her ability to communicate.[26] Take away her speech, his strategy runs, and you take away her violence, and hence her power. The exchanges between Captain Mirvan and Madame Duval always begin as verbal quarrels, and slowly escalate to physical assaults that leave Madame Duval speechless. And, as the relationship between Captain Mirvan and Madame Duval progresses, so, too, does the intensity of the violence and the humiliation increase. Their initial encounters are violent ones, but the violence becomes more severe as the two characters interact more, each time forcing the loss of Madame Duval's voice to a greater and more damaging extent. On the night of the Fantocini, for instance, before the Captain even knows who Madame Duval is, he first exercises his talent for wounding. Separated from her own party, Madame Duval pleads for assistance from the Mirvans. When the Mirvans admit the foreigner into their coach, the two strangers immediately begin bickering. The argument's hostility increases until Madame Duval calls the Captain "a low, dirty fellow." At that point, the Captain's anger becomes too great, and he "seiz[es] both her wrists," yelling, "hark you, Mrs. Frog, you'd best hold your tongue, for I must make bold to tell you, if you don't, that I shall make no ceremony of tripping you out of the window; and there you may lie in the mud till some of your Monsieurs come to help you out of it" (51). Shortly after this first meeting, on the night of the outing to Ranelagh, the Mirvan party finds itself separated from one another after their coach breaks down. Madame Duval remains missing, unable to be found, and only appears after Evelina is considerably worried. When she finally materializes with Monsieur Du Bois, both of them are filthy. Recalling the incident, Evelina relates that "She then entered,—in such a condition!—entirely covered with mud, and in so great a rage, it was with difficulty she could speak. We all expressed our concern, and offered our assistance,—except the Captain; who no sooner beheld her, than he burst into a loud laugh" (65). Madame Duval's rage, which makes it difficult for her to speak, is owing to a fall - a fall, the reader will later learn, initiated by the Captain. When she finally regains her ability to speak, Madame Duval explains that while Monsieur Du Bois was carrying her away from the fractured carriage, he accidentally fell, dropping both of them right into the middle of a large mud puddle. "This recital put the Captain into an extacy," Evelina will report, as, pleased at their misfortune, "he went from the lady to the gentleman, and from the gentleman to the lady, to enjoy alternately the sight of their distress. He really shouted with pleasure. . . . declaring repeatedly, that he had never been better pleased in his life" (65). The "extacy" that the Captain feels in their misfortune only sharpens Madame Duval's anger, which does not go unchecked for long, for she soon retaliates:

> The rage of poor Madame Duval was unspeakable; she dashed the candle out of his hand, stamped upon the floor, and, at last, spat in his face.
>
> The action seemed immediately to calm them both, as the joy of the Captain was converted into resentment, and the wrath of Madame Duval into fear; for he put his hands upon her shoulders, and gave her so violent a shake, that she screamed out or help; assuring her, at the same time, that is he had been one ounce less old, or less ugly, she should have had it all returned on her own face.

> Monsieur Du Bois, who had seated himself very quietly at the fire, approached them, and expostulated very warmly with the Captain; but he was neither understood not regarded, and Madame Duval was not released, till she quite sobbed with passion. (66)

The pleasure that the Captain takes in Madame Duval and Monsieur Du Bois' fall, an act of physical violence that the Captain actually committed, leaves Madame Duval speechless, filled with a "rage" that is "unspeakable." Unable to give voice to her feelings, Madame Duval can only manifest her emotions through actions, by "dash[ing] the candle out of his hand, stamp[ing] upon the floor, and, at last, sp[itting] in his face." Madame Duval is relegated to a child-like state, forced to use forms of nonverbal communication to represent her anger because the Captain has stripped her voice away from her.

The violence continues to slowly build after this encounter over Madame Duval's fall, until it finally crescendos in the fake robbery episode discussed earlier, an episode that also mirrors the movement of the novel, slowly building before it, too, reaches its final peak. In his desire "to convoy a crazy vessel to the shore of Mortification," the Captain stages an elaborate plan to put Madame Duval entirely at his mercy by pretending that her French companion Du Bois has been "taken up upon suspicion of treasonable practices against the government" (137). When she and Evelina set out in to learn what has become of Du Bois, the carriage is attacked by two 'thieves,' who are really Captain Mirvan and Sir Clement in disguise. The thieves enter the carriage, and, while one holds Evelina, "the other tore poor Madame Duval out of the carriage, in spite of her cries, threats, and resistance," causing Evelina to admit, "I was really frightened, and trembled exceedingly" (145). The elderly woman is taken "out of sight of the chariot" by one of the men (whom *we* know to be Captain Mirvan), who then abuses her. Madame Duval will later fill in the particulars of the incident, telling Evelina that the robber had violently shaken her: "he takes me by both the shoulders, and he gives me such a shake!—*Mon Dieu!* I shall never forget it, if I live to be an hundred. . . . So when he had shooked me till he was tired, and I felt all over like a jelly, without saying never a word, he takes me and pops me into the ditch" (150). When Evelina goes to look for her grandmother after her own release from Sir Clement, she finds Madame Duval

> seated upright in a ditch. I flew to her, with unfeigned concern at her situation. She was sobbing, nay, almost roaring, and in the utmost agony of rage and terror. As soon as she saw me she

> redoubled her cries, but her voice was so broken, I could not understand a word she said. I was so much shocked, that it was with difficulty I forbore exclaiming against the cruelty of the Captain, for thus wantonly ill-treating her; and I could not forgive myself for having passively suffered the deception. . . .
>
> Almost bursting with passion, she pointed to her feet, and with frightful violence, she actually beat the ground with her hands.
>
> I then saw, that her feet were tied together with a strong rope, which was fastened to the upper branch of a tree. . . . I assisted her to rise. But what was my astonishment, when, the moment she was up, she hit me a violent slap on the face! (147)

When Captain Mirvan earlier tripped Monsieur Du Bois, causing the Frenchman to land both himself and Madame Duval into the mud, the Captain laid his enemy low; this time, however, he lays her even lower, quite literally forcing her into a ditch. The Captain's penchant for fiercely shaking Madame Duval by the shoulders also reaches an extreme this time, for by the time he finishes maltreating her, Madame Duval is "sobbing, nay, almost roaring," capable only of producing the sounds of an animal. Her language abilities have been taken from her, for, as Evelina observes, Madame Duval's "voice was so broken, I could not understand a word she said." Unable to make herself understood through her broken cries and sobs, Madame Duval can only point to her source of discomfort, though in so doing, "with frightful violence, she actually beat the ground with her hands." Evelina's own sense of horror at her grandmother's condition is evident in this last remark in her use of the word *actually*; Evelina is extremely shocked to see Madame Duval act like an animal. Her extreme emotions also vent themselves in her treatment of Evelina, whom she viciously slaps. The Captain has thus succeeded once again in dehumanizing Madame Duval, and, although she is tempted to file suit against the thieves, Mrs. Mirvan dissuades her from doing so because there are no proper witnesses to the 'robbery.' The Captain had taken care to hide his own voice and face, even while doing such damage to Madame Duval's. *Her* voice was taken away from her by force, but *his* voice was taken away from him by choice. This important distinction once again points to the nature of their power relations, which always leave the Briton in the dominant position. Left with no form of retaliation, Madame Duval loses this final battle, leaving the Captain ultimately victorious.

*****

Although I have argued up until this point that the reader is cued to react to the Captain's violence in a sympathetic manner, seeing it as a humorous and even necessary way to deal with a national threat, a disturbing ambiguity still lies beneath the surface of this otherwise straightforward account of the Captain's treatment of Madame Duval. Violence against this French woman, violence committed by the very person who most closely represents the British state, is tolerated and even endorsed by the other characters, yet there is also something fundamentally unsettling about these acts of violence.[27] Our central narrator states this ambiguity concisely. Immediately after finding Madame Duval in the ditch and hearing her side of the tale, Evelina reflects on what has just occurred, remarking, "Though this narrative almost compelled me to laugh, yet I was really irritated with the Captain, for carrying his love of tormenting,—*sport*, he calls it,—to such barbarous and unjustifiable extremes. . . . Had I imagined he would have been so violent, I would have risked his anger in her [Madame Duval's] defence much sooner" (150-152). Torn between laughing at and grieving about Captain Mirvan's actions, Evelina raises two central questions regarding the Captain's violence: Is the violence even humorous? And, at what point does the violence become too excessive? The Frenchness of Madame Duval marks her as a prime target for nationalist prejudice and hence the Captain's forms of assault, but the violence still never quite sits right with the reader. The ambiguity revealed through these two questions owes its birth to two narrative strategies that Burney uses throughout the novel. The first strategy has to do with the nature of humiliation itself, which always works through the medium of comedy. That is, part of the difficulty in choosing whether or not to laugh stems from the Captain's use of humiliation as his method of devoicing Madame Duval. Explaining the differences between humiliation, shame, and embarrassment, Miller notes that

> Although both shame and humiliation work by lowering, in contemplating shame the observer is more likely to be moved to pity than glee. In a rough, but very crucial sense, shame involves tragic justice, humiliation comic justice. . . . humiliation's [genre] is comedy. . . . Humiliation is dark . . . . Humiliation is rough justice . . . . if humiliation has anything to do with amusement, that amusement would be dark indeed. The observers would get to indulge their malice, while the victim would suffer his fury and chagrin. . . . There is always a tinge of brutality in [humiliation], the delight of kicking someone who is down, a delight we can indulge in because the justice and desert of

> the humiliation excuses us from having to make excuses for our failure of fellow-feeling. We can even congratulate ourselves on the labor we devote to the administration of such justice as a service to the community.[28]

Humiliation needs comedy in order for it to function successfully. Psychologically, humiliation works by cultivating our desire to see justice served; it encourages us as witnesses to take pleasure in the sight of the victim brought low because of his or her claims to superiority. Madame Duval, with her condescending airs and her strong belief in the supremacy of her adopted nation, would thus seem to merit "the justice and desert of the humiliation" that the Captain ultimately dishes out.

The second and most sustained strategy comes from an implied critique of the Captain, where Burney's representation of the Captain reinforces this strong ambiguity about his use of violence. Burney uses humiliation as a strategy to induce us to laugh, but she uses the representation of the Captain to force us to catch that laughter in our throats. Too xenophobic, too extreme in his beliefs, the Captain is capable of producing some of the most socially embarrassing moments for Evelina and her group, and Evelina can rarely mention him in anything but a tone of disgust. His abrasiveness and savagery ultimately end up undermining his own authority by causing us to question the righteousness of all of his actions.[29] When first introduced to the Captain, for instance, Evelina describes him in purely negative terms:

> Captain Mirvan is arrived. I have not spirits to give an account of his introduction, for he has really shocked me. I do not like him. He seems to be surly, vulgar, and disagreeable.
>
> Almost the same moment that Maria was presented to him, he began some rude jests upon the bad shape of her nose, and called her a tall, ill-formed thing. She bore it with utmost good-humour; but that kind and sweet-tempered woman, Mrs. Mirvan, deserved a better lot. I am amazed she would marry him.
>
> For my own part, I have been so shy, that I have hardly spoken to him, or he to me. I cannot imagine why the family was so rejoiced at his return. If he had spent his whole life abroad, I should have supposed they might rather have been thankful than sorrowful. However, I hope they do not think so ill of him as I do. At least, I am sure they have too much prudence to make it known. (38)

Evelina's typically florid and spirited writing style has already been affected by her first meeting with the Captain. Direct and blunt, her first few sentences are simple ones, without any of her normal blandishments: "The Captain has arrived," "I do not like him," "He seems to be surly, vulgar, and disagreeable." Evelina's terse comments reflect her disapproval, and, knowing as we do her ability to accurately assess characters, we are trained to disapprove of the Captain also. Only a few pages later, Evelina makes her revelation even clearer: "I cannot bear that Captain; I can give you no idea how gross he is. . . . he seldom or never smiles but at some other person's expense" (48). These words appear before the group has even met Madame Duval or witnessed the Captain's acts of brutality against her, before the reader also realizes to how great of an extent the Captain derives pleasure from imposing pain and humiliation on others. Once again, then, one of Evelina's initial assessments of another character, this time Maria's father, prevails for the remainder of the novel. Knowing as we do both Evelina's and Burney's penchants for seeing the world as stable and transparent, as well as Evelina's facility in reading the world around her, it is difficult to see the Captain as anything but boorish and aggressive. First introduced to us as "surly, vulgar, and disagreeable," the Captain retains these same traits throughout our relationship with him.[30]

So why, then, does Burney undermine the Captain's power even while condoning it through his humiliating and yet humorous treatment of Madame Duval? The answer lies in Burney's own ambiguity about the nationalist project to which she tries to adhere. Although the novel readily makes use of the nationalist stereotypes and rhetoric of Burney's day, including a character like Madame Duval, who is so easy for readers to hate, it also reveals an underlying difficulty about believing in such falsified and exaggerated representations. The reader's sense of uneasiness with the violent encounters in *Evelina* reflects Burney's own nascent sense of uneasiness with extreme nationalism and violence against women, stirrings of uncertainty that will surface as outright criticism in her last novel, 1814's *The Wanderer*. The ambiguity evident in *Evelina* slips away in *The Wanderer*, leaving in its stead a direct and sustained critique of nationalist rhetoric and of violence against women conducted on behalf of the nation. Female community and protection also become paramount for Burney, as does the necessity for viewing the world and its inhabitants as ultimately complex and unknowable. Although in *Evelina* the French threat must be quelled, in *The Wanderer* Burney will come to recognize and appreciate French difference. Tolerance and compassion would become the hallmarks of Burney's new understanding of the world.

NOTES

1. Frances Burney, *Diary and Letters of Madame D'Arblay*, Ed. Charlotte Barrett (London, 1842–1846) 7: 154–163 and Fanny Burney, *The Wanderer*, Eds. Margaret Doody, Robert L. Mack, and Peter Sabor (New York: Oxford UP, 1991), 5.

2. Macaulay, *Edinburgh Review* 76 (January 1843): 559.

3. William Hazlitt, *Edinburgh Review* 24 (February 1815): 336.

4. Hazlitt, *Edinburgh Review*, 336.

5. Martha G. Brown offers a similar analysis of Burney's characters, arguing that Burney borrows character types, as well as plots and themes, from the romance tradition. For Brown, however, Burney's borrowing of romantic tropes is a sign that Burney is not a feminist writer. See Brown, "Fanny Burney's 'Feminism': Gender or Genre?," *Fetter'd or Free: British Women Novelists, 1670–1815*, Eds. Mary Anne Schofield and Cecilia Macheski (Athens, OH: Ohio UP, 1986), 29–39.

6. Both Margaret Anne Doody and Julia Epstein are notable exceptions, and refer to Burney's interest in issues of nationalism and national identity. Both critics mention that interest in passing, however, without developing the idea. See Doody, *Frances Burney: A Life in the Works* (New Brunswick, NJ: 1988), 23, 200, and Epstein, *The Iron Pen: Frances Burney and the Politics of Women's Writing* (Madison, WI: The U of Wisconsin P, 1989), 191. Some of the other critics who overlook these nationalist tones will be discussed later on in this essay.

7. See Benedict Anderson's important and influential text *Imagined Communities: Reflections on the Origin and Spread of Nationalism*. Rev. ed. (New York: Verso, 1991).

8. Linda Colley, *Britons: Forging the Nation 1707-1837* (New Haven: Yale University Press, 1992) 6.

9. Fanny Burney, *Evelina, or, The History of a Young Lady's Entrance into the World* (New York: Oxford UP, 1991), 29. All future references are to this edition and their page numbers will appear parenthetically in the text.

10. Even upon receipt of the false letter (actually written by Sir Clement Willoughby), Evelina's opinion of Orville is only temporarily clouded. The mix-up with the letter causes confusion, but is soon sorted out and even smoothed over by Evelina when Orville behaves so generously and kindly towards her afterwards.

11. It is also significant that the arranged marriage that Madame Duval tries to force upon her daughter Caroline would take place in France since the British had traditionally maligned France for this practice.

12. As Michèle Cohen explains, the term "Grand Tour" was coined in 1670 by Lassels to refer to extended voyages made to France. The term "Il Giro" was used to refer to travel to Italy. Cohen also traces the demise of the Grand Tour in more detail, explaining that it fell out of favor because it created frenchified and so effeminate men who often resorted to corruption and display. See Cohen,

Fashioning Masculinity: National Identity and Language in the Eighteenth Century (London and New York: Routledge, 1996), 54, 69–73.

13. Madame Duval's assessment of Evelina's education in this passage is also subject to Burney's critique, as are Madame Duval's own manners. Far from viewing Evelina as possessing a "*very bumpkinish air*," which Madame Duval claims she has, most of the characters in the novel see Evelina as intelligent. When Lady Howard first meets Evelina, for instance, she notes Evelina's upbringing: "She is a little angel! . . . . Had I not known from whom she received her education, I should, at fist sight of so perfect a face, have been in pain for her understanding" (21). At her first private ball, Evelina meets with a similar reaction from some of her gentleman admirers. Lord Merton will exclaim, "she is the most beautiful creature I ever saw in my life! . . . She looks all intelligence and expression" (35).

14. Writing as late as the third decade of the 1800's, Lady Morgan also noticed this tendency of the British to only consort with one another while traveling, although she viewed it as a negative trait of Englishmen abroad. In her *France in 1829–30*, Lady Morgan reports that

> The majority of Englishmen do not so much travel to acquire continental ideas, as to fortify and fix their own. They do not voyage for the sake of comparing British institutions, sentiments, and usages, with those of other countries; but for measuring all things foreign by the one infallible standard of all right and reason, "the custom of England." But the closer can be brought into juxta position, the easier is it to form a judgment between them. It is therefore a matter of unspeakable delight to the connoisseur to be thus enabled to bring home to the senses of the Parisians, the superiority of brown stout over champagne, and of muffins and twelfth cake over *brioches* and *gâteaus de Nantes*. . . . Englishmen generally travel for the sole purpose of congregating in foreign cities, and meeting the same faces which they habitually encounter in the Rotten-row and the round room at the Opera. . . .

Believing herself in the idea that "the closer things can be brought into juxta position, the easier is it to form a judgment between them," Morgan ridicules the extent to which the British take this idea when they only look to the false superiority of their own people. See Lady Sydney Owenson Morgan, *France in 1829–30*, (London, 1829–1830), 52–53.

15. Burney plays with the use of common names in her other works as well. In *The Wanderer*, for instance, Sir Jasper teasingly calls Juliet "Mrs. Betty" when she escorts him to the estate of Wilton. Sir Jasper picks this particular name for its commonality, while also choosing to tell the servants at Wilton that Juliet is a nursery-maid. See Fanny Burney, *The Wanderer; or, Female Difficulties*, Eds. Margaret Anne Doody, Robert L. Mack, and Peter Sabor (New York: Oxford UP, 1991), 759.

16. Edward W. Copeland connects this snobbery to Burney's own interest in economics and money, which, he argues, was a new concern for women novelists of the period. In all of Burney's novels, he claims, the lower classes are

treated with a "low, familiar comic style; the virtues of the admirable gentry (along with their estates) without fail involve her in reverent, if obscure, circumlocutions." See Copeland, "Money in the Novels of Fanny Burney," *Studies in the Novel* 8 (1976), 26.

17. Evelina is the only one of her circle to read Madame Duval as the possessor of a dual identity, since almost all of the other characters in the novel perceive Madame Duval as French. Madame Duval thus represents a threat to Evelina's own personal concerns, but a more general threat to the rest of the Britons in the novel. For example, on the same night of the Fantocini, right after Evelina first notices the "something foreign in [Madame Duval's] accent" discussed earlier, Maria Mirvan, Evelina's young friend and confidante, pleads to help the woman based on this very fact, urging her father to admit the unknown woman into their coach: "She is quite alone, and a foreigner" (50). Maria's father Captain Mirvan also believes that Madame Duval is French. He refers to her at various points as "Mrs. Frog" (51), "*the old French hag*" (54), "old Madam French" (64), and "the old French-woman" (136).

18. See John Andrews, *Remarks on the French and English Ladies, in a series of letters; interspersed with various anecdotes, and additional matter, arising from the subject* (London, 1783), 261.

19. Other critics read the purpose of this violence differently. The main argument of Julia Epstein's *The Iron Pen*, for instance, is that the episodes of violence that appear in Burney's novels represent Burney's "obsession with violence and hostility" (*Iron Pen*, 5). According to Epstein, Burney was not a "timid, prudish snob," as many critics have made her out to be, but rather an individual who masked her rage against society's constraints against women (4). "[S]urface propriety," Epstein writes, "was purchased at the price of internal rage" (5). Barbara Zonitch, on the other hand, reads the violence in Burney's texts as symptomatic of the declining aristocracy. In Zonitch's view, as British society moved away from being status-based and moved towards being class-based, violence broke out. Burney's fears about this new model of society emerged within her fiction as an investigation of the forms of protection that were now available for women. See Barbara Zonitch, *Familiar Violence: Gender and Social Upheaval in the Novels of Frances Burney* (Newark, DE: U of Delaware P, 1997).

20. Gellner admittedly borrows his definition from the theories of sociologist Max Weber. See Gellner, *Nations and Nationalism* (Ithaca, New York: Cornell UP, 1983), 3.

21. Miller, *Humiliation and Other Essays on Honor, Social Discomfort, and Violence* (Ithaca, NY: Cornell UP), 74. Miller himself points out, however, that "The state's claim to a monopoly on the means of violence has an uneven application in fact and even in some ways in theory" (80). Certain areas of society, for instance, such as the family, are allowed to exercise an unregulated violence.

22. In her otherwise insightful article "*Evelina*; or Female Difficulties," Susan Staves goes so far as to assert that Captain Mirvan is actually a positive character. Staves writes: "the Captain is a brave and essentially good-hearted man; he

exposes sham and administers his corporeal punishments only to those who deserve them." See Staves, "*Evelina*, or Female Difficulties," *Modern Philology* 73 (1976), 378. Julia Epstein also presents a negative portrait of Madame Duval by comparing her to the Captain. Madame Duval, according to Epstein, "is matched against Captain Mirvan as a character whose roughhewn sensibility makes it impossible for her to empathize with others" (*Iron Pen*, 113). If anything, however, Captain Mirvan is the character who possesses the "most roughhewn sensibility," not Madame Duval.

23. Walter Dorn, *Competition for Empire 1740–1763* (New York: Harper, 1940), 251.

24. It is also significant that Evelina generally refers to him as "the Captain" instead of as "Captain Mirvan." Her use of the definite article emphasizes the uniqueness of his position: he is *the* captain, *the* leader of their group.

25. Miller, *Humiliation*, 130–145.

26. By the time that *Evelina* was written, loquaciousness was a characteristic that the British perceived as being decidedly French. As critic Michèle Cohen explains, in the early part of the eighteenth century, the French had been represented as vocal and lively speakers, whereas the British had already been typecast as naturally taciturn and reluctant to speak. To develop their conversation skills more, British men were urged by popular writers such as Addison and Steele to engage in more conversation with women, who were also thought to be, like the French, natural talkers. Cohen, *Fashioning Masculinity,* 4–9.

27. Doody also notices this impression: "Burney uses farce and the licence farce gives to develop scenes of expressive violence. The odds are steadily raised until the laughing reader notices discomfort, protests that things have gone, as we say, beyond a joke" (*Frances Burney*, 56). Doody, however, links this unsettling nature of the violence, as mentioned in a previous footnote, to power relations, whereas I link it to Burney's own ambivalences about her nationalist project.

28. Miller, *Humiliation*, 137–149.

29. A discussion of the gender politics apparent in these acts of violence lies outside the scope of this essay. For thorough discussions of Burney's use of violence against women, however, see the recent work by Doody, Epstein, Staves, and Zonitch referenced earlier.

30. Besides possessing an extremely disagreeable personality, Captain Mirvan also uses some of the same violent tactics as he uses with Madame Duval in his relationships with his own family and their young guest. He never actually physically assaults his wife or daughter, but he continually abuses them verbally, in addition to repeatedly embarrassing them. See, for instance, pages 58, 73, 77, and especially 109, where the Captain commands Evelina and Maria to be silent.

The Critique of Originality in French Letters

REGINALD McGINNIS

The words *original* and *originalité* appear in eighteenth-century French dictionaries with two opposing meanings. The first definition of the noun *original* given in Diderot and d'Alembert's *Encyclopédie* is "the first drawing, or authentic instrument of something, & that is to serve as a model or example to be copied or imitated."[1] With respect to painting, the adjective is said to be taken both positively and negatively: "positively, when in a painting everything is grand, singularly new; & negatively, when one finds only a bizarrely grotesque singularity."[2] A similar ambivalence is mentioned in the short entry on *originalité*: "a way of executing a common thing, in a singular & distinguished manner: *originality* is very rare. Most men are in every genre but copies of other men. The title *original* is given both negatively & positively."[3] The laudatory meaning, expressing authenticity, or referring to a model to be copied or imitated, is well established. The following pages are concerned with the less familiar pejorative sense, relating to a bizarrely grotesque singularity.[4]

Though mentioned in dictionaries and at times in footnotes to literary works, the negative sense of the word has remained largely unstudied. Roland Mortier broaches the subject in his study of originality as a new aesthetic category in the eighteenth century,[5] but his observations on the negative sense are limited to showing the word's ambivalence. While he gives several examples of its usage, mostly in Marivaux and Diderot, he fails to draw the implicit conclusion for his thesis, the object of which is to show a separation occurring in the minds of Europeans during the period from 1740 to 1770 between originality and mimesis. [6] It follows from Mortier's observations on the negative sense of the word "originality" that the rise of its usage coincides with the period he assigns to the questioning of traditional mimesis. The texts we will consider in the following pages show that the negative sense contains a critique of originality conceived as separate from mimesis, so that the questioning of mimesis evolves in conjunction with a questioning of originality.

As stated in the *Encyclopedia* entries on originality, imitation can be considered either with respect to representation, as in painting for instance, or with respect to social relations, in which men are seen as copies of other men. The social aspect of imitation becomes prominent in the play with which we will begin, *Les Originaux* by Barthélemy Christophe Fagan, first performed in 1737. The object of the play, as stated in the introduction to the 1760 edition of Fagan's works, is "to rid a young man of quality of several flaws, & make them odious or ridiculous in his eyes by presenting them successively in the different people of his society who are affected by them."[7] The *originaux* are the characters affected by the flaws of which the young man, a marquis, is to rid himself. The project of correcting these flaws is not, however, that of the marquis, but rather of his mother, who despairs at his refusal, influenced by the fashion of the *originaux,* to marry the woman she intends for him. Convinced that "examples will be better than any lesson one could give," a chevalier, assisting the marquise, arranges for several *originaux*, each of whom has a very pronounced flaw, to visit the marquis. First in line is the ignorant seneschal, followed by a drunken baron, a slanderous chambermaid, a *faux brave,* and a profligate old man. Through the observation of his own flaws in the bizarre and ridiculous characters that come to visit him, the marquis ends up recognizing his errors and agrees to the wedding.

"Originality" in Fagan's play is linked with fashion, which is in turn linked with imitation. Its comic exploitation pertains to a destabilizing of relations between models and copies, whereby originals are shown to be copies, and copies appear as originals. The confusion of copies and originals is observed by the marquise in summarizing her son's imitation of fashion: "A slave to false airs, worshipper of the most outlandish silliness, he adopts so avidly the absurdities our young people bring into fashion, that it seems he alone would have created them, if, for the misfortune of society, others had not done so long before."[8] According to his mother, the marquis imitates so thoroughly the silly ways of fashion as to appear to have created them himself. His imitation could be confused with originality, though it should be observed in this instance that the confusion of models with copies is already at the second remove, since the "originals" he imitates are themselves imitations.

Though shown in the course of the play to be nothing but copies, and, moreover, flawed copies, the "originals" are seeking just the opposite: they endeavor to avoid imitation by refusing the models offered by society. The marquis' distaste for marriage is only one instance of his broader rejection of social norms, the most telling example of which is found in scene iii, where the marquis sits alone contemplating the morality and history books his mother has had placed on the desk next to him:

> Books! What a jumble of readings we are bothered with these days!
> Eh!, our first fathers, who were worthier than we, did they read?
> What are these volumes good for? For weighing down, for slowing
> down genius and making us copies, from originals we would be.[9]

According to the marquis, books are a hindrance, an impediment to originality. Implicitly, doing without books would liberate the marquis and those who think like him from models, making them more like their first fathers, who did not read, and yet were superior to them. In turning away from literary models, the marquis reverts to an anti-model, the illiterate first fathers, who are undoubtedly originals, since they come first, and yet offer no exit from imitation for the marquis who unwittingly evokes them as models. This visibly flawed theory, imitative in its rejection of imitation, reestablishes the very hierarchy of originals over copies it is trying to undo.

A distinctive trait of the "originals" is that, like so many traditional comic characters, they are unaware of their own flaws. In accordance with the play's pedagogical design, the marquis becomes aware of his flaws by confrontation with the "originals" he imitates. He ceases to be an "original" as soon as he recognizes "originality" for what it is, that is a flawed imitation.

"Originality," which Fagan refers to as a fashion in *Les Originaux*, becomes a fashionable subject for playwrights in the years that follow.[10] Though not indicated in the title, *Les Sincères* by Marivaux, first performed in 1739, is about originality. Sincerity in Marivaux' play is a false sincerity, the result of negative imitation. The marquise, having parted company with a group of "originals," complains of their various flaws, which she attributes broadly to an absence of sincerity (sc. iv). Like the marquise, Ergaste condemns the false airs of society, though in trying to avoid them he falls into the opposite excess. To avoid false appearances, he is led to adopt the appearances of avoiding false appearances, which are inevitably no less false than the appearances he wishes to avoid. "If, to appear frank," we are told, "it was necessary to lie, he would lie" (sc. ii). The search for sincerity dissolves into its opposite as the desire for truth is reduced to a desire for distinction. Ergaste does not want to persuade others that he is better than them, but that he is different from them. His "originality" consists of trying to distinguish himself from other "originals" who are visibly insincere. The negative imitation of a social model, which is a false model, results not in a true copy, but only in another false original.

The word itself appears again in the title of a play by Charles Palissot de Montenoy, *Le Cercle, ou Les Originaux,* first performed in 1755. Palissot's "originals" are similar to those of Fagan and Marivaux, the offspring of fashion and desire for distinction. His play reflects a shift in spirit, however, that has become meaner by the mid-1750's.[11] Whereas in *Les Originaux* by Fagan the aim is to instruct, in Palissot the aim is to amuse, and specifically to amuse at someone's expense. With Palissot, the question of "originality" becomes linked with "mystification," a kind of society game recently made fashionable, in which a group was made to laugh at the expense of a chosen victim.[12] Orphise and Ariste are practiced mystifiers who intend to make fun of some "originals" who, through oddity or trickery, are said to have eclipsed true talent and usurped a reputation. Taken literally, to usurp (*usurper*) is to appropriate by means of violence or fraud.[13] Just as violence is used to subvert the hierarchy, Orphise proposes violence as the means of restoring it. The comedy she wants to see played out at the expense of "originals" is presented as a just reprisal:

> My husband has the whim of holding a circle three days a week, of entertaining learned people, wits, all kinds of "originals"; and what to anyone other than himself would appear odd, bizarre, extravagant even, is precisely what pleases him most. I am good enough to go along with his whim, and often to feign great cheerfulness in the midst of these importunate characters. Today while he is in the country, I plan to amuse myself a bit at the expense of his society; I want to introduce it to you, enjoy the surprise you will feel at certain ridiculous traits I will see to exposing enough for us to have a laugh. So where is the crime in all that? Can I not avenge myself one time for all the ill humor these "originals" have given me in the two years I have had the generosity of letting them annoy me?[14]

Orphise's husband's circle constitutes an inversion of social norms: whatever would appear odd or bizarre to anyone else is what pleases him the most. Whereas Orphise usually goes along with her husband's whim, she has decided in turn to invert the already inverted order, exposing the "originals" for what they are. As in *Les Originaux* by Fagan, Palissot's play features a parade of bizarre characters: a poet, who wants to write plays that make the public laugh and cry at the same time; a *femme savante*, would-be author of an article for the *Encyclopedia;* a self-absorbed and pretentious financier; a philosopher who, in his quest for originality, goes so far as to oppose civilization; and finally a doctor who distinguishes between seeing *un malade* and *une maladie,* who sees patients, but not their illnesses.

The meaning of "originality" in the play, as well as the link between "originality" and "mystification," becomes clear with the first example, the poet. We immediately learn that he is in a bad mood because the public "has just mercilessly booed one of his plays, the success of which was making his head spin before the performance."[15] In the wake of his defeat, the poet tries to put a good face on things, attributing the public's reaction to his own failings:

> The poet, *with a very heavy tone of modesty:* I had tried to please the public; I had, as much as I was able, approached the great models, which we must look to as our masters. I was mistaken. I must have somehow deserved my misfortune, and it must be that the bias one naturally has for one's own works made me blind to my own flaws.[16]

The poet speaks here with a tone of false modesty in justifying the public for having booed his play. Unintentionally, he says the truth about himself: he is an "original" in the precise sense that he is a bad copy, a flawed imitation of his models.

Knowing the poet's weakness, Orphise begins caressing his vanity, using flattery as a means of making him do what she wants:

> Orphise, *maliciously to the poet:* Your modesty, monsieur du Volcan, cannot convince me that you received justice. I appeal to the public against the public itself; for, after all, true connoisseurs have assured me that the plan of your play was entirely within the rules; that it had interest, perfectly drawn situations, marvelous decoration, *coups de théâtre* in every scene . . .[17]

Mystification, which is a kind of comedy, is also a means of domination, of asserting one's mastery over others. In keeping with her plan, Orphise endeavors to bring out the flaws of the different characters. Her flattery draws the poet out of his false modesty, exposing him to ridicule as he begins praising his own play. The poet's role in the comedy is that of the victim. Though it seems like justice to Orphise, it has nonetheless the form of vengeance.

The spirit of vengeance characteristic of *Le Cercle* is not restricted to the theater and the actions of Orphise, but, rather, overflowed into the public sphere and accompanied the play from its first performance. Palissot's inclusion of Rousseau in his band of "originals" drew strong protests, not from Rousseau himself, but from other members of the philosophical camp, d'Alembert and the comte de Tressan, who led a vigorous campaign to have Palissot punished. Rousseau did not feel, however, as d'Alembert felt, that by attacking him his adversary had committed a serious offense against philosophy, and put an end to the affair by asking for Palissot's pardon.[18]

Though it ended without consequence, the episode began a cycle of vengeance that would soon continue. The following year, Palissot renewed his attack on the philosophers in his *Petites Lettres sur les grands philosophes,* stressing once again the question of originality. The beginning of the first letter refers to members of the "society of men of letters" associated with Diderot and d'Alembert's *Encyclopedia* in a way that recalls the "originals" of *Le Cercle*: "All these gentlemen say they are philosophers, and some of them are. But even amongst those in whom one recognizes the greatest talents, one is sorry to admit that there are some who have almost made reason and merit hateful in their writings."[19] Like Orphise in *Le Cercle,* Palissot draws a distinction in this passage between true and false talents. His view of the false philosophers resembles the characterization of the "originals" in *Le Cercle* who are said to have usurped a reputation through oddity or trickery.

Palissot's critique of philosophy in *Les Petites Lettres* remains closely tied to the question of originality. Prompted by what he considers a presmuptuous and delusive tone in the philosophers' writings, Palissot endeavors to show that works presented to the public as original are in fact copies. The confusion between originals and copies is said to pertain, moreover, to the philosophers' presentation of the project on which they founded their reputations, the *Encyclopedia*, in which erudition is made to appear as innovation. Following a line first used by Guillaume François Berthier in the *Journal de Trévoux,* Palissot argues that the authors of the *Encyclopedia* had copied other works without indicating the sources.[20]

The second letter is devoted to a critique of *Le Fils naturel* in which Diderot sets forth the principles of a new dramatic genre, which is neither tragedy nor comedy. Here again, Palissot maintains that Diderot's claim to originality is unfounded, pointing to models of the *genre sérieux* in ancient Rome, and alluding to unsuccessful efforts in this genre by the French: "May this author no longer imagine he has made a discovery by this so-called *genre sérieux* of which his play seems to him a model."[21] Diderot's confusion of models with copies is said to characterize not only *Le Fils naturel,* but his entire philosophical and literary output. Though the word itself is not used, Palissot implicitly accuses Diderot of plagiarism, citing *Les Pensées philosophiques,* copied from Shaftesbury, and *L'Interprétation de la nature,* copied from Bacon.

In discussing originality in the works of Diderot, Palissot uses both senses of the word. While arguing, on the one hand, that *Le Fils naturel* is a false original, and specifically a copy of Goldoni's *Verico Amico*, on the other hand he acknoweledges that certain characteristics of the play are "original" in the negative sense: "So is there nothing original in his play? I beg your pardon, Madame; and it is precisely the most finicky and worst thing. It is this cold philosophical jargon, always put in the place of what the characters should say."[22] That Diderot would have the characters of his bourgeois drama all speak like philosophers strikes Palissot as a serious error in taste, and every bit as bizarre as the theory of *conditions* which Diderot wishes to substitute for the analysis of *caractères*.

As with the attack on Rousseau in *Le Cercle,* Palissot's criticism of Diderot in *Les Petites Lettres* provoked a response from the philosophers. Daniel Delafarge considers at length an episode from the end of 1758 where Palissot was attacked as a protégé of Mme de Robecq and Mme de la Marck.[23] Two recently translated comedies by Goldoni, *Le Véritable ami* and *Le Père de famille,* were preceded by dedications that appeared insulting to Palissot's patronesses. The dedication to the second play was clearly a caricature of Palissot's dedication to *Les Petites Lettres,* inviting the conclusion that la princesse de * * * * * * was Mme de Robecq and the anonymous author Palissot. Leaving aside the intricacies of the affair, it seems certain that either Diderot or Grimm had written the dedications intended to disgrace him in the eyes of his patronesses. The accusation of plagiarism in *Les Petites Lettres* is answered by a different kind of false original. False attribution of authorship responds to the accusation of its opposite, the false appropriation of authorship, in an act of retaliation that is fundamentally imitative, though ultimately a negative imitation. Accusations of falsification and falsification of accusations fall one on the other in a pattern of mutual imitation that becomes generalized in the polemic of 1760 surrounding Palissot's satire, *Les Philosophes.*

Though not stressed the same way as in *Le Cercle,* "originality" remains very much a question in *Les Philosophes.* Palissot's philosophers are made to appear every bit as bizarre as his "originals" in the earlier play, and the adjective *original* maintains the same pejorative meaning.[24] The philosophers differ from the "originals" of *Le Cercle* chiefly in that they are meaner. They bring together the oddities of the "originals" and the maliciousness of their persecutors, Orphise and Ariste. The entire plot of *Les Philosophes* revolves around a "mystification" carried out by the philosophers at the expense of their hostess, Cydalise. Under the tutelage of Valère, Théophraste and Dortidius, Cydalise has been initiated into the most profound mysteries of philosophy. Her credulity is so extreme that she is led to believe she is the author of a book she has not even written herself, but rather that has been written by Dortidius. While the philosophers praise Cydalise in her presence, they laugh at her amongst themselves. And while Cydalise believes her book will establish her reputation in the world of letters, the philosophers know it will only expose her to ridicule. Significantly, as in the affair of 1758, Diderot, alias Dortidius, is assigned the role of penning a false original to someone else's detriment.

The question of originality becomes prominent in act II, scene iii where Cydalise meets with her secretary, M. Carondas, to write her preface. A former student of philosophy, Carondas admits he is still far from reaching his model, Valère.[25] His recognition of his shortcomings reveals, however, a degree of lucidity entirely lacking in Cydalise, whose knowledge of philosophy turns out to be very limited. From her discussion with Carondas, it becomes clear she is ignorant of ancient philosophy, and that she has read nothing but contemporary works. The entire scene reveals Cydalise's lack of originality, her utter inability to invent a thought. As she goes to dictate the beginning of her preface, the only lines she comes up with are taken from recent philosophy books, *Considérations sur les moeurs de ce siècle* by Duclos and *L'Interprétation de la nature* by Diderot. Her servile imitation of the new philosophy conveys the essence of Palissot's satire. In the context of the play, the philosophers are "originals" in the sense that they are flawed copies, and Cydalise is the copy of the copies.

The distinction between true and false talents drawn by Orphise in *Le Cercle* is echoed in *Les Philosophes,* where Palissot claims to ridicule not true philosophy, but rather the corruption or falsification of philosophy. The philosophers he satirizes have, like the "originals" in *Le Cercle,* used oddity or trickery to usurp a reputation. Like the "originals" in *Le Cercle,* moreover, they are punished for their trickery, as they end up being the victims of their own mystification. While the philosophers undertake to dupe Cydalise, the servants, Crispin and Marton, endeavor to trick the philosophers. The point of the entire play is to unmask the false philosophers, as stated by Marton in the final couplet:

> Des sages de nos jours nous distinguons les traits :

Nous démasquons les faux, et respectons les vrais. (III, xi)

It is, of course, unwillingly that the philosophers are exposed, and Palissot does not fail to include in his play its reception by the philosophers,[26] foreseeing their criticism, and the ways they would go about defending themselves.[27] Unable to stop the performance, the philosophers decide on a counter-offensive, which involves slandering both the author and his work, using acquaintances to carry out their vengeance for them. Palissot's prophecy in *Les Philosophes* did not take long to be fulfilled. Numerous polemical writings were published against Palissot in the weeks following the premiere, including *Les Originaux, ou les fourbes punis, parodie, scène par scène, des prétendus Philosophes* by André-Charles Cailleau. Though the author included music to produce a comic opera, the play imitates very closely Palissot's satire, quoting several verses almost textually.

While expressing opposite points of view, the two plays are structurally identical. Though the "originals" in Cailleau's play are no longer philosophers, but rather their enemies, they nonetheless resemble the philosophers in Palissot's satire in that they are shown above all to be "copies," and specifically plagiarists. Palissot was widely criticized for having put on the stage in his satire a person, Diderot, and not simply a type. But if the public recognized Diderot in Palissot's Dortidius, it could not have failed to see in Cailleau's "originals," Stipolas, Renfor and Tinpisone, the anagrams for Palissot, Fréron and Poinsinet. Cailleau's approach of a scene by scene parody only reinforces the symmetry. The famous bookpedlar's scene from *Les Philosophes,* for instance, that contains observations on books by Duclos, Grimm, Diderot and Rousseau is answered in Cailleau's play with observations on works by Palissot and Fréron, while Renfor makes a critique of *l'Ecossaise* by Voltaire.

The pattern of putting one's enemies on a public stage rapidly escalates in the weeks that follow the premiere of Palissot's satire, spreading to involve not only the principal actors, but also sympathizers on either side. The relation between opposing factions begins to resemble a vengeance cycle. Whereas Palissot attacks Diderot in *Les Philosophes,* he is attacked in return, not by Diderot, but by an associate, Cailleau, in *Les Originaux*. And Voltaire answers the satire of the philosophers by staging not Palissot but rather his erstwhile associate Fréron in l'*Ecossaise.*

Critics have traditionally drawn a distinction between Palissot and the philosophers, opposing mediocrity to genius, and blindness to lucidity. It would seem more accurate, though, to insist on the similarity between Palissot and the philosophers. From whichever side one considers this Enlightenment quarrel, what stands out is its anti-Enlightenment, attesting the triumph of the passions over reason. Whereas reason relies on distinctions between true and false, between cause and effect, the result of the polemic is to remove distinctions. Both Palissot and the authors from the philosophical camp claim to speak the language of reason, and they are equally lucid in portraying the deceptions of their adversaries. Yet they remain blind to their own deceptions, and particularly to the way in which they imitate each others' deceptions. As the violence of the polemic intensifies, authors on either side fall steadily into a pattern of copying, in which the adversary is always perceived as an "original," in the negative sense, but also with the implication that the other is at the origin of the conflict.

The polemic involving Palissot and the philosophers is a conflict between men, and more precisely between men of letters. Implicit at every point of the polemic, however, is a conflict between originality and mimesis. Palissot criticizes the encyclopedists for passing off as original material they have copied from other sources. When he refers to them as "originals" in *Les Philosophes* what he really means is that they are copies. Cailleau, in turn, does little more than copy *Les Philosophes* in *Les Originaux* where he applies Palissot's critique of the philosophers to Palissot and his cohorts.

We could say that the usage of "original" to signify "copy" is an example of antiphrasis. And while this is undoubtedly true, it does not really help to explain the pattern that emerges during the polemic around *Les Philosophes,* in which the aesthetic and social poles of mimesis converge. That the negative sense of the word "original" achieves ascendency in the context of a literary quarrel, that it belongs to a pattern of negative reciprocity, seems fundamental, and yet this point has been entirely overlooked in the history of both linguistic and literary criticism. The polemic between Palissot and the philosophers is radically destructive with respect to originality, that dissolves into a pattern of mutual negations. The violence of the polemic is reflected in the violence of the word used as a comic epithet. And just as the polemic is fundamentally critical, the usage of the word contains its criticism. What these authors imply through their mutual critiques is that what is put forth as original is never original in any pure sense, but always entails the imitation of models.[28]

The "original," who is always in this sense a false original, poses a threat to the established order. Destabilizing the relation between models and copies, "originality" undermines the foundations not only of reason, but also of morality and society. Rational, moral and social norms are replaced with an anti-model which takes the expression of exceptions to established norms. Philosophers and anti-philosophers refer to each other as "originals" in this very sense, implying that the threat is felt equally from either side. On the one hand, the history of the publication of the *Encyclopedia* shows the philosophers were perceived as a threat to the established hierarchy by religious leaders and by the court; yet, on the other hand, the philosophical movement soon becomes an institution in its own right, and becomes vulnerable as such to the kind of attacks it had itself made on the established hierarchy. The philosophers who are in this sense "originals" as long as they threaten the established order begin to fear "originals" once the legitimacy of their own reputations is called in question, as soon as other "originals" contest their authenticity.

It is often said that Diderot wrote *Rameau's Nephew* to take revenge on Palissot, and this is a very plausible interpretation, given that Palissot appears in Diderot's satire as an "original," and an associate of the nephew, who is presented in the opening pages as the prototype of the "original" as exception to established norms. The character of "originals" is said to contrast with that of others — "they break the tedious uniformity that our education, our social conventions and set politeness have brought about" —,[29] and if the philosopher, MOI, has no esteem for "originals" — "Je n'estime pas ces originaux-là"[30] —, this is because they subvert the rational, moral and social norms he embraces. Though referred to as an "original," the nephew stands out chiefly as a virtuoso imitator. The passages on pantomime and on music show the bizarre and often grotesque effects of his imitation issuing from a systematic perversion of models. The different parts he plays in the dialogue are so many variations of a first imitation in which the nephew is the flawed copy of his uncle, Jean-Philippe Rameau.

In playing his different roles — as many as twenty in one passage —, the nephew becomes entirely absorbed in the models he imitates, lost to the point of no longer recognizing where he is.[31] Unawareness is the consequence of a style of acting of which the distinguishing trait is passion,[32] in contrast to the style advocated by the first speaker in *The Paradox of Acting* demanding judgment and penetration, but no sensibility. That the inferior mode of imitation in *The Paradox of Acting* is constitutive of the nephew's "originality" is consistent with the theory of the first speaker, for whom impassioned actors are synonymous with "originals":

> In the great comedy, the comedy of the world, to which I always come back, all the passionate souls are on the stage, and all the men of genius in the pit. The former are called fools; the latter, who are busy copying the fools' follies, are called wise men. It is the wise man's eye that seizes upon the silliness of so many different characters, depicts it, and makes you laugh both at these annoying originals whose victim you have been and at yourself. It was the wise man who was observing

> you both, who was sketching the comic copy both of the annoyer and of your torture.[33]

The actors in this passage are referred to in turn as passionate souls, fools and "originals." Fools (*fous*) are synonymous with passionate souls and with "originals" in the sense that they are copies,[34] though the copies appear here as originals in the usual sense of the word since the fools are the models the wise men copy. The inversions of the relation between originals and copies from one moment to another or from one text to another — for instance from *Rameau's Nephew* where the original imitates genius to *The Paradox of Acting* where geniuses copy originals — ultimately dissolve originality to leave only copies. The absence of originals does not yield an absence of distinctions between different sorts of copies, however, as we are reminded by the first speaker proclaiming the superiority of reason over sensibility in matters concerning imitation. The superiority of reason pertains to mastery, firstly of oneself, and consequently of others. Though stated relative to actors, the rule holds also for dramatic poets, and specifically in this passage for the wise men. The opposition between fools and wise men reflects the negative and positive sides of mimesis. Good copies are opposed to bad copies in a manner suggestive of a danger in mimesis that can threaten society as soon as bad copies turn into bad models.[35]

The scenario depicted by the wise man is a violent one, in which the "original" is firstly a torturer and secondly a comic subject. A note in the Hermann edition of Diderot's *Oeuvres complètes* mentions a possible allusion in this passage to *Les Fâcheux* by Molière.[36] More plausibly Diderot is alluding to Palissot who alludes to *Les Fâcheux* in *Le Cercle.* Whether or not the allusion is intended, it elucidates the first speaker's usage of the term "annoying originals" (*fâcheux originaux*). Palissot's quarrel with the philosophers shows a pattern of mutual imitations and falsifications that is anti-philosophical. In the language of the polemic, "originals" are at once a source of violence and a corruption of the truth. In contrast to a scenario in which authors are in turn the perpetrators and the victims of a collective mystification, alternately representing their enemies and being represented by their enemies as false originals, the first speaker has the distance of an observer in proposing a theory of true copies and reasserting the philosophical claim to mastery.

While the period from 1740 to 1770 is said to have marked a separation between originality and mimesis, the works considered in the preceding pages show the opposite. The critique of originality contained in the usage of the negative sense of the word effaces the distinction, reducing originality to a form of mimesis.

NOTES

I wish to thank the College of Humanities at the University of Arizona for the grant that allowed me to complete research for the present article during the summer of 1999.

1. Translations from the *Encyclopedia* are my own. "ORIGINAL, s. m., est le premier dessin, ou instrument authentique de quelque chose, & qui doit servir comme de modele ou d'exemple à être copié ou imité."

2. "Peinture, tableau *original,* se prend en bonne & en mauvaise part; en bonne, lorsque dans un tableau tout y est grand, singuliérement nouveau; & en mauvaise, lorsqu'on n'y rencontre qu'une singularité bisarrement grotesque."

3. "ORIGINALITÉ s. f, *Gramm.,* maniere d'exécuter une chose commune, d'une maniere singuliere & distinguée: l'*originalité* est très-rare. La plupart des hommes ne sont en tous genres, que des copies les uns des autres. Le titre d'*original* se donne en bonne & en mauvaise part."

4. Usage of the substantive in this sense can be found as early as 1657 in *Les Historiettes* by Tallemant des Réaux — "Joyeuse estoit un original. Il avoit je ne sçay quelle fille avec laquelle il couchoit, mais il juroit qu'il ne luy faisoit rien, et qu'en cela il n'offensoit point Dieu" (Paris: Gallimard, 1961, collection de la Pléïade, ed. Antoine Adam, t. II, 368) — and is mentioned both in Furetière's *Dictionnaire universel* (1690) — "On appelle proverbialement & ironiquement un *original,* un homme qui est ridicule & singulier en ses manieres, qui fait rire par la nouveauté de ses actions" — and in the *Dictionnaire de l'académie française* (1695) — "On dit par raillerie, d'un homme qui est singulier en quelque chose de ridicule, que *c'est un original, un vray original."* The negative sense of the word is also found in the title of a play by Antoine Houdar de la Motte, performed in 1693, *Les Originaux ou l'Italien.* Paul Dupont summarizes the comic plot as follows: "Colombine, fille de Goguet, aime le charmant Octave. Son père veut la contraindre à faire un choix parmi des prétendants plus ridicules les uns que les autres *(les originaux).* Elle se dérobe à ces odieuses poursuites en feignant une aversion pour le mariage. Le valet Pasquariel vient à son aide, ménage des entrevues aux deux amants et fait si bien qu'il amène le père à les marier ensemble» (*Un Poète-Philosophe au commencement du dix-huitième siècle: Houdar de la Motte, 1672-1731* [Paris: Hachette, 1898], 80). *Les Originaux ou l'Italien* is included in *Le Théâtre italien de Gherardi ou le Recueil de toutes les comédies & Scenes Françoises jouées par les Comediens Italiens du Roy, pendant tout le temps qu'ils ont été au Service, tome IV* (Amsterdam, Elzevir, 1707), 393-471. The notion of "original" as flawed copy underscored in the present article is implicit in a comedy by Voltaire, *Les Originaux, ou Monsieur du Cap Vert*, first performed in 1732: "Un petit freluquet idolâtre de sa figure, et qui est plus longtemps que nous à sa toilette, *qui copie tous les ridicules de la cour sans en prendre une seule bonne qualité"* (II, i; my emphasis).

5. *L'Originalité : une nouvelle catégorie esthétique au siècle des Lumières* (Genève : Droz, 1982), 31-37.

6. *L'Originalité,* 9-11.

7. Translations from Fagan are my own. "Elle a pour objet de corriger un jeune homme de qualité de plusieurs défauts, & de les rendre à ses yeux odieux ou ridicules en les lui présentant successivement dans les différentes personnes de sa société qui s'en trouvent affectées" (*Théâtre de M. Fagan, et autres oeuvres du mesme auteur,* tome I [Paris: Duchesne, 1760], xxxi-xxxiii).

8. "Esclave des faux airs, adorateur des travers les plus outrés, il adopte si avidement les ridicules que nos jeunes gens mettent à la mode, qu'il semble que lui seul les auroit tous créés, si, pour le malheur de la société, on ne l'eût dès long-temps prévenu" (sc. i).

9. "Des livres! De quel fatras de lectures on nous assomme aujourd'hui! Eh!, nos premiers pères, qui valoient mieux que nous, lisoient-ils? A quoi servent ces volumes? à appesantir, à retarder le génie et à nous rendre copies, d'originaux que nous serions."

10. The same subject is depicted, though less successfully, by Philippe Néricault Destouches in *L'Homme singulier*, published in 1745. Like Ergaste in *Les Sincères,* Sanspair's rejection of fashionable errors leads him to the errors of singularity. Jean Hankiss, in *Philippe Néricault Destouches, L'Homme et l'oeuvre,* says that *L'Homme singulier* was written between 1736 and 1753 (Genève-Paris: Slatkine, 1981, 242). Judging from Destouches' own explanation, which must have been unavailable to Hankiss, the play was written at least a year prior to its publication in 1745: "Cette piéce a été lue aux Comédiens, qui l'ont reçue avec applaudissement. Les rôles ont été copiés & distribués. J'ai fait faire une répétition; la seconde étoit indiquée pour le lendemain, & huit ou dix jours après la Piéce eût été représentée; mais un obstacle que je ne prévoyois pas, a suspendu les autres répétitions; & la longue maladie d'une célèbre Actrice, nous a obligés de remettre la partie à l'année suivante. Dans cet intervalle de temps j'ai changé de résolution, & j'ai pris le parti de ne faire paroître ma Comédie, que dans le recueil de mes ouvrages dont on préparoit une nouvelle édition" (*Oeuvres de théatre de M. Destouches, de l'académie française. Nouvelle édition, Revûe, corrigée, & augmentée par l'Auteur,* tome V [Paris: Prault, 1745], 243). Given that an edition of his works was published in 1742, Destouches must have written the play between 1742 and 1744.

11. In a recent study on the evolution of the word *persiflage* in the eighteenth century, Élisabeth Bourguinat outlines a shift during this time from a playful to a cruel kind of humor. *Le Siècle du persiflage* (Paris: Presses universitaires de France, 1998), 83-97.

12. On the origins of *mystification,* see Jean-François Jeandillou, *Esthétique de la mystification* (Paris: Minuit, 1994), 11-20; John Vincent-Benn, "Historique du mot *mystifier",* *Revue de philologie française et de littérature,* 1925, vol. 37, no. 1, 33-42.

13. "S'approprier sans droit, par la violence ou la fraude" (*Petit Robert).*

14. Translations from Palissot are my own. "Mon mari a la fantaisie de tenir cercle trois jours de la semaine, de recevoir des savans, des beaux-esprits, des

originaux de toute espèce; et ce qui à tout autre que lui paraîtrait singulier, bizarre, extravagant même, est précisément ce qui lui plaît davantage. J'ai la complaisance de me prêter à son goût, et souvent de feindre beaucoup de gaîté au milieu de ces importuns qui m'excèdent. Aujourd'hui qu'il est à la campagne, je me propose de me réjouir un peu aux dépens de sa société; je veux vous la faire connaître, jouir de la surprise que vous causeront certains ridicules que j'aurai soin de faire sortir assez pour qu'ils nous donnent la comédie. Où donc est le crime de tout cela? Ne puis-je me venger une fois de toute l'humeur que m'ont donné ces originaux depuis deux ans que j'ai la générosité de m'ennuyer avec eux?" (I, i)

15. "C'est un petit ressentiment qu'il a contre le public, qui vient de siffler impitoyablement une de ses pièces, dont le succès lui tournait la tête avant la représentation" (I, i).

16. "Le poète, *d'un ton de modestie très-chargé*: J'avais tâché de plaire au public; je m'étais, autant que je l'avais pu, rapproché des grands modèles, que nous devons regarder comme nos maîtres. Je me suis trompé. Il faut bien que j'aie mérité mon malheur par quelque endroit, et que la prévention qu'il est si naturel d'avoir pour ses ouvrages, m'ait aveuglé sur mes défauts."

17. "Orphise, *malignement au poète*: Votre modestie, monsieur du Volcan, ne peut me convaincre que l'on vous ait rendu justice. J'en appelle du public au public même : car enfin de véritables connaisseurs m'ont assuré que le plan de votre pièce était absolument dans les règles ; qu'il y avait de l'intérêt, des situations parfaitement dessinées, une décoration merveilleuse, des coups de théâtre à chaque scène . . ." (I, ii).

18. Daniel Delafarge, *La Vie et l'oeuvre de Palissot (1730-1814)* (Genève: Slatkine, 1971), 43-68; E. Méaume, *Palissot et les philosophes* (Nancy, 1864), 11-29.

19. "Tous ces Messieurs se disent philosophes, et quelques-uns le sont. Mais parmi ceux même d'entre eux à qui l'on accorde le plus de talents, on est fâché d'avouer qu'il s'en trouve qui ont presque rendu le mérite et la raison haïssables dans leurs écrits" (*Oeuvres complètes* [Genève: Slatkine, 1971], vol. 1, 269).

20. Regarding Berthier's critique of the *Encyclopedia* see John N. Pappas, *Berthier's Journal de Trévoux and the Philosophes*. In *Studies on Voltaire and the Eighteenth Century,* ed. Theodore Besterman, vol. 3 [Genève: Droz, 1957], 163-196.

21. "Que cet auteur n'imagine donc plus avoir fait une découverte par ce prétendu genre sérieux dont sa pièce lui paraît un modèle" (*Oeuvres complètes,* 296).

22. "N'y aurait-il donc rien d'original dans sa pièce? Je vous demande pardon, Madame; et c'est précisément ce qu'il y a de plus minutieux, ou de plus mauvais. C'est ce jargon philosophique et glacial, mis toujours à la place de ce que les personnages devraient dire" (*Oeuvres complètes,* 297).

23. *La Vie et l'oeuvre de Palissot,* 103-110.

24. As in *Le Cercle* the adjective is used in *Les Philosophes* with reference to Rousseau: "Il est *original* du moins dans son système" (III, ix).

25. "Je suis encor trop loin d'atteindre mon modèle" (II, ii).

26. "Certain auteur, dans une comédie, veut, dit-on, nous jouer" (III, 4).

27. Le pis-aller, messieurs, c'est d'attendre l'orage;
Jusque-là diffamons et l'auteur et l'ouvrage;
Armons la main des sots pour nous venger de lui;
Portons des coups plus sûrs en nous servant d'autrui. (III, 4)

28. On the relevance of contemporary critical theories, particularly those of René Girard and Jacques Derrida, to Enlightenment reflection on violence and imitation, see Pierre Saint-Amand, *The Laws of Hostility: Politics, Violence, and the Enlightenment* (Minneapolis: University of Minnesota Press, 1996).

29. *Rameau's Nephew and D'Alembert's Dream,* tr. L.W. Tancock (Penguin, 1966), 35. "Ils rompent cette fastidieuse uniformité que notre éducation, nos conventions de société, nos bienséances d'usage ont introduite" *(Oeuvres,* Paris: Gallimard, bibliothèque de la Pléiade, ed. André Billy, 1951, 396).

30. *Oeuvres,* 1951, 396.

31. "Sa tête était tout à fait perdue. Épuisée de fatigue, tel qu'un homme qui sort d'un profond sommeil ou d'une longue distraction; il resta immobile, stupide, étonné. Il tournait ses regards autour de lui, comme un homme qui cherche à reconnaître le lieu où il se trouve" (*Oeuvres,* 1951, 456).

32. "Il commençait à entrer en passion, et à chanter tout bas. Il élevait le ton, à mesure qu'il se passionnait davantage . . ." (*Oeuvres,* 1951, 454).

33. My translation, based on *Diderot's Selected Writings,* tr. Derek Coltman (New York: Macmillan, 1966), 321, the most literal translation I have found of this passage, which is altered here to render more exactly the French vocabulary, for instance *qui s'occupent à copier leurs folies* as "who are busy copying the fools' follies" rather than "taking notes of the madmen's follies" and *fâcheux originaux* as "annoying originals" rather than "tiresome eccentrics." I render "fou" as "fools" to convey the continuity in Diderot's vocabulary that can be lost in translation, for instance alternating between "jester" and "madman." "Dans la grande comédie, la comédie du monde, celle à laquelle j'en reviens toujours, toutes les âmes chaudes occupent le théâtre; tous les hommes de génie sont au parterre. Les premiers s'appellent des fous; les seconds, qui s'occupent à copier leurs folies, s'appellent des sages. C'est l'oeil du sage qui saisit le ridicule de tant de personnages divers, qui le peint, et qui vous fait rire et de ces fâcheux originaux dont vous avez été la victime, et de vous-même. C'est lui qui vous observait, et qui traçait la copie comique et du fâcheux et de votre supplice" (*Oeuvres,* 1951, 1009).

34. In *Rameau's Nephew* LUI plays the fool, that is mock double, to a number of characters, from the financier Bertin to the philosopher MOI, though ultimately the roles are reversible, as LUI suggests that MOI may also be his fool: "Il n'y a point de meilleur rôle auprès des grands que celui de fou . . . Moi je suis le fou de Bertin et de beaucoup d'autres, le vôtre peut-être dans ce moment; ou peut-être vous le mien" (*Oeuvres,* 1951, 438).

35. Regarding the Platonic question of danger in mimesis, see Paul Woodruff's article, *Plato on Mimesis,* in the *Oxford Encyclopedia of Aesthetics*, vol. 3. See also Iris Murdoch, *The Fire and the Suns: Why Plato Banished the Artists.* Oxford, 1977.

36. *Oeuvres complètes*, ed. H. Dieckmann-J. Varloot, tome XX (Paris: Hermann, 1995), 54, note 22.

The First French Literary Centenary: National Sentiment and the Molière Celebration of 1773

JOHN R. IVERSON

When was the first French literary centenary? Pierre Nora has called our times the "era of commemoration," and William M. Johnston has defined the "cult of anniversaries" as one of the hallmarks of the modern age.[1] Celebrations are staged around even rather trivial cultural dates; commemoration has become a major industry in France, as elsewhere.[2] Despite the magnitude of this phenomenon, however, no one has stopped to ask precisely where these practices originated, what first inspired them, what types of rationale were applied to their earliest manifestations. The self–evident nature of the modern commemorative impulse has prevented us from looking towards the past or, more precisely, back to the celebration of Molière's death in 1773—France's first literary centenary.[3]

Given the lack of commemorative precedent in France, the significance of the 1773 celebration extends far beyond Molière.[4] In order for this literary tribute to take place, multiple factors had to converge, some of which had little to do with Molière specifically.[5] The prominence of the "cult of great men," an emerging tendency to treat the passing of a hundred-year interval as a significant occurrence, a growing concern for cultivating the heritage of the French literary tradition, and a growing sense of cultural rivalry with England, particularly aggravated by the example of the Shakespeare Jubilee of 1769, all contributed to the birth of the centenary. In combination, these elements make the commemorative observance of 1773 a key moment in the formation of a French national literature. More than a simple sign of veneration for Molière, this event emblematized the emergence of French literature and French writers as vital components of national identity.

The Molière Centenary

On 17 February 1773, the actors at the Comédie Française celebrated the one hundredth anniversary of Molière's death by performing a one-act comedy entitled *L'Assemblée*.[6] Written for the occasion by the abbé Le Beau de Schosne, this work was hardly a theatrical masterpiece. The form it assumed, however, was significant because it established a model for subsequent celebratory spectacles in France.

As indicated by the title, *L'Assemblée* depicts a meeting of the actors of the Comédie Française who must decide whether to accept a new play for their repertory. An aspiring playwright proposes an idea which, he says, will certainly please the troupe,

> Puisque je veux célébrer le retour
> Et de l'année & du jour séculaire
> Qui vit Moliere éclipsé de la terre (33).

The plan meets with general acclaim, but the actors are at a loss as to how they might best honor their founder. A sorcerer is called; the ghost of Molière appears and explains why the comic genre has fallen on hard times in France. When the ghost finally departs, a curtain rises and, "la statue de Moliere paroît posée sur un piédestal" (34). The play ends as the entire company gathers around this bust, crowning it with laurels. This was the "Apothéose de Molière" referred to in the full title of the work.[7]

The following evening, 18 February 1773, a second one–act play dedicated to the Molière centenary premièred, Jean–Baptiste Artaud's *Le Centenaire de Moliere*.[8] In this case, the scenario involves the arrival of Thalie and Momus in France, where they have been sent by Jupiter to gauge whether the great comic author is still properly appreciated in his homeland. One by one, characters from Molière's comedies come forth to lament the loss of their creator. Again, as in Lebeau de Schosne's *Assemblée*, the work concludes with the crowning of a bust of the dead playwright. The "apotheosis" of the writer is thus established as an obligatory element of the commemorative celebration.

During the following weeks, each of these two works was given several performances, often in conjunction with one of Molière's works. Of the two, *La Centenaire de Moliere* was the more successful. Compared with the five performances of *L'Assemblée, La Centenaire* was performed 12 times in 1773 and then revived in 1774 for 3 more performances at the Comédie Française. Even more notably, its first run in 1773 included a performance for Louis XV at Versailles. According to H. Carrington Lancaster, a total of more than 15,000 spectators attended the two plays. [9]

In addition, the events of the Molière centenary were publicized in many periodicals and critical works, including the *Mercure de France, L'Année littéraire, Le Journal encyclopédique, L'Avantcoureur, L'Almanach des Muses,* the *Correspondance littéraire*, and, at a further remove, the *Mémoires secrets*.[10] Both plays were available in print to readers in the provinces as well as in the capital. Le Beau de Schosne's *Assemblée* appeared in Bordeaux as well as in Paris, and the two Parisian editions of Artaud's *Centenaire* were supplemented by a third edition issued in Avignon. The Molière celebration, though it did not dominate the cultural calendar of 1773, was clearly an event that generated public interest on a number of levels.

The Cult of Great Men in Eighteenth–Century France

The celebration of the Molière centenary attests to the strength of the *culte des grands hommes* in France during the second half of the eighteenth century. As Jean-Claude Bonnet has demonstrated, this period witnessed a dramatic increase in the attention accorded to French intellectual and cultural heroes, giving rise to a variety of artistic monuments and literary works.[11] The philosophy that informed this trend was quite simple: the example of great men would inspire new acts of courage and virtue in the nation's citizens. Proponents of this "cult" argued that society could greatly encourage future great deeds by propagating images and monuments of individuals worthy of emulation.

This veneration for great Frenchmen produced two extremely prominent initiatives. Beginning in 1758, the French Academy reconfigured its eloquence prize, choosing to center its biannual competition around the *éloge* of one of the nation's great men. In 1775, the Marquis d'Angiviller, as the newly appointed director of the Bâtiments du Roi, ordered the first four in a series of full–sized portrait statues portraying military and governmental figures as well as writers and artists. Coming at four–year intervals, these commissions "put the enormous patronage power of the crown firmly behind the celebration of great Frenchman." As David Bell argues, the cult of great men was a central element in the monarchy's attempts to shape national sentiment during the second half of the eighteenth century, contributing to the luster of the crown by celebrating France's most illustrious citizens.[12]

Molière was among the individuals who most benefited from these practices. In 1769, he was designated as the subject of the essay competition at the Académie Française, and in 1783 the sculptor Caffieri was selected to complete his portrait for the d'Angiviller series. He was also celebrated in many projects of lesser prominence. Louis–Sébastien Mercier and Michel de Cubières, among others, dedicated theatrical works to episodes from his life.[13] In response to a commission received in 1776, Houdon created a bust of Molière for the Comédie Française. In 1778, d'Alembert donated a copy of Houdon's work to the Académie Française, thereby granting Molière a sort of posthumous welcome into the institution that had denied him membership during his lifetime.[14] The celebration of 1773 at the Comédie Française was obviously part of these efforts to honor France's greatest comic writer.

In several significant ways, however, the Molière centenary marked a departure from standard treatment of France's great men. Firstly, the two celebratory comedies differed substantially from the type of literary work that typically served to celebrate great men. In contrast to the formal rhetoric of the academic *éloges*, the centenary plays sought to generate a more spontaneous type of enthusiasm and applause. The works by Le Beau de Schosne and Artaud ended with song, dance and the crowning of Molière's bust. Secondly, the open forum of the public theater lent a markedly different resonance to the celebratory spectacles. At their conclusion, the stage became a sort of shrine to Molière, as actors and spectators joined in a communal act of homage, aided by impressive scenographic effects. The theatrical experience would have produced a powerful impression of unanimous admiration for Molière's genius. Lastly, and most obviously, the centenary celebration was determined by a precise year. In contrast to academic competitions and sculptural programs, for which the subjects were chosen for philosophical, political or artistic reasons, with no thought to precise dates, this particular kind of commemoration could only take place in 1773. Given this attention to the quantitative imperative of the calendar, the Molière centenary was an important innovation within the context of the eighteenth–century *culte des grands hommes.*

The Invention of the Centenary

In 1773, the notion that a hundred–year anniversary was an event worthy of celebration had only recently taken shape. The novelty of this idea is reflected in the title of Artaud's play, where "centenaire" is preceded by the feminine article "la," indicating that modern usage of the masculine form had not yet been established. Indeed, all eighteenth–century dictionaries define "centenaire" exclusively as "une personne qui a cent ans," making no mention of the idea of centenary celebrations. Only in the mid-nineteenth century did lexicographical works begin to include definitions of "centenaire" as an "anniversaire qui revient de cent ans en cent ans."[15] In the mid–eighteenth century, there was as yet no commemorative practice that required the existence of such a term.[16]

The contemporary *Almanach des centénaires* clearly documents the emergence and evolution of the concept of the centenary at this time. Originally conceived in 1761 as an annual register of all persons who had attained the age of one hundred years, this publication quickly expanded to incorporate other meanings of "centenaire."[17] In the second volume, the editors included a "*Supplément* des faits anecdotes de l'Année 1662," stating that, "Ce sera, si l'on veut, une espéce de *Gazette Centénaire*" ("Avertissement," 1762). As justification for this broadening of the *Almanach*'s mission, the editor noted: "On aimera sans-doute à revoir ceux qui occupoient la scène du monde, il y a cent ans; à relire les noms des Souverains de l'Europe, l'état sur-tout de la Famille Royale, des Princes du Sang d'alors; à comparer les usages de ce temps passé avec celui-ci." Over the next ten years, this portion of the *Almanach* gained greater importance. Comprising fewer than sixty pages in 1762, and shrinking to fewer than 10 pages in 1764, it eventually expanded to more than one hundred pages.[18] The contents of this "gazette" also shifted over time; although originally focused on political and religious events, it gradually devoted more and more attention to profiling the remarkable individuals who had died one hundred years previously. Among others, the 1773 edition included notice of the Molière centenary: "17 *Février*. Mort de *Jean-Baptiste Pocquelin de Molière*, à la quatrième Représentation de son *Malade imaginaire*."[19] The *Almanach* had become, in a sense, an instrument for annual renewal of the French historical memory.

The editors and readers of the *Almanach des centénaires* also began to recognize that events occurring precisely one hundred years earlier could become the occasion for celebrations and commemorations. In 1771, for example, a reader submitted a "Lettre sur un Fait *Centénaire* ou *Séculaire*," describing a centennial observance in the Netherlands: "Voici, Monsieur, un Extrait de la Gazette d'Amsterdam qui prouve l'attention que l'on donne dans ce pays-là aux *Faits centénaires* ou séculaires."[20] On this point, the *Almanach's* authors concurred with other writers at the time. Notably, the *Correspondance littéraire* devoted an impassioned article to the bicentenary (referred to as the "second jubilé") of the Saint Bartholomew's Day Massacre, just six months prior to the Molière centenary. Deploring French insensitivity to this milestone, this text argued that the periodical commemoration of significant events could play an important role in forming public morals.[21]

Literary events and lives also began to receive special treatment on the basis of significant anniversary dates. The chevalier Du Coudray, directly inspired by the Molière centenary, composed a *Cinquantaine dramatique de M. de Voltaire* in 1774:

> Il me semble que je dois dire quelque chose de la *Cinquantaine*; c'est une cérémonie qui se célebre entre deux époux, au bout de cinquante ans de mariage; on a adopté cette dénomination pour tous les événements heureux. Nous avons fait la *Cinquantaine* du regne de notre Monarque, surnommé à si juste titre, Louis *le Bien-Aimé*. J'ai donc cru qu'il me seroit permis de l'adapter à mon sujet; & comme il y a différentes *Cinquantaines*, j'ai ajouté le mot de *Dramatique*.[22]

The idea of the commemorative celebration was still novel enough to require careful justification from this author. But it is clear that by the early 1770's the idea of celebrating special anniversaries had already made significant headway in France. The Molière centenary was thus both the culmination of a heightened awareness of the significance of centenary dates and a precedent that would later produce other notable celebrations.

French Anxieties and the Cultivation of Literary Tradition

The emergence of the centenary impulse during the second half of the eighteenth century coincided with a period of heightened national sentiment. As Edmond Dziembowski has powerfully argued, a humiliating defeat in the Seven Years' War and widespread perceptions of English superiority spawned new feelings of patriotism among the French.[23] As part of this general tendency, many writers, journalists and publishers expressed growing anxieties about the decadence of French literature.[24] Critics commonly denounced the decay of literary standards, lamenting that the traditional genres had been stricken with sterility and charging that new tendencies like the *drame* and the sentimental novel had introduced inferior, foreign standards destructive of good taste.[25]

Voltaire, among others, stridently advocated more careful cultivation of the nation's literary heritage, railing against the insidious influence of the English theater and claiming that "la gloire de la France" was imperiled by attacks against the nation's great writers. Beginning in 1761, in the midst of the military conflict with Great Britain, he launched a massive epistolary campaign to generate support for his annotated edition of Corneille, promoting this project as a key to maintaining the reputation of French letters: "J'aime passionnément à commenter Corneille, car il a fait l'honneur de la France dans le seul art qui mette la France au dessus des autres nations."[26] He pursued his work on the *Commentaires sur Corneille* for several years, despite severe health problems, convinced that he was creating an important literary "monument." Even after the end of the Seven Years' War, Voltaire continued his editorial work. Expressing a desire to render "quelque service à la scène française," he updated Mairet's *Sophonisbe*, both in its language and in its dramatic structure. In presenting this text to the duc de La Vallière, he recommended that other flawed works from the nation's past be reworked in similar fashion.[27]

Many other significant editorial projects appeared during the 1760's and 1770's, including an edition of Racine that closely adhered to the model established by Voltaire.[28] A number of other undertakings focused on the history of the theater,[29] and dictionaries and almanacs chronicled the history of theatrical performance.[30] Several multi–volume collections sought to create a comprehensive survey of the French theater by reprinting the most important works in the national repertoire.[31] Marmontel, who had revised Rotrou's *Venceslas* for performance at the Comédie Française in 1759, pursued his interest in this area by issuing the first volume of a collection of *Chefs-d'oeuvre dramatiques ou Recueil des meilleures Pièces du Théâtre François, tragique, comique et lyrique* (1773).[32] Collé, best known as the author of the *Partie de chasse de Henri IV*, also "retouched" four works from the previous century in a collection of *Anciennes comédies*.[33]

Although these projects did not all make explicit arguments about the need to defend the French tradition against foreign incursions, they were generally informed by a sense that the literary heritage of the preceding century was an essential, particularly positive component of national identity. Charles Palissot, among others, very strongly articulated the idea that great literary works were part of the national patrimony. Prevented from editing Molière's works by a group of publishers, he contended that no individual or group should hold the exclusive rights to such an important part of the French past: ". . . Les productions du génie d'un grand homme, ne lui appartiennent pas de la même maniere que l'héritage de ses peres. Elles deviennent après lui, une des branches de la gloire nationale. . . ."[34] His edition, he claims, would have been "une entreprise honorable pour Moliere, & précieuse pour la Nation." These statements typify the motivations behind many of the editorial projects from the 1760's and 1770's. Although the canon of French classics would not be defined and edited in a systematic way until the nineteenth century,[35] the push to solidify a certain vision of the nation's literary heritage and to build a support apparatus to preserve it was already in motion.

Antoine Bret's *Molière* (1773) and the Interplay between Writer and Nation

One reason that Palissot's editorial plans had been blocked was that a second–rank author by the name of Antoine Bret had already been hired to prepare a complete edition and commentary of the works of Molière.[36] There is no indication whether this project was originally conceived as a centenary tribute, but the fact that the edition coincided with the one hundredth anniversary of Molière's death was duly noted in the "prospectus" that appeared in the *Journal historique* late in 1772: "Cette Edition, qui paroîtra en 1773, sera, de la part de ses Coopérateurs & de la Nation, une espece d'hommage centenaire bien dû au grand homme que la France a pleuré un siecle avant nous, & dont elle n'a point encore réparé la perte."[37] In the edition itself, Bret first mentions the centenary celebrations only at the end of the last volume. When he finally composed his commentary on *Le Malade imaginaire* (Molière's last play), the celebratory performances at the Comédie Française had been staged, and the editor was able to report on the enthusiastic response of the Parisian audience.[38]

The Molière edition of 1773 thus represents the convergence of the new interest in centenary dates and the desire to promote the national literary heritage. Bret's commentary develops the idea that Molière was a quintessentially French author and carefully connects his plays to the court at Versailles and the particular occasions for which they were written. The editor further asserts that Molière was driven by a desire to be useful to his nation and that, to fulfill this mission, he sought to correct social vices by making them appear ridiculous. Bret is not content, however, simply to assign a moral function to Molière's plays, in accordance with the Horatian precept, *castigat ridendo mores*. More pointedly, he maintains that Molière's comic style was perfectly adapted both to the French character and to the strongly centralized government of Louis XIV.

By stressing this consonance between Molière and his public, Bret reveals that one of the aims of his edition is to protect the French theater against the destructive influence of English drama:

> C'est par là sur-tout que cette édition peut être de quelque utilité, en ramenant les esprits aux principes d'un art qui se perd tous les jours

> parmi nous, & qu'une admiration peu raisonnée des hardiesses de nos voisins dans ce genre a dénaturé, au point d'être entièrement méconnaissable (1: 8).

Like Voltaire in his commentary on Corneille, Bret justifies his editorial work in terms of national interest. If, as was commonly believed, France owed a considerable portion of its international prestige to the literary accomplishments of the seventeenth century, then it was extremely important to protect that tradition. Bret could safely argue that Molière, as the greatest of all comic writers, was particularly deserving of special veneration from his compatriots.

Molière's privileged position with relation to the French nation becomes even clearer when Bret describes the centenary celebration at the Comédie Française. After lamenting Molière's death during the initial run of the *Malade imaginaire* in 1673, the editor turns to the recent commemorative events: "C'est ici le lieu de féliciter la Nation de l'ivresse avec laquelle elle a partagé, après cent ans expirés, depuis la mort de ce Grand Homme, le zèle de deux Auteurs qui se sont disputé la gloire de consacrer cette époque par deux piéces également précieuses par leur objet" (6: 493). In commenting on the general preference given to Artaud's *Centenaire*, Bret also refers to similar celebrations that were staged in England to honor Shakespeare in 1716. By drawing this connection, the Molière editor suggests that the French have shown themselves to be as faithful as the English to their own theatrical tradition. He substantiates this point by approving the initiative of the troupe at the Comédie Française. Their plans to erect a statue of Molière should result in a monument expressing the public's lasting gratitude: "Elle est décernée dans un moment de transport & d'amour par un acte public qui la rend digne de ce Grand Homme" (6: 494). This spontaneous public display of affection for Molière reinforces Bret's general notion of a perfect identification between this writer and the French nation.

Further testimony from actors, journalists, and government officials fully substantiates Bret's description of the 1773 centenary as an expression of national sentiment. As the actors at the Comédie Française formulated their plans, Lekain, their leader, wrote to the duc de Duras to explain that they wished to use the proceeds from the centenary performance to commission a statue of their founder. In his missive, he argued that, "Une détermination de cette nature ne peut qu'honorer le spectacle national et tous les gens de lettres."[39] In a second document, the troupe declared its desire to record for posterity the profound veneration it felt for this "grand homme": ". . . Il ne doutait nullement que la partie la plus éclairée de la nation française ne contribuât grandement à l'exécution d'un pareil projet . . . ."[40] Commenting on this initiative, the *Mercure de France* voiced great enthusiasm:

> Si les personnes les plus considérables, si les amateurs des lettres & des arts se réunissaient pour faire achever ce monument de la gloire de Molière, cet exemple serait peut-être suivi en faveur des grands hommes qui ont illustré la scène; les statues de Corneille, de Racine, de Voltaire orneraient le péristyle de la nouvelle Salle que l'on projette de bâtir; & la France, depuis long-temps la plus heureuse rivale d'Athènes dans les beaux arts, le serait aussi dans les honneurs rendus à ceux qui les cultivent.[41]

The *Correspondance littéraire* also approved, alluding to the national literary significance of the spectacle and projected statue. This commentary went even further, however, in suggesting that centenary celebrations could become a regular practice in France: "On insinua en même temps qu'on célébrerait dorénavant l'année séculaire de tous les grands hommes qui ont illustré la scène française."[42] In all of these cases, the celebration of Molière's death was viewed not simply as a personal tribute paid to one individual, but as an important public gesture that would contribute to the prestige of French letters.

The French Response to the Shakespeare Jubilee

The cult of great men, the advent of the centenary impulse, French concern for cultivating the national literary heritage, and public veneration for Molière: even in combination, these elements would not necessarily have resulted in the centenary celebration at the Comédie Française in 1773. An even stronger, more immediate impetus came from a foreign source, as indicated by Antoine Bret in his intriguing, though erroneous, reference to a previous celebration in England. As we have seen, he compared Artaud's *Centenaire*—which consisted primarily of a parade of characters from Molière's comedies—with a similar play that had been staged in honor of Shakespeare: "C'est ainsi qu'à Londres en 1716, pour célébrer la centenaire de Shakespear, on fit passer en revue sur le Théâtre les plus beaux morceaux des piéces du Sophocle Anglois" (6: 493–4). The editor mistakenly assumed that this play was part of a centenary celebration; accordingly, he assigned it to the year 1716, which would have marked the one hundredth anniversary of Shakespeare's death. There can be little doubt, however, that Bret was actually referring to the more recent events of the Shakespeare Jubilee, which had taken place in Stratford–upon–Avon in 1769.

The program for this three–day Jubilee included concerts, fireworks, banquets, a masquerade ball, and a lavish ceremony for the coronation of a new statue of Shakespeare.[43] Sponsored by local dignitaries in Shakespeare's hometown, and organized by the famous Shakespearean actor, David Garrick, the extensive preparations included road improvements, the construction of a new "Shakespeare Hall," and a subscription campaign to raise adequate funds. The *Shakespeare Jubilee* was also the title of the theatrical work that Garrick and his troupe performed dozens of times in London during the months following the celebration in Stratford. (Based on a procession of characters from Shakespeare's plays, this is most probably the work to which Bret was referring in his commentary.) All in all, as Michael Dobson has argued, the Shakespeare Jubilee of 1769 was an unabashed expression of national pride, closely allied in spirit to the ongoing process of British imperial expansion in the wake of the Seven Years' War.[44] Given that the French were already on the cultural defensive at this time, it is not surprising that the Shakespeare Jubilee quickly attracted attention in France and eventually inspired a French response in the same vein.

In December 1769, the *Mercure de France* gave a brief but glowing account of the events of the Shakespeare Jubilee, culminating in a description of the ceremony that was supposed to bring the week-long celebration to a close:

> A ce divertissement devoit en succéder un autre dont on se promettoit la plus grande satisfaction; c'étoit une mascarade composée de tous les personnages de Shakespear, qui devoient promener sa statue par la ville dans un char de triomphe; s'arrêter ensuite dans la principale place, où M. Garrick étoit chargé de couronner de laurier l'effigie du poëte.

This final event had been cancelled due to rain, but the *Mercure* had nothing but praise for the enterprise as a whole: ". . . L'hommage qu'on vient de rendre à la mémoire de ce grand homme est sans doute inoui; il doit faire honneur à la nation qui en a donné l'exemple; un pays où l'on honore ainsi les talens, doit les voir naître & multiplier dans son sein."[45]

In these terms, the French periodical emphasized two aspects of the Jubilee that would clearly resonate with the future Molière celebration. First, the detailed account of the final ceremony very closely defined a form of spectacle that would resurface in the two plays of 1773. The parade of characters from the author's plays, the crowning of his statue by the actors, and the accompanying poetic tribute were all later recreated in Paris at the Comédie Française. By honoring the English Bard in this contemporary, public setting, the Jubilee reenacted and modernized the ancient tradition of crowning great poets and dramatists, thereby establishing a model for many other commemorative celebrations in subsequent years.[46] Secondly, the *Mercure* immediately interpreted the Jubilee in patriotic terms, stating specifically that the tribute did honor to the entire nation and that such admiration for a literary hero would inspire other talents. These were lessons and examples that were not lost on the French. The Shakespeare Jubilee almost immediately generated calls for a similar event in France.

Voltaire was among those who reacted most quickly, referring to the Jubilee even before the description in the *Mercure* had appeared. In a letter to Chamfort, who had recently won the prize at the French Academy for his *Éloge de Molière* (1769), the old philosophe alluded to English veneration for Shakespeare:

> Les Anglais nous avaient donné cent ans auparavant un autre éxemple; ils avaient érigé dans la cathédrale de Strafort, un monument magnifique à Shakespear, qui pourtant n'est guères comparable à Molière, ni pour l'art ni pour les moeurs. Vous n'ignorez pas qu'on vient d'établir une espèce de jeux séculaires en l'honneur de Shakespear en Angleterre (D15921, 27.9.1769).

By closely associating Molière and Shakespeare, Voltaire seemed to anticipate the idea of staging a ceremony in France that would respond to the Jubilee. Writing to mademoiselle Clairon, the famous actress, he more explicitly mentioned the possibility of a parallel French celebration: "Les Anglais ont établi une fête annuelle en l'honneur du fameux comédien poète Shakespear. Nous n'avons pas encore parmi nous la fête de Molière."[47]

In attempting to apply the English model to France, the philosophe was not alone. Madame Riccoboni informed Garrick himself, with whom she maintained a regular correspondance, that the Jubilee had in effect created a stir throughout French literary circles: "L'apothéose de votre poète chéri a tenté les François, peuple imitateur, de consacrer un temple à leurs plus fameux auteurs."[48] She continued by saying that the discussion had come to nothing because of divisions in public opinion, but that finally, a full year after the Jubilee, an alternative project had been formulated: "Cependant, on aura la statue de Voltaire par souscription." The resulting statue, of course, was Pigalle's famous nude portrait of Voltaire, and Riccoboni's comment suggests that the public campaign to finance its creation was, at least in some measure, a response to the Shakespeare Jubilee.[49] In more general terms, her observations demonstrate that the idea of paying tribute to the nation's great writers had taken on greater urgency and had assumed a more concrete form as a result of the English precedent.

The precise sequence of events that led from these early reactions to the Shakespeare Jubilee of 1769 to the Molière centenary of 1773 remains unknown. Unfortunately, there is nothing in the texts surrounding Lebeau de Schosne's *Assemblée* and Artaud's *Centenaire* that links the observance at the Comédie Française directly back to the events at Stratford–upon–Avon. In 1775, however, when Pierre Le Tourneur published the prospectus for his *Shakespeare traduit de l'Anglois*, a tremendous flare-up in cross-Channel literary tensions resulted, and comparisons between English and French commemorative practices surfaced anew.[50] Le Tourneur himself certainly helped to provoke this reaction, for in the prospectus for his translation, he very deliberately disparaged the Molière centenary as a mere copy of the Shakespeare Jubilee:

> L'Angleterre est plus glorieuse d'avoir produit Shakespeare, que Newton lui-même; & l'on a oui parler de cette Fête fameuse récemment instituée en son honneur, & que l'enthousiasme des Anglais a nommé le *Jubilé* de Shakespeare. . . . C'est aussi le nom de la Piéce qui fut faite à sa gloire . . . Cette Piéce se joue très-fréquemment, & c'est le premier monument dans l'univers qui ait été élevé au Théâtre à la gloire d'un Acteur. La Centenaire de Molière n'est que le second, & n'en est que l'imitation.[51]

Not content simply to praise the English for devotion to their great playwright, Le Tourneur denounced the imitative nature of the French commemoration, suggesting that the ceremonies in honor of Molière were inspired primarily by a desire to counter the English precedent. He thereby asserted the ascendancy of his hero, who enjoyed great popular support, over the comic writer who had been pushed forward as a sort of French antidote to English literary superiority. Le Tourneur clearly perceived that the literary centenary, already at its inception, had become a tool for propaganda, a weapon in a burgeoning cultural war.

Subsequent Eighteenth–Century Centenaries

When the actors at the Comédie Française resurrected Artaud's *Centenaire* in February 1774, one year after the initial performances, they took a second step toward making the centenary celebration an annual occurrence, as was noted by the *Mercure de France*: "Le vendredi 18 Février, époque de la mort de Molière, les Comédiens François ont donné une représentation de la *Centenaire*, comédie en un acte de M. Artaud, qui a l'avantage d'avoir fondé, en quelque sorte, une fête en l'honneur du grand homme, le génie, le père & le modèle de la bonne comédie."[52] The following year, however, Linguet reported that the anticipated ceremony had been canceled despite "la bonne volonté de la Comédie, qui désiroit de renouveller annuellement ce témoignage de son respect & de sa reconnoissance pour son Fondateur."[53] Thus, after a mere two years, the Molière celebrations came to a halt and would resume on a regular basis only at the time of the Molière birth bicentenary in 1822.[54]

Nevertheless, the centenary of 1773 did have some more lasting effects. In 1774, as we have seen, the chevalier Du Coudray honored Voltaire on the momentous occasion(!) of the fiftieth anniversary of the first performance of the tragedy, *Mariamne*. In response to objections that it might have been more appropriate to celebrate the première of the philosophe's first tragedy, *Oedipe*, one of the characters in the *Cinquantaine dramatique* naively admitted that the idea simply had not occurred to the author at the appropriate time. Only the Molière celebration had given him the idea of feting his illustrious contemporary: "Non, je n'en fais point le fin; je dédaigne une gloire qui ne m'appartient pas: j'avouerai avec ma franchise ordinaire . . . que ce fut *la Centenaire*, qui me fit naître l'idée de *la Cinquantaine*."[55] The passage points out the extent to which the young author, even at this early stage in the evolution of commemorative practice, felt constrained by a temporal imperative. Since he had decided to use the idea of the anniversary to justify his homage to Voltaire, he was also compelled to find a date of some significance, large or small, that fell at a convenient moment. Du Coudray's text also gave a sense of the extent to which ceremonial form had already been fixed by the Molière celebration: ". . . Je desire que l'on représente Mariamne, & qu'on la [*La Cinquantaine dramatique*] joue après en guise de petite Piece, de même après Brutus, Zaïre, Alzire, &c." (9). The anticipated menu—one of Voltaire's plays, then a shorter play written in his honor, and the crowning of his bust—replicated the spectacle at the Comédie Française the previous year and anticipated the recipe that would be followed at the time of Voltaire's death in 1778–79.[56] Although the *Cinquantaine dramatique* was never performed, it contributed to the standardization of the commemorative formula.

In March 1784, the *Journal de Paris* published a letter from a reader who hoped to regularize commemorative practice in a more rigorous way. Indicating that, "la Nation sent aujourd'hui plus vivement que jamais le mérite des grands hommes qui ont fait sa gloire," the anonymous author of this letter asked: ". . . Pourquoi les Comédiens François n'honoreroient-ils point tous les ans, par une fête particulière, le jour de la mort de chacun de ces hommes célèbres? . . . Il ne s'agiroit que de représenter ce jour-là un de leurs chef–d'oeuvres, & d'indiquer sur l'affiche que c'est pour honorer l'anniversaire, soit de *Corneille*, soit de *Molière*, soit de *Racine*, &c."[57] This patriotic reader felt that "ceux qui aiment sincérement la gloire de leur pays" would certainly approve his plan. In his eyes, this type of celebration was a logical corollary to other initiatives in honor of the nation's great men, like d'Angiviller's statue series and the academic eulogies. He further insisted, however, on the benefit that would derive from the ceremonial performance of the works of these great writers in the presence of "une assemblée nombreuse, qui n'en sortiroit point, je crois, sans une admiration plus sentie." According to this author, the standardization of the commemorative performances at the Comédie Française would serve to reinforce a sense of national literary identity.

Perhaps in response to the proposal in the *Journal de Paris*, the Comédie Française staged an open competition in connection with the Corneille centenary in October 1784. Eleven celebratory plays were written as a result, from which the troupe selected a work entitled *Corneille aux Champs-Élysées*.[58] Predictably, this work and its rivals closely adhered to the model of 1773; each of the surviving examples stages the triumph of the honoree in requisite fashion, with the crowning of Corneille's bust by the actors. The occasion also served to reaffirm the rivalry with England. Artaud, encouraged no doubt by the success of his *Centenaire de Moliere*, again created a work befitting the circumstance. In his *Fête séculaire de Corneille*, he stridently vindicated the cause of French letters, denouncing the Anglomania of his compatriots:

Ariste: Tel est le caractere
De nos Anglomanes fougueux;
Fatigués des talens qui naissent autour d'eux,
Ils ne prisent que ceux d'une terre étrangere;
Et leur orgueil, plus que leur goût préfere,
Dans la liste des noms fameux,
Shakespir à Corneille, & Congreve à Moliere.
Thalie: Que ne vont-ils en Angleterre,
C'est-là qu'ils doivent réussir;
Et chez le brave Anglois une Fête annuelle,
Fait revivre à son souvenir
Les grands noms, revêtus d'une gloire immortelle,
De Handel & de Shakespir.[59]

The obvious solution to this problem, as Artaud stated in his "Avertissement," was to appropriate English celebratory practice and to institute similar festivals in France.[60] The anxieties voiced in the play demonstrated, however, that even as the centenary gained a firmer position on the French cultural calendar, lingering concerns about the neglect of the nation's great writers persisted. As the French saluted Corneille, the founder of their tragic tradition, they still struggled against the specter of Shakespeare.

National Sentiment and the Birth of the Centenary

If the abbé Le Beau de Schosne were to learn of the long–term fate of his *Assemblée*, he would certainly be disappointed. In 1773, he claimed in the preface to his work that its performance at the Comédie Française, precisely one hundred years after the death of Molière, would be remembered as an important date in the history of the theater: "Cette représentation fera époque dans les Annales du Théâtre." As history has shown, he largely overestimated the impact of *L'Assemblée*. His play and the first Molière centenary have long disappeared from view.

The events of 1773 did, however, lay the foundations of a cultural tradition that has continued unabated into the twenty-first century. Given the role played by historical contingency in determining the timing of this celebration, we must resist the temptation to interpret the choice of Molière as the subject of the first centenary celebration strictly on the basis of literary merit. Rather, the Molière centenary served to designate the greatest comic writer in the French tradition as a founding member of the nation's cultural lineage, reinforcing the idea of historical continuity between the eighteenth century and the "Grand Siècle." In this sense, the two commemorative plays reflected much broader and enduring concerns about national identity.

Spurred by the example of the English Shakespeare Jubilee, the French viewed the Molière centenary as a way of responding to a challenge from their cross–Channel rival. In this context, the tribute at the Comédie Française functioned conceptually as the enactment of a shared identity, founded in a common veneration for the nation's cultural heroes. During the second half of the eighteenth century, writers and critics alike enthusiastically embraced the literary and artistic accomplishments of these heroes as a manifestation of national virtue. It is no accident that the birth of the literary centenary in France coincided with a rise in anxiety about the decadence of French literature and morals. Defeat in the Seven Years' War had badly bruised the nation's ego. The resulting sense of national humiliation generated calls for revitalization and inspired plans for more systematic expressions of devotion to France's great men. The literary centenary of 1773 was thus embedded in a discourse of national glory, a premise that would be replicated numerous times throughout the nineteenth century and well into the twentieth.[61] Even in its origins, commemorative practice in France combined positive and negative impulses, seeking to enhance the prestige of French letters while reaffirming French resistance to foreign influence.

NOTES

1. Pierre Nora, "L'Ère de la commémoration," in *Les Lieux de mémoire*, dir. Pierre Nora, 7 vols. in 3 parts (Paris: Gallimard, 1984–92), 3.3: 977–1012. William M. Johnston, *Celebrations: The Cult of Anniversaries in Europe and the United States Today* (New Brunswick, New Jersey: Transaction Publishers, 1991).

2. For an analysis of recent celebrations, see Thierry Gasnier, "La France commémorante. Les célébrations nationales (1986–1993)," *Le Débat* 78 (janvier–février 1994): 89–98. Françoise Mosser notes that, "beaucoup plus importants qu'on pourrait le penser sont ceux qui exploitent les anniversaires à des fins économiques et commerciales (maisons d'édition, organismes de tourisme—offices de tourisme, mais aussi agences de voyage—, établissements commerciaux (producteurs de 'produits dérivés')" ("Pour un guide de la commémoration. Publics et projets," La Fédération des maisons d'écrivain et des patrimoines littéraires, 27 novembre 1999 <http://www.litterature–lieux.com/pdf/comm1.pdf>).

3. Previous scholarship on the Molière centenary has not inquired whether there had been any previous centenary celebrations in France. See Francis W. Gravit, "The First Centenary of Molière's Death," in *Molière and the Commonwealth of Letters: Patrimony and Posterity*, eds. Roger Johnson, Jr., Editha S. Neumann, Guy T. Trail (Jackson: University Press of Mississippi, 1975), 547-56; and E. Déborde de Montcorin, "Les Centenaires de Molière dans l'Histoire," *Revue des études historiques* 88 (1922): 151-60. For a descriptive overview of Molière celebrations through the years, see Noëlle Guibert, "Le culte et les lieux," *Cahiers de la Comédie Française* 3 (1992): 51-61.

4. Previous works dealing with the historical reception of Molière have paid little attention to the centenary observances. See Monique Wagner, *Molière and the Age of Enlightenment, Studies on Voltaire and the Eighteenth Century* 112 (1973); and Maurice Descotes, *Molière et sa fortune littéraire* (Bordeaux: Éditions Guy Ducros, 1970). The catalogue for the tricentenary exposition at the Musée des Arts Décoratifs makes only a passing reference to the centenary *(Exposition du IIIe centenaire de la mort de Molière* [Paris: Musée des Arts Décoratifs, 1973], 72).

5. My approach here is informed by Peter Uwe Hohendahl's conception of literary reception. Drawing on Tony Bennett's notion of "reading formations," Hohendahl advocates a more synthetic type of reception study, emphasizing the role of social, political and institutional influences in determining the ways in which readers (or spectators) think about literature. See Peter Uwe Hohendahl, *Building a National Literature: the Case of Germany, 1830-1870*, trans. Renate Baron Franciscono (Ithaca and London: Cornell University Press, 1989 [1985]), 1-43.

6. Augustin–Théodore–Vincent Lebeau de Schosne, *L'Assemblée, comédie en un acte et en vers; avec l'Apothéose de Moliere, Ballet Héroïque* (Paris: L. Cellot, 1773). Beyond a modest list of theatrical and poetic works, the standard biographical sources contain little information regarding Lebeau de Schosne's activities. The title page of *L'Assemblée* indicates that he was the member of learned societies

in Nîmes and Auxerre.

7. The first edition of the *Dictionnaire de l'Académie Française* (1694) defines "apothéose" as "deification, ceremonie que faisoient les Romains Idolastres, pour mettre leurs Empereurs au nombre des Dieux" (1: 44). In the fifth edition (1798), this definition had been expanded to include modern commemorative practice: "Apothéose, se dit aussi par hyperbole Des honneurs extraordinaires rendus à un homme que l'opinion générale et l'enthousiasme public élèvent au–dessus de l'humanité" (1: 65).

8. Jean Baptiste Artaud, *La Centenaire de Moliere, comédie en un acte, en vers et en prose; Suivie d'un Divertissement relatif à l'Apothéose de Moliere* (Paris: Veuve Duchesne, 1773). Artaud held a position as royal censor in 1773; he later served as editor for the *Courrier d'Avignon*. For additional information, see René Moulinas, "Artaud, Jean Baptiste (1732-1796)," *Dictionnaire des Journalistes, 1600-1789*, ed. Jean Sgard, 2 vols. (Oxford: Voltaire Foundation, 1999), 1: 23.

9. H. Carrington Lancaster, *The Comédie Française, 1701-1774, Plays, Actors, Spectators, Finances*, in *Transactions of the American Philosophical Society*, new series, 41 (1951): 835-38.

10. *Mercure de France* (mars 1773), 172–81*; L'Année littéraire* (1773), 3: 73–85,145–63; *Journal encyclopédique* (mars 1773), 490–94; *L'Avantcoureur* (22 février 1773), 122–26; *L'Almanach des Muses* (Paris: Delalain, 1774), 225; *Correspondance littéraire, philosophique et critique par Grimm, Diderot, Raynal, Meister, etc.*, ed. Maurice Tourneux, 16 vols. (Paris: Garnier frères, 1872–82), 10: 182–88; *Mémoires secrets pour servir à l'histoire de la République des lettres en France, depuis MDCCLXII jusqu'à nos jours*, 36 vols. (London: John Adamson, 1784–89), 6: 289–91, 24: 234-35.

11. Jean-Claude Bonnet, *La Naissance du Panthéon. Essai sur le culte des grands hommes* (Paris: Fayard, 1998).

12. I thank David Bell for sharing with me a chapter from his forthcoming study, *The Cult of the Nation in France: Inventing Nationalism, 1680–1800* (Cambridge: Harvard University Press, 2001). See also the contributions by Bell and Bonnet in the recent issue of *MLN* dedicated to the "Culte des Grands Hommes," ed. Jacques Neefs (116: 4 [September 2001]). For a useful summary of the role of statuary, see James David Draper and Guilhem Scherf, *Augustin Pajou, Royal Sculptor, 1730–1809* (New York: The Metropolitan Museum of Art, 1997), 300–03.

13. Louis-Sébastien Mercier, *Molière, drame en cinq actes en prose, imité de Goldoni* (Amsterdam, 1776). Mercier later reworked this play and presented it under the title, *La Maison de Moliere* (1788). Michel de Cubières, *La Mort de Moliere* (Londres: chez Knapen et fils, 1788). Like Molière, Cubières revised his play, republishing it in 1803.

14. Louis Réau, *Houdon, sa vie et son oeuvre*, 2 vols. (Paris: F. de Nobele, 1964), 1: 348–50. For further commentary on the bust at the Academy, see also the article in the *Année littéraire* (1778, 8: 202–11).

15. According to the *Trésor de la langue française* (5: 385), Pierre Larousse, in the *Grand dictionnaire universel du XIXe siècle* is the first lexicographer to include

the modern definition of the *centenaire* as a periodic celebration (1867; 3: 720). For commentary on the idea of "siècle" as a temporal marker, dating from the late seventeenth century, see Joan DeJean, *Ancients against Moderns: Culture Wars and the Making of a Fin de Siècle* (Chicago: University of Chicago Press, 1997), 18-24.

16. Pierre Nora cites three events in particular that strongly favor regularization of the term *centenaire*—le centenaire de l'indépendance américaine (1876), le centenaire de la Révolution française, et le centenaire du siècle lui-même (1900)" ("L'Ère de la commémoration," 982).

17. The title of the first volume is *L'Almanach de la Vieillesse, ou Notice de tous ceux qui ont vécu cent ans et plus* (Paris: A. M. Lottin, 1761). In 1764 and continuing through 1773, the title becomes *Almanach des Centénaires; ou Durée de la Vie Humaine au-delà de Cent Ans, démontrée par des Exemples sans nombre, tant anciens que modernes*.

18. In reviewing the 1773 edition, *L'Année littéraire* indicates that this section of the *Almanach* has become the most interesting part: "Cette galerie, où sont rangés par ordre ces hommes extraordinaires qui ont reculé les limites de la vie, n'est pas la partie la plus intéressante du Recueil. . . . L'auteur a sçu y insérer une *Gazette Centénaire*, c'est-à-dire, un choix des principaux événemens & des anecdotes arrivés précisément il y a cent ans" (1773, 1: 112-13). The journalist further notes that "il semble que l'intervalle d'un siècle donne du prix aux moindres choses" (115).

19. "Troisième partie, contenant la Gazette centénaire," 43. The entry on Molière runs ten pages, including the history of his troupe after 1673, several epitaphs written to deplore his death, and an announcement of the forthcoming edition of his works.

20. 1771, 68. The following year, the editors added their own "Remarques sur les Années Séculaires," again drawing on the *Gazette d'Amsterdam* to announce a bicentennial commemoration of the battle of Lepantc: "Voici une nouvelle preuve de l'attention que l'on donne aux *Années séculaires*, ou *centénaires*, ou *jubilaires*" (1772, 96). The emphatic triple designation (séculaire, centénaire, jubilaire) reflects obvious hesitancy in the nomenclature to use when designating this newly emerging phenomenon.

21. "Que nous sommes encore loin de cette réformation salutaire de nos moeurs, où les réjouissances publiques d'une nation auront pour objet la commémoration des grandes actions de ses ancêtres, et où leurs forfaits publics seront expiés par des jours solennels d'humiliation, qui inspirent à la nation une juste horreur pour les crimes dont ses annales sont souillées!" (*Correspondance littéraire*, [septembre 1772] 10:51).

22. *La Cinquantaine Dramatique de M. de Voltaire, suivie de l'Inauguration de sa statue, Intermede En un Acte, orné de Chants & de Danses. Par l'Auteur du Poeme du Luxe* (Paris: Durand & Despilly, 1774), "Avertissement." For a description of the celebrations held in Rheims to celebrate the fiftieth year of Louis XV's reign, 28 December 1772, including a *Te Deum*, a feast, a performance of Collé's *Partie de chasse de Henri IV*, free wine and fireworks, see *Journal historique et politique*

des prinicipaux évènemens des différentes Cours de l'Europe 1773, 2 (20 janvier): 55-56.

23. Edmond Dziembowski, *Un Nouveau Patriotisme français, 1750–1770. La France face à la puissance anglaise à l'époque de la guerre de Sept Ans, Studies on Voltaire and the Eighteenth Century* 365 (1998).

24. Jeffrey Ravel identifies the theater as an important venue for the formation of national identity during the 1770's; see *The Contested Parterre: Public Theater and French Political Culture, 1680-1791* (Ithaca and London: Cornell University Press, 1999), particularly chapter 6. My analysis here in no way contradicts his arguments, but my perspective is significantly different. Rather than looking at theatrical performances as social events having significant political ramifications, I focus here on the eighteenth–century perception that France's literary heritage, particularly the theatrical tradition, was one of the nation's most important and unimpeachable claims to greatness.

25. See Roland Mortier, "L'idée de décadence littéraire au XVIIIe siècle," in *Le Coeur et la raison. Recueil d'études sur le dix–huitième siècle* (Oxford: Voltaire Foundation, 1990), 53–67.

26. D10162, 18 November 1761. All quotations from Voltaire's correspondence refer to *Correspondence and Related Documents*, ed. Theodore Besterman, 51 vols. (Oxford: Voltaire Foundation, 1968–1977). For analysis of Voltaire's epistolary campaign in support of the *Commentaires sur Corneille*, see the introduction to this text by David Williams in *Complete Works of Voltaire* (Oxford: Voltaire Foundation, 1968-present), vol. 53; and, by the same author, "Voltaire's War with England: The Appeal to Europe, 1760-1764," *Studies on Voltaire and the Eighteenth Century* 179 (1979): 79-100. Voltaire's concern with French decadence during the period of the Seven Years' War also manifests itself in his views on language; see my essay, "Voltaire's Militant Defense of the French Language," *Romance Notes* 40 (2000): 313-24.

27. "A Monsieur le duc de La Vallière," dedicatory epistle to *Sophonisbe* (*Oeuvres complètes de Voltaire*, ed. Louis Moland, 52 vols. [Paris: Garnier frères, 1877-1885], 7: 29-30). La Vallière himself had been part of a project to compile a *Bibliothèque du théâtre français depuis son origine* (1768).

28. David Williams, "Luneau de Boisjermain's *Racine*: A Voltairean Emulation?" *Studies on Voltaire and the Eighteenth Century* 90 (1972): 1773-89.

29. Pierre Peyronnet, "Y eut-il des historiens du théâtre au XVIIIe siècle?" *L'Histoire au dix-huitième siècle: colloque* (Aix-en-Provence: Edisud, 1980), 173-86.

30. The "Avertissement" of the *Dictionnaire dramatique* promoted the importance of the French theater in typical terms: "On a beaucoup écrit sur le genre Dramatique, une des plus intéressantes parties de notre Littérature, une de celles où le Génie François a pris le plus grand essor, où il a déployé le plus de ressources, franchi le plus d'obstacles; en un mot, où il a fait éclore un plus grand nombre d'excellens modéles" ([Sébastien Roch-Nicolas Chamfort and Joseph de Laporte], *Dictionnaire dramatique, conentant l'histoire des Théâtres . . .*, 2 vols. [Geneva: Slatkine Reprints,

1967; Paris, 1776]).

31. Samuel Taylor, "La Collaboration de Voltaire au *Théâtre français* (1767-1769)," *Studies on Voltaire and the Eighteenth Century* 18 (1961): 57-75.

32. This volume, including Du Ryer's *Scévole* and Mairet's *Sophonisbe* along with *Venceslas*, was the only one of the sixteen projected volumes to appear. According to Jacques Gury, Marmontel's preliminary discourse "offre un panorama du théâtre occidental et affirme la suprématie de la tragédie classique française" (*Préface du Shakespeare traduit de l'anglois*, ed. Jacques Gury [Geneva: Librairie Droz, 1990], 227).

33. This collection, including Quinault's *La Mère coquette*, Hauteroche's *L'Invisible*, Baron's *L'Andrienne* and Corneille's *Le Menteur*, is reviewed in *L'Année littéraire* (1773, 8: 3-53). Fréron declares that, "M. *Collé* ne s'est proposé d'autre but que de conserver & de faire rester au Théâtre nos anciennes bonnes Comédies," motivated by "un zèle ardent & pur pour la gloire de la Scène Françoise" (10-11). The journalist praises "l'idée qu'il [Collé] donne aux Amateurs actuels & futurs d'entreprendre d'âge en âge le même travail, & de rendre par ce moyen nos anciennes Comédies toujours nouvelles" (52).

34. Charles Palissot de Montenoy, "Mémoire contre une Compagnie de Libraires, qui s'est opposée au projet qu'avait l'Auteur de donner une Edition commentée des Oeuvres de Moliere," in *Oeuvres complêtes*, 6 vols. (Liège: J.–F. Bastien, 1778), 6: 247.

35. On the subject of the classics in nineteenth–century France, see Daniel Milo, "Les Classiques scolaires," in *Les Lieux de Mémoire*, 2.3: 517–62.

36. *Oeuvres de Molière, avec des Remarques Grammaticales, des Avertissmens, & des Observations sur chaque Pièce, par M. Bret*, 6 vols. (Paris: Compagnie des Libraires Associés, 1773). For an overview of Bret's activities, see A. C. Keys, "An eighteenth-century editor of Molière: Antoine Bret," *Studies on Voltaire and the Eighteenth Century* 98 (1972): 219-30. Like Voltaire's *Corneille*, this *Molière* was a beautiful piece of printing: "En général, cette nouvelle & magnifique Edition me paroît digne du grand homme qui en est l'objet. Elle est ornée d'excellentes estampes, toutes dessinées par l'habile M. *Moreau*, & exécutées par les meilleurs Graveurs" (*L'Année littéraire* 1773, 6: 172). Bret's edition was reprinted at least twice: *Oeuvres de Molière, avec des Remarques Grammaticales. . .*, 8 vols. (Paris: Compagnie des Libraires Associés, an XIII [1805]); and *Oeuvres de Molière, avec des Remarques Grammaticales. . ., nouvelle édition, imprimée sur celle de 1773*, 6 vols. (Paris: Tardieu–Denesle, 1821).

37. "Prospectus d'une nouvelle Edition de Moliere, avec Figures," *Suite de la Clef, ou Journal Historique sur les matières du tems* 112 (October 1772): 254.

38. Certain printings of the two celebratory plays provide further evidence linking Bret's edition with the centenary. At the end of Le Beau de Schosne's *Assemblée*, an "Avis du Libraire" announces: "Plusieurs personnes ayant paru désirer que cette pièce pût être jointe à l'édition des Oeuvres de Moliere qu'on imprime *in 8°*. on s'est conformé à leurs vues, en choisissant le même format, qui, d'ailleurs, est d'un usage plus universel" (48). At the end of *La Centenaire* (in the 70–page edition), a

similar "Avis" states: "M. Bret, Auteur du nouveau Commentaire des *Oeuvres* de Molière, dont l'édition va paraître incessament ayant paru désirer que cette pièce fût imprimée dans le même format, on s'est empressé de satisfaire à son désir."

39. "Lettre du sieur Lekain à M. le duc de Duras," in *Mémoires de Lekain, précédés de Réflexions sur cet acteur, et sur l'art théâtral, par F. Talma* (Paris: Ponthieu, 1825), 36-7.

40. "Délibération des comédiens du roi, prise à l'occasion de la centenaire de Molière," in *Mémoires de Lekain*, 34.

41. *Mercure de France* (mars 1773), 180.

42. *Correspondance littéraire* (février 1773), 10: 184.

43. The standard accounts of these events are Christian Deelman, *The Great Shakespeare Jubilee* (London: Michael Joseph, 1964); and Martha W. England, *Garrick's Jubilee* (Columbus: Ohio State University Press, 1964).

44. Michael Dobson, *The Making of the National Poet: Shakespeare, Adaptation and Authorship, 1660-1769* (Oxford: Clarendon Press, 1992).

45. *Mercure de France* (décembre 1769), 184-86. The article in the *Mercure* also attracted the attention of a young Goethe who was inspired to stage his own celebration in 1771 ("Zum Schäkespears Tag," in *Der Junge Goethe, neu bearbeitete Ausgabe in fünf Bänden*, ed. Hanna Fischer-Lamberg, 5 vols. [Berlin: Walter de Gruyter, 1999], 2: 83-86, 327-29).

46. The Antique tradition of crowning poets was certainly not unknown in Europe, as evidenced by the Petrarchian precedent and numerous engraved images of laurel–crowned poets. The *Encyclopédie* article "Poëte couronné" (12: 844–45, by Jaucourt, published in 1765) clearly indicates, however, that this tradition had no currency in eighteenth–century France.

47. D12832, [?August 1765]; the dating of this letter is highly uncertain. Theodore Besterman places it in 1765 on the basis of textual evidence but does not consider the reference to the Shakespeare Jubilee. It seems more probable that Voltaire was writing in 1769.

48. "57. to David Garrick, 1 October 1770," in *Mme Riccoboni's letters to David Hume, David Garrick and sir Robert Liston, 1764-1783* ed. James C. Nicholls, *Studies on Voltaire and the Eighteenth Century* 149 (1976): 161. Riccoboni also relays an anecdote concerning Antoine Bret (who had unwittingly offended Jean-Jacques Rousseau) and discusses political tensions between the French and the English. The contingencies of epistolary discourse thus bring together, in a happy coincidence, the primary threads of our discussion here—Molière (by association with his editor), Shakespeare, commemorative practice, and the Franco–British rivalry.

49. For a reading of this campaign as an attempt to publicize the integrity of the Republic of Letters, see Dena Goodman, "Pigalle's 'Voltaire nu': The Republic of Letters Represents Itself to the World," *Representations* 16 (1986): 86–109.

50. Largely instigated by Voltaire, the Shakespearean quarrel eventually spread to the Académie Française and involved authors in both countries. For a summary

of this episode, see Haydn Mason, "Voltaire versus Shakespeare: the *Lettre à l'Académie Française*," *British Journal for Eighteenth–Century Studies* 18 (1995): 173–85. Within the context of this ongoing dispute, the crowning of Voltaire at the Comédie Française after his return to Paris in 1778 must be interpreted as a sort of ultimate response to English Bardolatry. The reproduction of precisely the same type of ceremony—the famous engraving by Moreau shows the actors on stage, gathered around the bust of the author—grants a final victory to the French writer against the English enemy whom he had been combating for some twenty years. I am indebted to Russel Goulbourne for sharing with me an unpublished essay in which he traces this genealogy.

51. "Prospectus" for Le Tourneur's *Shakespeare traduit de l'Anglois*, quoted in [d'Aquin de Château-Lyon], *Éloge de Molière, en vers, avec des Notes curieuses, par le petit-cousin de Rabelais* (London and Paris: chez les Libraires qui débitent les Nouveautés, 1775), 45. The very first "note curieuse," appended to the second line of this poem, deals with the 1773 centenary. The passage from Le Tourneur's prospectus is cited in an "Addition à la premiere note," suggesting that it was added immediately before publication.

52. *Mercure de France* (mars 1774), 154.

53. *Journal de politique et de littérature*, no. 7 (5 mars 1775), 1: 262. The *Mémoires secrets* also records this cancellation (14 mars 1775), 7: 310.

54. See Guibert, "Le Culte et les lieux," 57.

55. *La Cinquantaine Dramatique*, 10. A further footnote cites the two plays of 1773: "Cette année, les Comédiens donnerent la *Centenaire de Molière*, Comédie, en un acte, en vers & en prose, ornée de couplets & de vaudevilles, par M. *Artaud*. La seconde fut *l'Assemblée*, Comédie en un acte, en vers, suivie de l'Apothéose de Moliere, Ballet héroïque, par M. l'Abbé *de Schosne*" (64-65).

56. Most notably, see Jean-François de La Harpe, *Les Muses rivales, ou l'apothéose de Voltaire*, in *Oeuvres de La Harpe*, 16 vols. (Paris: Firmin Didot, 1820), 2: 199–229.

57. "Aux Auteurs du Journal," *Journal de Paris*, no. 85 (25 mars 1784), 379.

58. For a negative review of the performances, see *Correspondance littéraire* (janvier 1785), 14: 85-87; the work is attributed to "un fort jeune homme, M. Laurent." This article also reports on performances of *Le Triomphe du Génie* in Rouen, the birthplace of Corneille. *Le Triomphe* was one of two centenary plays written by Michel Cubières-Palmezeaux, published as *Les Deux Centenaiires de Corneille, pièces en un acte et en vers. Représentées à Rouen, Bordeaux, le Havre, Tours, Grenoble, &c., &c. Par M. le Chevalier de Cubieres, de l'Académie de Lyon* (Paris: Cailleu, 1785). The full title points to a significant expansion of the centenary phenomenon to the provinces.

59. *La Fête Séculaire de Corneille, Comédie, en un acte et en vers* (Paris: Hardouin & Gattey, 1785), 14.

60. "Parmi les modes qui nous viennent d'Angleterre, celle de célébrer annuellement les grands Génies qui illustrent les Nations, ne nous est pas encore arrivée. Mais il est possible qu'elle arrive enfin. Tout le monde sçait qu'à Londres le

Musicien Handel a sa Fête annuelle; ainsi il n'y auroit rien de bien étrange, si le pere de la Scene tragique jouissoit un jour à Paris du même honneur" ("Avertissement," n.p.).

61. For commentary on one of the most notable nineteenth–century centenaries, see Georges Benrekassa, Michel Delon, Jean-Marie Goulemot, Jean Jiou, Jean Sgard and Eric Walther, "Le Premier Centenaire de la mort de Voltaire et de Rousseau: Significations d'une commémoration," *Revue d'histoire littéraire de la France* 79 (1979): 265-85; and Jean–Marie Goulemot and Éric Walter, "Les Centenaires de Voltaire et de Rousseau," in *Lieux de mémoire*, 1:1: 381-420.

Philosophical Reflection, Happiness, and Male Friendship in Prévost's *Manon Lescaut*

JOE JOHNSON

Although there is no dearth of important texts concerning idealized male friendship in French literature in any given century, it is no exaggeration to assert that the eighteenth century was more intensely taken with the matter than any previous or subsequent era in French literature. Whether considered in the light of Ancients like Aristotle or Cicero, or French Moderns such as Montaigne, La Fontaine, and Saint-Évremond, friendship became in the Age of Enlightenment a common subject in all aspects of French cultural life and literary forms of discourse. It was much reflected upon in salons, in correspondences, and in numerous philosophical treatises. It was the inspiration for poetry, for the stage, for novels, *nouvelles* and *contes* and was grist for all of the major writers of the Enlightenment, including Antoine-François Prévost d'Exiles (1697-1763).

Published first in 1731, and with important revisions made for the 1753 version, the *Histoire du chevalier des Grieux et de Manon Lescaut*, or more simply, *Manon Lescaut*, has largely eclipsed the rest of Prévost's voluminous corpus.[1] Moreover, it has gone on to become the most reprinted work of French literature with, as Jean Sgard notes, "more than two hundred and fifty editions published between 1731 and 1981"(xxxii).[2] Outside the bounds of French literature classes, it is probably fair to say that, in the United States at least, the story is best known in its rather different, operatic versions by

Jules Massenet (1842-1912) and Giacomo Puccini (1858-1924), both of which remain in the modern repertory. Encouraged by the operas, the predominant image of *Manon Lescaut* is that of its famous lovers. Joining Lancelot and Guinevere, Tristan and Yseut, Paolo and Francesca, Romeo and Juliet, Pelléas and Mélisande in the pantheon of thwarted great lovers, Manon, the "bad" girl with the "heart of gold," and Des Grieux, the young man ruined, yet exalted by his love, are an overwhelming image threatening the exclusion of all else. Perhaps this explains why the complicated figure of Tiberge disappears altogether from both operatic versions of the tale, for late-Romantic opera rarely pays much attention to the exigencies of male friendship, particularly of the exclusive sort required by Tiberge.[3]

Dwelling too exclusively on the overpowering image of Manon and Des Grieux does an injustice to Prévost's masterwork, for it clouds the extent to which *Manon Lescaut* is also one of the noteworthy treatments on male homosocial desire and idealized male friendship in the first half of the eighteenth century.[4] Going against the grain of contemporary ethics that tended to oppose friendship and passion, this novel depicts friendship and passion as ambiguous doubles and finds that love is just as apt to exalt and bring about happiness as is male friendship, which, at least in Des Grieux's reformulation on the matter, best serves as a vehicle for realizing his passion for Manon. An analysis of the novel's prefatory "Avis au lecteur" will reveal the underlying, yet tenuous, connection of friendship with happiness and virtue, especially as this linkage informs the novel's manifestations of male homosocial desire in the relationship between Des Grieux and the "homme de qualité." The depiction of their relationship, which illustrates the nature of friendship posited in the "Avis," is echoed in the subsequent one of the young M. de T…, an ambiguous figure who serves as a double for Tiberge, the figure most associated in the text with idealized male friendship, yet whose brand of friendship fails at the end of the tale, despite the death of Manon.

One reason Des Grieux's attempt to reformulate the idea of friendship is so striking is that eighteenth-century ethics concerning friendship pervade Prévost's text. Although written for a different context, Charles G. Smith's summation of the widespread, proverbial discourse of friendship remains appropriate for Prévost's novel and could easily figure as a synopsis of any of the more prolix treatises of friendship so common in the eighteenth century. Smith lists them as such:

> 1. Friendship is based on virtue. 2. Friendship is based on equality.
> 3. Friendship is based on similarity. 4. Friends have but one soul.

> 5. A friend is a second self. 6. False friendship cannot last. 7. Friends' goods are common goods.[5]

Though not necessarily in Smith's order, these ethics of friendship figure almost from the first of Prévost's work in the "Avis au lecteur," one of two distinct frame-elements preceding Des Grieux's own account. This passage is notable for more than one reason. On the one hand, there is its aspect of moral self-justification on the basis of Horatian utility and pleasure. As Richard Smernoff opines, such claims were "often little more than ploys designed to convince the censor of the author's moral probity," as typical of the day as the novel's claim to be a true memoir to protect it against the attacks of classically minded critics hostile to the novelistic genres.[6] As the impressive amount of critical consideration devoted to it might indicate, the "Avis" is far more than a simple subterfuge, for its justification purports to be the exposition of the story's central conflict.

> [Le public] verra dans la conduite de M. des Grieux, un exemple terrible de la force des passions. J'ai à peindre un jeune aveugle, qui refuse d'être heureux, pour se précipiter volontairement dans les dernières infortunes; qui, avec toutes les qualités dont se forme le plus brillant mérite, préfère, par choix, une vie obscure et vagabonde, à tous les avantages de la fortune et de la nature; qui prévoit ses malheurs, sans vouloir les éviter; qui les sent et qui en est accablé, sans profiter des remèdes qu'on lui offre sans cesse et qui peuvent à tous moments les finir; enfin un caractère ambigu, un mélange de vertus et de vices, un contraste perpétuel de bons sentiments et d'actions mauvaises. (M, 21-22)

One standard interpretation of this passage is the Christian, allegorical one whereby Des Grieux embraces the "wrong" path exemplified by his passion for an earthly Manon and rejects the "right" path exemplified by an Augustinian Tiberge who represents "l'amitié vertueuse," as Frederick Gerson puts it in his treatment on friendship in Prévost's text. In a similar vein, Marie Wellington opts for a psychological analysis of a text-long back and forth struggle between Manon and Tiberge for the maladjusted Des Grieux. While it is true that this passage primarily concerns Des Grieux, through the course of the novel one discovers that, in a profoundly Christian manner, the admixture of virtue and vice taints every character in the novel. For instance, as Sgard notes, "Tiberge n'est pas simplement le pieux ecclésiastique, le séminariste doux, sentencieux et un peu mélancolique que l'on serait tenté de voir en lui."[7] Sharing many of the same experiences, the two men are, to a considerable extent, doubles of one another, and are themselves doubled in other characters with an ultimate effect of problematizing the notion of idealized friendship and the linkage with it of happiness and virtue.

For now, however, if we look at the central conflict in the "Avis" and in the story proper as being one opposing friendship and love, this conflict is a traditional one. After all, by the time Prévost penned *Manon Lescaut*, the rivalry of same-sex friendship and heterosexual passion had long constituted a *topos* in French literature going back to such medieval texts as *Ami et Amile*, *Yvain, ou le chevalier au lion*, and the Prose *Lancelot*. In the Renaissance, Montaigne's essay concerning La Boétie can similarly be reduced to such a formulation.[8] Like Montaigne, moreover, treatises on friendship in the eighteenth century typically argue their case to the detriment of love as is evident in Caraccioli's account of the characteristics of friendship.

> Quelle différence entre l'amitié & l'amour! L'amitié devient la mère des plaisirs innocens, l'amour est la source du trouble & des chagrins; l'amour ne respecte aucunes Loix, l'amitié les observe toutes; l'amour est l'ouvrage du caprice, l'amitié le fruit de la réflexion; l'amour s'éteint aussi vite qu'il s'allume, l'amitié se forme peu à peu, & elle ne meurt jamais; l'amour se plaint, l'amitié se tait; l'amour tourmente, l'amitié tranquillise.[9]

Even though it does not make such a bald opposition, the "Avis au lecteur" would have implicitly evoked the subject of friendship to any well-read eighteenth-century reader. Moreover, as has been noted by more than one critic, Prévost likely intended such a connection to male friendship when he accepted for publication in *Manon Lescaut* an illustration by Pasquier, already used in copies of Fénélon's *Télémaque*, showing Mentor leading Telemachus away from the destructive appeal of love toward the summit of virtue and happiness.

It is this search for virtue and happiness that the "homme de qualité" uses in his appeal to a presumptive audience "d'un certain ordre de l'esprit et de politesse" who enjoy engaging in moral considerations. Indeed, the willingness to engage in such discourse is the first explicitly mentioned hallmark of friendship in the text. According to the "homme de qualité,"

> les plus doux moments de leur vie sont ceux qu'ils passent, ou seuls, ou *avec un ami*, à s'entretenir à cœur ouvert des charmes de la vertu,

> *des douceurs de l'amitié*, des moyens d'arriver au bonheur, des faiblesses de la nature qui nous éloignent, et des remèdes qui peuvent les guérir. Horace et Boileau marquent cet entretien comme un des plus beaux traits dont ils composent l'image de la vie heureuse. (M, 22, emphasis added)

While these observations mirror the usual cant concerning friendship, in light of subsequent events in the novel, the passage comes to ring a decidedly ambiguous note. For one thing, in a conversation with Tiberge where he disputes the route to virtue and happiness, Des Grieux argues that his happiness, dependent on Manon, does not lie with Tiberge, thus refuting the erstwhile superiority of ideal friendship as proposed by Montaigne, Caraccioli, and Tiberge. Moreover, the value attached in the "Avis" to philosophical reflection and friendship is put into question because almost all of the moralistic "entretiens" depicted in the novel include Des Grieux himself. The narrator foreshadows the subsequent course of events when he opines that moral consideration is problematic because "on craint de devenir dupe en voulant être bienfaisant et libéral; de passer pour faible en paraissant trop tendre et trop sensible"(M, 23). Des Grieux persistently attempts to dupe, to defraud, or to manipulate the men around him by exploiting the very qualities that create class solidarity and male homosocial desire in the text.

The importance of male homosocial desire in *Manon Lescaut* cannot be exaggerated. Throughout the novel, Des Grieux, although he resists, rejects, and inevitably exploits the other men involved, is ever the object of male desire. This pattern begins in the opening pages of the novel in the second, prefatory frame that introduces the episode into the context of the "homme de qualité's" larger novel. The scene is memorable, among other reasons, because of the pornographic objectification of the silent Manon who, chained and guarded by male guards, is exposed to the eyes of all. While an old woman expresses her horror before this vision, the reaction of the "homme de qualité" is markedly different. Moved first by curiosity, he experiences a vague sentiment of "quelque chose d'assez touchant"(M, 26), which is finally transformed into "du respect et de la pitié"(M, 26). Upon questioning the guards, he learns of a young man who has followed Manon "depuis Paris, sans cesser presque un moment de pleurer. Il faut que ce soit son frère ou son amant"(M, 26-7). Not only implying the potential for Manon's sexual availability to the "homme de qualité," the guard's statement casts Des Grieux in an ambiguous light, feminizing him by both his strong passion and his lack of emotional control and his lack of a clearly defined role vis-à-vis Manon.

Just as he has done with Manon, the "homme de qualité" views and objectifies Des Grieux, but here with a much stronger emotional reaction as evidenced by the moment's shorter declarative statements.

> Il paraissait enseveli dans une rêverie profonde. Je n'ai jamais vu de plus vive image de la douleur. Il était mis fort simplement; mais on distingue, au premier coup d'œil, un homme qui a de la naissance et de l'éducation. Je m'approchai de lui. Il se leva; et je découvris dans ses yeux, dans sa figure et dans tous ses mouvements, un air si fin et si noble que je me sentis porté naturellement à lui vouloir du bien. (M, 27)

His instinctual response to assist Des Grieux is partly based on class solidarity, yet it also verges on the homoerotic because it is, after all, Des Grieux's physical appeal that inspires the interest of the "homme de qualité." Anne Vila persuasively describes this scene as an example of the way "*Manon Lescaut* reflects not only the dynamics of erotic desire but also the equally complex, but more enduring, mechanism by which sensibility, sympathy, and benevolence operate within the privileged confines of the upper class."[10]

Further accentuating the ambiguity of the two men's encounter is the narrator's subsequent question: "voulez-vous bien satisfaire la curiosité que j'ai de connaître cette belle personne, qui ne me paraît point faite pour le triste état où je la vois?"(M, 27). It cannot simply be a lapse that there is no clear referent in the question posed by the "homme de qualité," for the "belle personne" in a "triste état" could refer to either Des Grieux or Manon or to both. In his response, Des Grieux opts for understanding the narrator to be referring to Manon, thus symbolically deflecting the narrator's gaze back onto Manon and thereby displacing the homoerotic potential of the moment. The deflection is only symbolic, however, for Des Grieux's elaboration makes it clear who shall prove to be the center of this tale: "il ne pouvait m'apprendre qui elle était sans se faire connaître lui-même"(M, 27). Des Grieux thus keeps himself, rather than Manon, squarely under the gaze of the male narrator in this encounter and the one two years (and two paragraphs) hence in Calais.

The narrator's reaction to Des Grieux's good looks is not a singular event in *Manon Lescaut*. Indeed, Des Grieux is ever conscious of his ability to alter circumstances via his solidarity with men based on his physical appeal. For instance, after he has been kidnapped by his father and is lodged in the same hotel where he had heretofore absconded with Manon, he notes the reaction of the innkeeper and his servants, "j'entendis dire à l'hôte: Ah! c'est ce *joli* monsieur"(M, 41, emphasis added). His "pretty" looks even work in his attempt during the deportation to manipulate Manon's guards and their leader who permit him to accompany Manon because "je lui paraissais néanmoins *si joli homme* que lui et ses compagnons se relâcheraient un peu de leur devoir"(M, 157, emphasis added). Another notable instance where Des Grieux's good looks stand him in good stead are when the bishop proposes to him a career as a priest. Des Grieux makes it clear that the offer is, in part, the result of his appearance: "ma naissance, le succès de mes études *et quelques agréments extérieurs* m'avaient fait connaître et estimer de tous les honnêtes gens de la ville"(M, 30, emphasis added).

Moved like so many other men, both by the vision of Des Grieux and Des Grieux's melancholic narrative, the narrator proffers his services, then implicitly his friendship, since the revelation of secrets is a traditional sign of friendship: "je ne vous presse pas de me découvrir, lui dis-je, le secret de vos affaires, mais, si je puis vous être utile à quelque chose, je m'offre volontiers à vous rendre service"(M, 28). Des Grieux does not accept the narrator's offer outright, but does soon mention the word "amis" for the first time. He notes that a friend to whom he has written will provide for his financial needs at Le Havre, but that in the meantime, he needs funds to continue the trip and to ensure Manon's comfort. By implication, for Des Grieux, rather than confidence, the act of offering money will constitute the most desired gesture of friendship. The narrator immediately responds by giving Des Grieux money and also effects a better treatment of Des Grieux and Manon by bribing the guards. The narrator, perhaps evoking the fear of being duped expressed in the "Avis," seems relieved to note that "la bonne grâce et la vive reconnaissance avec laquelle ce jeune inconnu me remercia, achevèrent de me persuader qu'il était né quelque chose, et qu'il méritait ma libéralité"(M, 29).

Parting company, the two do not encounter one another for some two years when, at Calais accompanied by another young nobleman his student, the narrator espies Des Grieux. Once again, the "homme de qualité" is drawn by Des Grieux's looks. "Il était en fort mauvais équipage, et beaucoup plus pâle que je ne l'avais vu la première fois [. . .] cependant, *comme il avait la physionomie trop belle* pour ne pas être reconnu facilement, je le remis aussitôt"(M, 29, emphasis added). Note the effusive physicality of their joyous reunion. "Ah! monsieur, s'écria-t-il en me baisant la main"(M, 29). The narrator, meanwhile, is equally affectionate, "je lui fis mille caresses"(M, 29), and invites Des Grieux to the inn where he is currently lodging and attends to all his needs. Des Grieux, citing his sense of noble obligation for monies spent before and now, proposes, in a barter-like exchange, to recount his entire story to the narrator: "je veux vous apprendre, non seulement mes malheurs et mes peines, mais encore mes désordres et mes plus honteuses faiblesses"(M, 30). Although neither the narrator nor Des Grieux expressly label their relationship as a friendship, the notion of friendship as laid forth by the "Avis" serves to imply such a relationship, for the two men will proceed to reflect upon issues of morality, happiness, and virtue. Once more, however, it is important to recall that the value of such an exercise becomes dubious over the course of the novel. Throughout the novel, Des Grieux repeatedly reveals his misadventures to the men in his life because as he says to the "homme de qualité:" "je suis sûr qu'en me condamnant, vous ne pourrez pas vous empêcher de me plaindre"(M, 30). Here, although Des Grieux can no longer acquire money to maintain Manon, he can make his passion for Manon live again in his relation of it to the "homme de qualité."

In the end, despite his omnipresence, the narrator exists merely as a vehicle for Des Grieux to re-live his passion for Manon. Like all of Des Grieux's male friends, he largely disappears from the novel, only reappearing in asides by Des Grieux and to mark the brief interlude between the first and second parts of the book. Yet, it should be clear that he represents the only sort of male friendship that Des Grieux is finally willing to accept. This interpretation runs counter to those that view Tiberge as gaining the upper hand at the end of the novel following Manon's death.[11] However, that Des Grieux ends the novel in the company of the "homme de qualité," rather than Tiberge, speaks volumes. Moreover, as we shall see from a comparison of M. de T… and Tiberge, the "homme de qualité," at least as he is presented in the one example from Prévost's corpus, is exactly the kind of friend that Des Grieux desires, the kind who enables Des Grieux's passion for Manon monetarily, sentimentally, or emotionally.

The depiction of Tiberge undermines the traditional notion of exclusive idealized friendship. Juxtaposing Des Grieux's initial description of Tiberge with Des Grieux's fantasy concerning one M. de T…, a character introduced late in the first part whose name patently evokes Tiberge, will make this pattern more obvious. "Fantasy" is not too strong a word: Des Grieux, who discovers the existence and name of M. de T… under false pretenses with the intent of meeting him and forming a relationship with him in order to effect Manon's release, imagines beforehand what kind of person he will prove to be. This gesture, in effect, redefines the notion of idealized friendship in order to make it conducive to the furtherance of heterosexual desire.

In Des Grieux's narration, Tiberge makes his first appearance on the fateful day when Des Grieux meets Manon. The two men are wandering about Amiens feeling sad because Des Grieux is to leave soon. His father intends for him to become a Knight of Malta, although Des Grieux has the possibility of becoming a priest. Both of these careers, at least symbolically, represent what Pierre Saint-Amand characterizes as "a homosocial morality, which implies a rejection of sexuality and women."[12] The virginal seventeen-year-old Des Grieux's sole regret in leaving Amiens "était d'y laisser un ami avec lequel j'avais toujours été tendrement uni"(M, 30). Des Grieux then launches into a long description of this man and their relationship without, however, naming him in the paragraph until after the description.[13]

Concerning Tiberge, Sgard emphasizes his common ties with his friend: "élévé avec des Grieux, lié à lui depuis l'enfance, il est passé par les mêmes expériences." Similarly, Wellington believes the fact "that Tiberge and Des Grieux are together and share a common future at the start of the story highlights an essential similarity often overshadowed by an apparent dissimilarity."[14] However, it must be emphasized that their dissimilarities run contrary to the era's proverbial understanding of friendship and reveal immediate points for questioning the veracity of the two men's friendship. First there is the matter of a difference of age. "Il était de quelques années plus âgé que moi"(M, 30-31). Des Grieux later mentions that the friend is "âgé seulement de trois ans plus que moi"(M, 34). Though Des Grieux implies otherwise, there is nonetheless a significant difference of physical and mental maturation between the ages of seventeen and twenty. This difference is all the more accentuated when the two men meet after Des Grieux's kidnapping and Des Grieux is shocked by Tiberge's change in appearance or, perhaps, by his change of perception concerning friendship, either of which make Tiberge assume the role of an elder, exploitable mentor. By way of contrast, let us consider Des Grieux's fantasy for a new friendship, which anticipates that M. de T… will share with Des Grieux "un certain goût de plaisirs, comme la plupart des jeunes gens de son âge"(M, 94). Once in the company of the M. de T…, Des Grieux appeals specifically on the basis that "la ressemblance de nos âges me fait espérer qu'il s'en trouvera quelqu'une dans nos inclinations"(M, 95).

Without yet commenting on the importance of common inclination, the next important difference shared by Tiberge and Des Grieux is that of financial means and social status. Although Tiberge and Des Grieux had "été élevés ensemble, . . . le bien de sa maison étant des plus médiocres, il était obligé de prendre l'état eccelésiastique, et de demeurer à Amiens après moi, pour faire les études qui conviennent à cette profession"(M, 31). Des Grieux, on the other hand, has the opportunity to join one of the great, noble religious orders of crusading knights.[15] Equality, social and financial, was one of the proverbial conditions of friendship proposed by the treatises of the day, as is clear in the *Encyclopédie*'s entry on the issue. "On éclaircira au sujet de l'*amitié*, une maxime importante; savoir, que l'*amitié*, doit entre les amis, trouver de l'égalité ou l'y mettre."[16]

It is not at all obvious that both men are of the same social caste. While Des Grieux is clearly an aristocrat, he has a particule in his name, is called "chevalier," and is destined for a noble career. Tiberge's name is worthy of some consideration. Previously, I had always thought of it as his given name, perhaps because I wanted such usage to reflect an intimacy in their relationship. Moreover, the usage of Tiberge's first name would offset the use of Manon's by Des Grieux. It is also possible that "Tiberge" is intended to be a seeming acronym for the conventional purposes of novelistic obfuscation that purports to lend credibility to the story, much like the use of an ellipsis in M. de T… implies that a true identity is being concealed. As far as I can determine, however, there are no saints by the name "Tiberge", with the possible exceptions of two saints by the name of Tibertius. Furthermore, a Web search revealed that "Tiberge" is, in fact, a surname in France and in Quebec.[17] Moreover, in literature of the eighteenth century, male characters, *if they are noble*, are identified by their surname. In any event, by simply referring to Tiberge, the usage marks a social distinction between Des Grieux and Tiberge. When speaking to Tiberge or referring to him, Des Grieux never uses any sort of honorific or title except for "Tiberge" or "ami." Tiberge, on the other hand, like Manon, always addresses Des Grieux as "chevalier," "mon cher chevalier," or simply, "mon ami."

The difference concerning the wealth of the two friends also makes obvious that there is also no mention of the two sharing their belongings, a proverbial element in previous centuries' texts and contemporary treatises concerning idealized friendship. Nor do Tiberge and Des Grieux, as we discover subsequently, share lodgings or a bed, as male friends might have done in medieval and Renaissance times. In addition to this disparity of means, there is Des Grieux's systematic exploitation of Tiberge's mediocre resources. Although Tiberge recognizes that he is abetting Des Grieux's disorder, he agrees to provide Des Grieux with funds, one hundred pistoles to be exact, but on one condition, that Des Grieux reveal his whereabouts and consent to visits by Tiberge who hopes thus to bring his friend back into the fold.

As opposed to Tiberge, M. de T…is, by virtue of the particule in his name, defined by, even reduced to, his nobility. More importantly, Des Grieux fantasizes that M. de T… "est riche et de bonne famille, est dans un certain goût de plaisirs, comme la plupart des jeunes gens de son âge"(M, 94). While I cited the second part of this line earlier, I want to emphasize it differently here. Des Grieux, whatever his pecuniary motives, himself stands to inherit some funds when he reaches adulthood and is also of good family. M. de T… satisfies Des Grieux's every hope when, after the two become fast friends, M. de T… immediately offers his purse to Des Grieux who, uncharacteristically and temporarily only, refuses. Later, Des Grieux is content to accept M. de T…'s largesse in purchasing clothing for Manon because "cette galanterie se fit de si bonne grâce que je crus pouvoir en profiter sans honte"(M, 107). Later, however, the disinterested generosity of M. de T… comes to resemble that of Tiberge when, in Des Grieux's moment of need, M. de T… also loans him one hundred pistoles, on the condition that Des Grieux pay him back later. That the two men provide Des Grieux with the same amount of money is surely not coincidental.

The taste for pleasure shared by young men of a certain age is precisely a characteristic that Tiberge does not share. This points to another element missing in their friendship: theirs is not a true marriage of like minds or a division of souls where the two men comprise one self. Extra-textual elements of the novel accentuate this point. As Raymond Picard points out concerning the illustration serving as frontispiece for the 1753 edition of the novel, the difference of age and profession colors this friend more as a Mentor-like figure leading Des Grieux toward salvation, rather than a soul mate *à la* Montaigne.[18] According to the codes of the day, however, friendship presupposes a preexisting similarity of character and morals. If the two men were truly friends, then Tiberge would have no need of leading Des Grieux back to his vocation. In fact, logically, they should share the same sexual desires as do the male protagonists of the other literary depictions of friendship in the eighteenth century, for instance, Marmontel's moral tale "L'Amitié à l'épreuve" and Saint-Lambert's "Les Deux amis, conte iroquois." All the more ironically, as René Démoris has astutely noted, from the very beginning of Des Grieux's praise, Tiberge's mentoring abilities are already put in question, "faisant oublier que sa tendresse déjà en dérangeait l'ordonnance, engageant sur une voie que n'avait pas fixée le père"(M, 20).

Linked with these dissimilarities undermining the case for ideal friendship is Des Grieux's own expression of the century's discourse linking friendship and happiness: "si j'eusse alors suivi ses conseils, j'aurais toujours été sage et heureux"(M, 31). As noted earlier, however, the worth of such philosophical discourse is undermined precisely because of the dubiousness of friendship. This ambiguity continues when Des Grieux likens Tiberge's zeal and generosity in friendship to "les plus célèbres exemples de l'antiquité"(M, 31). On the first read, one might take this as a compliment. However, describing the events following his deception of Tiberge in Amiens, such terminology sounds more equivocal when Des Grieux notes, "son zèle n'en devint pas moins ardent. Vous verrez à quel *excès* il le porta"(M, 35, emphasis added).

Varying interpretations are possible. On the one hand, the reference to

Antiquity evokes a pagan notion of exclusive friendship that is not only discordant with Tiberge being a priest, it runs counter to Des Grieux's desire for a friendship that will allow for the presence of Manon. This need is evident, once again, in his fantasy concerning M. de T...'s hoped-for qualities, characteristics he clearly does not associate with Tiberge. "Il ne saurait être ennemi des femmes, ni ridicule au point de refuser ses services pour une affaire d'amour"(M, 94). Tiberge is, at one point, likened to an enemy of love when he doubles for the elderly man guarding Manon on her way to the convent in the beginning of the tale. This character, whom Des Grieux describes as "un vieil Argus"(M, 32) is like Tiberge. Both are hostile to the love of Des Grieux and Manon, both are deceived by their subterfuge. This Classical reference, like the previous one, is not innocent and is, in fact, ominous. The Argus Panoptes of a hundred eyes, memorialized in the peacock's tail, was lulled to sleep by Hermes and murdered because he was thwarting Zeus' lust for Io.

While Tiberge is never explicitly labeled as an enemy of women, the lack of women in his life is addressed at two points in the text. The first such instance occurs after Des Grieux's kidnapping and imprisonment by his father. When he pays his call, Tiberge begins by advocating a renunciation of the "vanité des plaisirs,"(M, 47) that is, a renunciation of the world sought after and symbolized by Manon. Tiberge mentions that "j'avais autant de penchant que vous vers la volupté"(M, 47). Other than a dismissive jest by Des Grieux later, this is the only mention in the text of any kind of sexuality on the part of Tiberge. Sgard makes much of this comment, seeing in it the shared experience of the two men.[19] It should merely be stressed that there is no specific mention of a woman. The admission might be merely one of admitting lust or simply a maladroit effort by Tiberge to give the two men some common ground despite the divergence of their apparent commitments. Tiberge remarks that he had been graced with "du goût pour la vertu"(M, 47). Of course, the notion of virtue was inextricably linked with friendship in the eighteenth century. Thus, in that allegorical vein, the opposition of virtue and vice is the opposition of a commitment to a world of vice symbolized by men's sex with women or a world of virtue symbolized by men's exclusive commitment to other men. In short, Tiberge is admitting his preference for Des Grieux over "volupté."

Tiberge is so strongly drawn to Des Grieux, he admits that the only thing stopping him from adopting a misanthropic pose toward the world are his feelings for Des Grieux: "ce qui me retient . . . et ce qui m'empêche de courir à la solitude? C'est uniquement la tendre amitié que j'ai pour vous"(M, 47). Pleading the need for Des Grieux to follow the path of virtue, i.e., to stay with him, Tiberge goes on to recount how Des Grieux's departure had not left him with any peace during their separation. Des Grieux describes their conversation almost in the terms of a seduction: "il me flatta si adroitement sur la bonté de mon caractère et sur mes inclinations, qu'il me fit naître, dès cette première visite, une forte envie de renoncer comme lui à tous les plaisirs du siècle pour entrer dans l'état ecclésiastique"(M, 48).

The second occasion alluding to Tiberge's sexuality comes when Tiberge has given Des Grieux money, but on the condition of being receptive to (frequent) visits that place him in direct, rather than simply symbolic, conflict with Manon. Des Grieux listens to Tiberge's admonitions out of a sense of gratitude, but does not heed them. Indeed, "quelquefois je le raillais agréablement, dans la présence même de Manon"(M, 66). Not content with mocking the precepts of his friend, Des Grieux says, "je l'exhortais à n'être pas plus scrupuleux qu'un grand nombre d'évêques et d'autres prêtres, qui savent accorder fort bien une maîtresse avec un bénéfice"(M, 66). There is something implicitly homophobic about this moment. Des Grieux is telling Tiberge to get a girlfriend and to spend his money on her rather than spending it on another man, that is, Des Grieux. As far as the text itself is concerned, Tiberge, for all his admission of voluptuousness, has no romantic interests in women. His sole interest and consuming passion is Des Grieux. Des Grieux drives his point home when he thrusts his mistress literally between the two men. "Voyez, lui disais-je, en lui montrant les yeux de la mienne, et dites-moi s'il y a des fautes qui ne soient pas justifiés par une si belle cause"(M, 66).[20] When, after a subsequent confrontation, in the presence of Manon, where Tiberge temporarily breaks with Des Grieux, Manon completes the rout of Tiberge by saying that "c'était un fou"(M, 67). As for any temporary remorse on the part of Des Grieux, "les caresses de Manon dissipèrent, en un moment, le chagrin que cette scène m'avait causé"(M, 67).

These two scenes emphasizing the absence of women in Tiberge's life implicitly raise the specter of sodomy, one of the other traditional, negative associations with idealized male friendship. Not unlike writers of the Renaissance, eighteenth-century writers were intensely aware of sodomy and, as Jacob Stockinger notes, "nearly all the great Enlightenment writers did address the question."[21] Although same-sex desire occupied a place of moral, legal, and social proscription that dated back to the days of the late Roman Empire and the gradual ascension of Catholic theology as the defining moral force in Western European thought, the eighteenth-century establishment in France was relatively tolerant of homosexual behavior and gender deviance, especially among the aristocracy and the priesthood.[22]

Insofar as Modern stereotypes went, nuns, e.g. Diderot's *La Religieuse*, and priests were often associated with sodomy and priests were frequently arrested for solicitation by undercover "vice cops" called *mouches*. In fact, the Church's hypocritical tolerance of priestly sodomy, and intolerance of the laity equivalent, more than once drew the ire of the philosophes and was an issue in the Revolutionary repeal of sodomy statutes. Tiberge, caught in the ambiguous associations of his profession, when likened by Des Grieux to the famous friends of Antiquity, may well evoke sodomy, too.[23] Of the major writers of the century, both Diderot, in his "Suite de l'Entretien" in *Le Rêve de d'Alembert*, and Voltaire, in the essay in the *Dictionnaire philosophique* entitled "L'Amour nommé socratique" and, more pertinently, at the conclusion of his entry concerning friendship, connect sodomy with Antiquity and Classical notions of friendship.

Consider, then, the episode following the fire that nearly bankrupts Manon and Des Grieux. Des Grieux resorts to asking Tiberge for money and invites him to meet him in the "jardin du Palais-Royal"(M, 62). As Bryant Ragan points out, "Parisian sodomites looked for sexual partners on the banks of the Seine, along the northern boulevards, and in the gardens of the Tuileries, *Palais-Royal*, and Luxembourg, the same places female prostitutes usually worked."[24] Tiberge's effusiveness marks this meeting, "Il vint m'embrasser…me tint serré longtemps entre ses bras, et je sentis mon visage mouillé de ses larmes"(M, 62 emphasis added). Des Grieux does not mention any similar reaction on his own part and merely uses the occasion to hustle Tiberge, agreeing to make himself available if Tiberge will lend him money, in essence prostituting himself. While this episode does not necessarily mean that Tiberge and Des Grieux have or had had a sodomitical relationship, it seems nonetheless clear that Prévost is deliberately evoking an equivocal atmosphere. After all, this scene obviously foreshadows Manon's liaisons with the Italian prince in the Bois de Boulogne, another long-time, popular zone for assignations in the vicinity of Paris. Thus, as disguised as it is, Prévost links idealized male friendship with sodomy.

No less venerable than the association of sodomy and male friendship is the passionate, triangular rivalry of Tiberge and Manon for the beloved Des Grieux common to earlier French depictions of friendship like *Ami et Amile*, *Yvain*, and François de Rosset's sixteenth *histoire tragique* , which concerns the rape of a young Polish nobleman by an Italian monk and a knight. Des Grieux, despite his moral ambiguities, is something of an eighteenth-century avatar of Lancelot, endlessly humiliating, yet exalting, himself on the cart of his love for Manon. As Henri Coulet puts it in *Le Roman jusqu'à la Révolution*, "plus il se dégrade socialement et, selon le jugement commun, moralement, plus son amour s'approfondit et s'épure jusqu'à devenir une charité rayonnante par laquelle Manon est enfin métamorphosée."[25] Des Grieux even has his own Galehaut played by Tiberge. Yet, as Coulet also notes, in part because of its moralistic nature and in part because of its scandalous nature, this novel bears a striking resemblance to "nouvelles tragiques."[26] Here Des Grieux and Manon are not the only moral counter-examples, so is Tiberge. He stalks Des Grieux the length of this novel no less determinedly than Flaminio does toward Eranthe in Rosset's tale from a century earlier.

In his redefinition of friendship involving the young M. de T…, Des Grieux also fantasizes about the possibility of replacing the triangle focusing on himself as the desired object with the one more typical of *Tristan et Yseut*.

> S'il est honnête homme, et qu'il ait des sentiments, il nous accordera son secours par générosité. S'il n'est point capable d'être conduit par ce motif, il fera du moins quelque chose pour une fille aimable, ne fût-ce que par l'espérance d'avoir part à ses faveurs. (M, 94)

While it is not at all clear whether Des Grieux would accept such an arrangement, the intersection of concepts here is striking because it links Des Grieux's relationship to the "homme de qualité" with his relationship to M. de T… and thus to Tiberge. As he in fact does with the "homme de qualité," Des Grieux hopes that he will be able to appeal to M. de T… on the affective bases of generational solidarity against old men and, more importantly, on the class solidarity that, of itself, constitutes an essential aspect of male homosocial desire in this novel. Barring that, Des Grieux believes he can appeal to the other man erotically by sexually sharing Manon, or at least arousing the other man by raising such a possibility. Des Grieux thus toys with the idea of living a ménage à trois where, rather than himself, Manon is the object of desire. This paradigm of affective rivalry, deflecting as it does the potential for sodomy, but linking men sexually through normative heterosexuality, is the stereotypical paradigm of male homosocial desire as explicated by Eve Sedgwick.

As things work out, Des Grieux's skillful manipulation of male homosocial desire wins the day. This time, Des Grieux is the one studying another man, as we see when he reads the other man's features much as he himself is read by the "homme de qualité" in the beginning. Just as with the "homme de qualité," Des Grieux resorts to the marks of friendship, here total confidence, as he recounts his story in such a way as to successfully appeal to the other young man. Exposed to the same kind of speech as the "homme de qualité," M. de T..., whose appreciation of Des Grieux's looks is not noted surprisingly enough, is soon seduced by Des Grieux. His reaction is effusive, "il me dit qu'il mettait ma visite au rang de ses bonnes fortunes, qu'il regarderait mon amitié comme une de ses plus heureuses acquisitions"(M, 95).

M. de T..., in turn, wins over Des Grieux upon offering to serve as an *entremetteur* for the lovers: "il m'offrit de me procurer le plaisir de la voir, et de faire tout ce qui serait en sa puissance pour la remettre entre mes bras"(M, 95). Their bond is sealed not in the evoked arms of Manon, but in M. de T...'s arms: "nous nous embrassâmes avec tendresse, et nous devînmes amis"(M, 95). After that homoerotic moment, Des Grieux then lapses into the language of friendship of the elect claiming their friendship results "sans autre raison que la bonté de nos cœurs et une simple disposition qui porte un homme tendre et généreux à aimer un autre homme qui lui ressemble"(M, 95). As R.A. Francis has pointed out, however, what "looks like the same communion of souls which draws Renoncour (the "homme de qualité") to Des Grieux"(15) is not at all disinterested and was born of a false pretense. Francis goes on to label this new friendship a "debased parody of noble friendship," because "the advice M. de T... subsequently gives Des Grieux pushes him further and further into bad behavior."[27] This one scene, however, links three of the important male protagonists of the novel. After all, the "homme de qualité," then Tiberge, and finally M. de T... all offer their purses as the mark of friendship to the indigent Des Grieux. In a sense, all three men become interchangeable.

The new ménage à trois formed by M. de T..., Manon, and Des Grieux is only reinforced in ambiguous scenes involving the trio. For instance, in the scene where M. de T... enables Des Grieux to meet the imprisoned Manon and leads the way into Manon's room, he voyeuristically observes their passionate reunion, which frankly sounds like a quick sex scene between the two lovers.

> Nous nous embrassâmes avec cette effusion de tendresse qu'une absence de trois mois fait trouver si charmante à de parfaits amants. Nos soupirs, nos exclamations interrompues, mille noms d'amour répétés languissamment de part et d'autre, formèrent pendant un quart d'heure, une scène qui attendrissait M. de T.... (M, 97)

The veiled words of M. de T..., after watching this scene, "je vous porte envie, me dit-il, en nous faisant asseoir; il n'y a point de sort glorieux auquel je ne préférasse une maîtresse si belle et si passionnée"(M, 97) seem almost a veiled invitation to Des Grieux to share his mistress. Thus when M. de T...

buys expensive cloth to make clothing for Manon, an action Des Grieux describes as a "galanterie"(M, 107), it seems like the opening salvo in a seduction of the pleasure-loving Manon. Albeit more pleasantly, like Tiberge, M. de T…, continues to spend much of his time with the two lovers. Here, however, Des Grieux is content with the situation: "je me croyais si heureux, avec l'amitié de M. de T…. et la tendresse de Manon (M, 115).

In the end, of course, the friendship with M. de T…, like Des Grieux's other attempts at friendship, proves a deleterious failure. M. de T… proves less than the worthy friend of the young G…M…, his supposed "ami intime"(M, 117), once he betrays the latter's love for Manon to Des Grieux.[28] Later, thinking that G…M… has seduced Manon, he uselessly offers his sword to assist Des Grieux. Then it is M. de T…'s disastrous stratagem for Des Grieux to defraud G…M… and regain Manon that sets into motion the pair's capture and Manon's deportation. In his last appeal to M. de T…, Des Grieux is once more disappointed for M. de T…proves pusillanimous. He offers Des Grieux a hundred pistoles, the same amount offered by Tiberge on an earlier occasion, but breaks the rules of friendship by requesting that Des Grieux repay him later. Bowing out of any attempted rescue, M. de T…'s last betrayal is a refusal to assist Des Grieux fully, claiming "si le soin de sa réputation lui eût permis d'entreprendre lui-même la délivrance de ma maîtresse, il m'eût offert son bras et son épée"(M, 151). Promising to intercede with the younger M. de G…M…, who now harbors his own suspicions concerning M. de T…, the latter thereupon disappears from the story.

The disappearance of an alternate Tiberge coincides with the gradual renewal of the psychological presence in the tale of Tiberge who himself disappears as Manon gains ultimate ascendancy. When, however, the two men are reunited in Louisiana after Manon's death, Tiberge still evinces his physical attraction to Des Grieux, "ce fidèle ami me remit de loin, malgré les changements que la tristesse avait faits sur mon visage"(176). Now that Manon is dead, Des Grieux briefly acquiesces to Tiberge's dream of homosocial bliss in a scene that evokes a lovemaking reconciliation.

> Je ne pouvais marquer trop de reconnaissance pour un ami si généreux et si constant. Je le conduisais chez moi. Je le rendis maître de tout ce que je possédais. Je lui appris tout ce qui m'était arrivé depuis mon départ de France, et pour lui causer une joie à laquelle il ne s'attendait pas, je lui déclarai que les *semences* de vertu qu'il avait jetées autrefois dans mon cœur commençaient à prodire des fruits dont il allait être satisfait. Il me protesta qu'une si douce assurance le dédommagea de toutes les fatigues de son voyage (M, 177, emphasis added).

Although Saint-Amand waggishly notes, "Des Grieux will bear Tiberge's child…," the two men spend but two months more in New Orleans before returning to France.[29]

As the novel concludes, their brief homosocial idyll is likewise at an end, for as in so many works concerning idealized male friendship, exclusive male friendship can only exist, if at all, in exotic locales, as Louisiana must have then seemed. Once returned to "civilization" in France, Des Grieux is alone when he meets the "homme de qualité" and en route to rejoin his family. Des Grieux makes no mention of any plans for the future, except for mourning Manon. It is not at all clear if he has really joined the path of virtue and friendship and intends to rejoin Tiberge. Perhaps Des Grieux will take on the vocation of a writer/scholar, a possibility that he had envisioned once before while imprisoned by his father. The only thing that is clear is that he is presently caught up in reliving his passion for Manon, for now, via the "homme de qualité." As during Manon's life, there is no room for Tiberge in such a situation. As the story comes full circle, the very first sentence in the novel introducing Tiberge ultimately attests to the failure of their friendship in the end. "Mon seul regret, en quittant Amiens, était d'y laisser un ami avec lequel j'*avais* toujours *été* tendrement *uni*"(M, 30, emphasis added). The use of the pluperfect tense, rather than a past progressive one, in the beginning of Des Grieux's account to the "homme de qualité," but only shortly after his separation from Tiberge in the chronology of the story, implies that the two men's relationship is no more. The failure of friendship in this novel is historically important if for no other reason than the fact that the novel has proven to be lastingly popular. There can be no doubt that its perspective speaks more loudly concerning the legitimacy of male friendship than other, more ephemeral works of the era that had more positive perspectives toward male friendship.

NOTES

1. I am grateful to Doug Bonneville and Read Baker for their help in editing this essay. All citations of the text are to l'Abbé Antoine-François Prévost d'Exiles, *Histoire du chevalier des Grieux et de Manon Lescaut*, ed. Henri Coulet (Paris: Garnier-Flammarion, 1967). All further references to this text will be given using the abbreviation "M".

2. Sgard, Jean, "Introduction," in *Manon Lescaut*, Abbé Prévost. (London: Penguin, 1991), xxiii. In a subsection of the same introduction "Manon in the Age of Louis XIV" and also in a similarly titled, though somewhat modified, version in *L'abbé Prévost: Labyrinthes de la mémoire* (Paris: PUF, 1986), 56-63, Sgard argues that the novel is set in the latter years of the reign of the Sun King instead, as is more generally accepted, of taking place during the Regency of the duc d'Orléans.

3. Ironically, as Marie Wellington notes in "Unity and Symmetry of the Character of Tiberge," in *Romance Quarterly* 38.1 (1991): 27-37, Tiberge tends to similarly disappear from critical analyses of the work, much as he does in the second half of Prévost's novel!

4. Male friendship, like every human relationship, is a function of discourse. This central tenet in my study has been established by a number of heterogeneous sources inspiring or inspired by the modern academic trend known as "men's studies." The men's, or masculinity, studies movement, not to be confused with the "men's movement" *à la* Robert Bly, is frequently subsumed under the broader rubric of gender studies and is an offshoot of feminist theory, gay studies, and cultural studies. As I understand and implement it, a men's studies perspective adheres to the notion that masculinity, like femininity or sexuality, is an ever-shifting, ever-evolving construct often growing out of, or reacting against, that which came before. While recognizing the importance of continued, historical patterns, this perspective maintains that discursive constructs must be recognized as contingent. They vary within and without borders, among races and ethnic groups, and across generations of humankind. Their shifts are ascertainable in varied forms of cultural expression such as the plastic arts and literature. Accordingly, a study using this approach must strive to be at once historical, in that it requires a historical and cultural contextualization of the works to be studied, and critical, in that it requires the close reading of primary texts.

In the course of this study, I will frequently call on Eve Kosofsky Sedgwick's notion of "male homosocial desire" to characterize the gamut of affective associations of men that includes idealized male friendship. In *Between Men: English Literature and Male Homosocial Desire* (New York: Columbia University Press, 1985), one of the Ur-texts of queer studies in particular, Sedgwick proposes the notion of a continuum of male homosocial desire, which she characterizes as the "affective or social force, the glue, even when its manifestation is hostility or hatred or something less emotively charged, that shapes an important relationship"(1-2). Such forces are not specifically sexual. In fact, Sedgwick claims that concomitant changes in the structure of the continuum of male "homosocial desire" were tightly, often causally bound up with . . . other more visible changes; that the emerging pattern of male friendship, mentorship, entitlement, rivalry, and hetero- and homosexuality was in an intimate and shifting relationship to class; and that no element of that pattern can be understood outside of its relationship to women and the gender system as a whole. (1)

Sedgwick goes on to define homosocial desire as a contradictory, complicated term coined by disciplines seeking to describe various same-sex social relationships.

Obviously formed by analogy with 'homosexual,' [it is] just as obviously meant to be distinguished from 'homosexual.' In fact, it is applied to such activities as 'male bonding,' which may, in our society, be characterized by intense homophobia, fear and hatred of homosexuality. (1)

By way of contrast, in different times and different places, homosexuality and homosocial desire have not necessarily been viewed as mutually exclusive. Indeed, the two can be complementary forces or, as notes John Rowland in *"Swords in Myrtle Dress'd": Toward a Rhetoric of Sodom: Gay Readings of Homosexual Politics and Poetics in the Eighteenth Century* (Cranbury, NJ: Associated University Presses, 1998), 54, homosexuality can be "*subordinate* to the homosocial" and therefore serviceable to the predominant order.

5. Charles G. Smith, *Spenser's Theory of Friendship* (Baltimore: Johns Hopkins UP, 1935), 27.

6. Richard A. Smernoff, *L'Abbé Prévost* (Boston: Twayne, 1985), 44-5.

7. Gerson, Fredrick, *Le Thème de l'amitié dans la littérature française au dix-huitième siècle* (Ann Arbor: UMI, 1967), 224. Sgard, *Labyrinthes*, 68.

8. In his essay "De l'amitié" concerning La Boétie, Montaigne calls "l'affection envers les femmes" a "feu . . . plus actif, plus cuisant et plus aspre. Mais c'est un feu téméraire et volage, ondoyant et divers, feu de fiebvre, subject à accez et remises, et qui ne nous tient qu'à un coing." Friendship on the other hand, "est une chaleur generale et universelle, temperée au demeurant et égale, une chaleur constante et rassize, toute douceur et pollisure, qui n'a rien d'aspre et de poignant." Michel de Montaigne, *Œuvres complètes*. Ed. by Albert Thibaudet and Maurice Rat. (Paris: Gallimard, 1962), 184.

9. Louis-Antoine de Caraccioli, *Les Caractères de l'amitié* (Liege: Chez J.F. Bassompierre, 1762), 2.

10. Anne C. Vila, *Enlightenment and Pathology: Sensibility in the Literature and Medicine of Eighteenth-century France* (Baltimore: Johns Hopkins University Press, 1998), 119.

11. According to Pierre Saint-Amand in *The Libertine's Progress: Seduction in the Eighteenth-Century French Novel*, trans. Jennifer Curtis Gage (Hanover and London: Brown University Press, 1994), 46-47, "Manon's death allows Des Grieux to return to his first tendencies, to his original asceticism [...] Naturally, Tiberge is the person who welcomes his friend back to morality and family responsibility."

12. Saint-Amand, 41.

13. Des Grieux does, in fact, makes oblique mention of this friend during the course of his first encounter with the narrator at Pacy. He is the unnamed friend who will provide him with money upon arriving at Le Havre.

14. Sgard, *Labyrinthes*, 68. Wellington, 28.

15. According to Desmond Seward in *The Monks of War: The Military Religious Orders* (London: Penguin, 1995), 300, in the eighteenth century, "the Order of Malta's standing remained high in every Catholic country, its priors and bailiffs ranking with the great nobles of the land." Furthermore, "the seventeenth and eighteenth

centuries were far from being a Baroque sunset for military orders. They flourished right up to the destruction of the *ancien régime.*"(306). Seward's perspective is largely shared by H.J.A Sire in *The Knights of Malta* (New Haven, CT: Yale UP, 1994). Sire admits, however, that the Order in eighteenth-century France itself, particularly in Paris, was more than a little worldly and was very much involved in salons and "glittering society"(133).

16. "Amitié" in *Encyclopédie, ou dictonnaire raisonné des sciences, des arts et des métiers, par une société de gens de lettres* (Elmsford, NY: Pergamon, 1969), 362.

17. According to Charles Fell in *The Lives of Saints* (London, 1729), the two saints are associated with Saints Cecilia and Sebastian and their feast days are on April 14th and August 11th. During my web search, besides turning up examples of the family name Tiberge in modern times, I also located a genealogy chart listing a woman named Jeanne Tiberge who lived in France from 1657-1750 (see the following site: http://solo.abac.com/johnmcg/gendata/dat39.htm).

18. Raymond Picard and Frédéric Deloffre, eds. in *Histoire du Chevalier des Grieux et de Manon Lescaut*, Abbé Prévost (Paris: Garnier Frères, 1965), i-clvi.

19. Sgard, *Labyrinthes*, 68.

20. This moment is also echoed in Manon's humiliation of the Italian prince, an episode where she is the contested object of desire.

21. Jacob Stockinger "Homosexuality and the French Enlightenment," in *Homosexualities and French Literature: Critical Contexts/Critical Texts*. (Ithaca, NY: Cornell UP, 1979), 161-185. Citation is from page 162. A short list of such works would include: Montesquieu in *De l'esprit des lois*; Voltaire in the *Anti-Giton*, *Candide*, *Le Dictionnaire philosophique*, and *La Pucelle*; Rousseau in his *Confessions;* and Diderot in *Le Rêve de d'Alembert* and *La Religieuse*. Sade's *La Philosophie dans le boudoir* includes a defense of sodomy, a topic that appears in all of his novels. As far as I know, Prévost never discusses male sodomy openly. However, Alan Singerman, in *L'Abbé Prévost: L'Amour et la Morale* (Geneva: Droz, 1987), does refers to a scene with incestuous and lesbian overtones from the seventh book of the *Cleveland* series where Cleveland observes Fanny and Cécile asleep together in a convent bed, with Fanny's mouth on the breast of her unbeknownst daughter by Cleveland.

22. As Bryant Ragan notes in "The Enlightenment Confronts Homosexuality" in *Homosexuality in Modern France* (Oxford: Oxford University Press, 1996), 8-29, there were extensive sodomitical subcultures in eighteenth-century France, especially Paris, as various taverns and cabarets there gained reputations as areas patronized by sodomites, while other areas were frequented by those people "cruising" for sexual partners. The police kepts records of the men and women arrested, often in vice stings with undercover officers called *mouches*, much like the Office of the Night had done centuries before in Renaissance Florence. Ragan reports, "the *mouches* certainly kept busy. In the year 1749 alone, for example, they arrested 234 people"(13). Most of these people received relatively light sentences despite draconian laws concerning sodomy. Those people who were executed were often convicted of

other crimes, usually of a violent nature. In the same volume as the Bryant article can be found a useful one by Jeffrey Merrick entitled "The Marquis de Villette and Mademoiselle de Raucourt: Representations of Male and Female Sexual Deviance in Late Eighteenth-century France, 30-53. A fuller treatment of the issue is included in Gary Kate's *Monsieur d'Eon is a Woman: A Tale of Political Intrigue and Sexual Masquerade* (New York: BasicBooks, 1995), an engrossing account concerning the Chevalier d'Eon, a renowned, decorated war veteran and diplomat to the British and Russian courts, who in 1776 and to great public consternation, was declared by Louis XVI to actually be a woman. Obliged to don women's clothing and to sacrifice his public offices, Eon nonetheless was able to retain his military decorations and assumed the title of "Chevalière." In 1810, after the impoverished Eon's death, it was discovered that he was physiologically a man after all.

23. This ambiguous association might also account for Tiberge's disappearance from the operatic versions of the story.

24. Ragan, 12, emphasis added.

25. Henri Coulet, *Le Roman jusqu'à la Révolution, Tome I: Histoire du roman en France* (Paris: Colin, 1967), 360.

26. Coulet, *Roman*, 361.

27. R.A. Francis, *Prévost: Manon Lescaut* (London: Grant-Cutler, 1993), 15-16.

28. Frederick Gerson also notes this point. "Puisqu'il [M de T…] se targue d'être l'ami intime de G…M… la règle la plus fondamentale de l'amitié aurait exigé qu'il lui fasse part de sa désapprobation et essaie de l'en dissuader. Au lieu de cela, il s'encourt divulguer des renseignements […]"(219).

29. Saint-Amand, 47.

Et in Arcadia Ego?: Thomas Amory, Mary Hamilton, and the (Re)Construction of Arcadia

J. DAVID MACEY, JR.

In the opening scene of Thomas Amory's idiosyncratic first novel, *Memoirs: Containing the Lives of Several Ladies of Great Britain* (1755), the anonymous narrator employs the esthetic vocabulary of the eighteenth-century landscape arts, including pastoral poetry, painting and landscape design, in order to describe the novel's heroine, Miss Marinda Bruce, and her rural estate, Hali-farm.[1] The narrator assimilates Miss Bruce and her green retreat in his verbal portrait by representing the lovely heroine as a figure in—and for—the no less lovely landscape. In doing so, he repeats a characteristic gesture of eighteenth-century artists, whether novelists, poets, painters or landscape architects, by treating both women and the supposedly female "body" of nature as passive objects of esthetic pleasure and by evaluating them in terms of their ability "to titillate the imagination and satisfy the senses while at the same time remaining within carefully prescribed moral, aesthetic, and territorial limits."[2]

Amory (?1691-1788) uses this scene to explore the power of culturally conditioned esthetic sensibilities to shape—and distort—our understanding of the relationship between human beings and their environment. The narrator's verbal portrait of Miss Bruce is, in fact, misleading; she is not the passive and inarticulate esthetic object that he imagines her to be but rather a landscape artist in her own right who is engaged in revising a well-known pastoral scene, Nicolas Poussin's *Arcadian Shepherds* II (*c.* 1638-40). Miss Bruce transforms Poussin's painting by depicting a Utopian community in which women, no longer ornamental figures in a landscape constructed by a male artist, act as teachers and spiritual guides to their male companions (22-25). Her *Arcadia* corrects the narrator's verbal portrait of Hali-farm by demonstrating the full range of roles available to women as artists and as subjects of the landscape genre. Her revision of Poussin's painting, which requires her to work both within and against the conventions of an established genre, typifies the approach of eighteenth-century women writers to a literary tradition which provided them with a limited thematic and stylistic vocabulary in which to express their hopes, anxieties and lived experiences. Amory's fictional account of Miss Bruce and her painting offers a useful paradigm for interpreting the work of such writers as Eliza Fowler Haywood (?1693-1756), Sarah Robinson Scott (1720-95) and Lady Mary (Walker) Hamilton (1739-1816) because it provides a richly symbolic (and exceptionally lucid) example of the way in which marginalized artists learn to speak in their own voices by entering into dialog with traditions that both shape and constrain their artistic development.

Amory's *Memoirs*, now largely forgotten by critics and readers, may seem an unlikely point of departure for a discussion of intertextuality, artistic appropriation, and the social function of the landscape arts during the eighteenth century. Influenced by the oral narratives of Amory's native Ireland as well as by picaresque fiction and contemporary travel narratives, the digressive and episodic *Memoirs* resists generic classification.[3] While Amory's *Memoirs* and his second, no less digressive novel, *The Life and Opinions of John Buncle, Esq.* (1756-66) tend to puzzle (if not frustrate) twentieth-century readers, they delighted some of the most sophisticated readers of an earlier age, and these readers' assessments of Amory's work ought not to be taken lightly. Hazlitt, for example, enthusiastically proclaims Amory "the English *Rabelais*," while Charles Lamb finds in Amory's writing "an infinite fund of pleasantry."[4] One recent critic has even suggested that Amory's diffuse and digressive narrative style, with its "blend of landscape description, tourism, and philosophical debate," may have served as one of Wordsworth's models for the design of *The Excursion* (1814).[5]

This diffuse and digressive style makes the *Memoirs* an ideal site at which to begin examining the role that artists played in shaping—and challenging—the social, political and sexual *status quo* in eighteenth-century England. Trained as a physician, Amory was also an amateur philosopher, theologian and antiquarian, a connoisseur of painting and an inveterate apologist for his own Christocentric brand of Unitarianism. He brings all of these interests to bear in the *Memoirs*, producing a text which ranges widely over a dazzling (and at times dizzying) variety of subjects and offers a singularly comprehensive if quixotic compendium of cultural knowledge. At the same time, Amory—as an Irishman, a Unitarian, and a persistent and vocal advocate of women's rights as well as of a modified form of monasticism—viewed eighteenth-century English society from the perspective of an outsider.[6] In the *Memoirs*, Amory's unrestrained intellectual curiosity and his perspective as an intelligent but critical outsider observing English society from its intellectual and cultural margins contribute to a fresh and revealing analysis of the strategies used by other socially and culturally marginalized authors to comment upon and revise the esthetic, religious and social codes that both shaped and constrained their artistic development.

Within the copiously annotated *Memoirs*, Amory incorporates passages from the works of eminent philosophers, theologians and scientists, and in the process he both comments upon and corrects their representations of the spiritual, social and material world. He represents Miss Bruce as engaging in a similar process in her revision of Poussin's painting. This form of artistic reproduction, in both literature and the visual arts, conforms to a common eighteenth-century practice. From Pope's sophisticated "imitations" of the *Satires* and *Epistles* of Horace to Fielding's lighthearted revision of Richardson's *Pamela* (1740), eighteenth-century texts routinely imitate and transform earlier texts. Aspiring painters also routinely copied the works of established artists as a means of developing their own technique, while popular demand for reproductions of famous artworks sustained a growing number of artisans whose primary activity consisted in copying well-known sculptures and painting such as Poussin's *Arcadian Shepherds*. Poussin's painting, in particular, was a popular subject for imitation and was reproduced in paintings and sculptural reliefs and even on snuff-box covers. Miss Bruce's painting differs from other eighteenth-century variations on the pastoral theme because it challenges the understanding of Arcadian society that informs Poussin's Arcadian vision. Amory, a cultural and religious outsider, uses the no less marginalized Miss Bruce and her painting to explore the complex ways in which marginalized artists transform alien and potentially alienating artistic traditions into fruitful media for self-expression, a process all too often overlooked by observers situated closer to the cultural center.

* * * * * *

Amory's unnamed narrator—identified in the sequel as John Buncle, Esq.—begins his *Memoirs* by describing his first encounter with the devout and erudite Unitarian recluse Marinda Bruce. The narrator, an amateur antiquarian traveling alone through the "vast hills" of Northumberland in search of "ancient monuments and curious things," happens one evening upon Hali-farm, which he describes as "the sweetest retirement my eyes have ever beheld." Nestled in the upper reaches of a sheltered valley, Hali-farm boasts

> the prettiest thatched cottage in the world, and a garden of the most artful confusion I had ever seen. The little mansion was covered on every side with the finest, flowery greens. The streams, all around, were murmuring and falling a thousand ways. All the kinds of singing birds were here collected, and in high harmony on the sprays. (2)

The narrator describes Hali-farm in terms that exemplify the category of the "beautiful" constructed by the eighteenth-century estheticians who preceded Burke.[7] The "little mansion" (previously described as a "pretty thatched house"), the shallow and gently murmuring streams, the sweet, soft singing of the birds and the profusion of delicate flowers anticipate Burke's identification of beauty with smallness, smoothness, movement, and delicacy and variety of coloration.[8] Amory also draws upon his knowledge of the landscape arts in constructing the imaginary landscape of Hali-farm. The great English gardens created during the first half of the eighteenth century, including those at Stowe and at Stourhead in Wiltshire, invited visitors to linger in shady groves and leafy arbors in order to puzzle out the meaning of complex emblems and satirical allusions encoded in inscriptions, sculptures and ingeniously contrived grottoes, hermitages and temples—architectural elements which, according to Ronald Paulson, "were used like words to make new sentences," transforming the garden into a "poem manqué" or "a page from an emblem book."[9] Such gardens were influenced by and frequently alluded to allegorical landscapes such as those painted by Poussin and his contemporary Claude Lorrain (1600-82). Hali-farm, to which the narrator attributes a palpably "artful" confusion, is itself a hermitage, and although it boasts no ornamental temples or sculptures, it possesses a speaking statue in the stationary and statuesque Miss Bruce. The tableau the narrator describes, a pastoral "poem manqué," cries out for interpretation and could well figure as a "set-piece" within one of the larger estate gardens of the period or as the background for an allegorical painting such as Poussin's.

The greatest beauty of Hali-farm, however, is not the garden but the gardener, Miss Bruce, whom the narrator assimilates to the garden in his attempt to describe and interpret the scene. The narrator attributes to Miss Bruce "the charms of an angel" (2) and offers a Hogarthian catalog of qualities that distinguish her as an epitome of beauty in its human form:

> Her person appeared faultless, and of the middle size; between the disagreeable extremes: Her face a sweet oval, and her complexion the brunette of the bright rich kind: Her mouth, like a rosebud, that is just beginning to blow, and a fugitive dimple, by fits, would lighten, and disappear: The finest passions were always passing on her face; and in her long, even, chesnut eyes, there was a fluid fire sufficient for half a dozen pair. (2-3)[10]

The narrator's comparison of Miss Bruce's pursed lips to a rosebud provides a key to the interpretation of the passage: Miss Bruce is, from the narrator's perspective, the fairest flower in the garden of Hali-farm. Her physical size, "between disagreeable extremes," mirrors that of the garden, large enough to offer the weary traveler refuge from the expansive wilderness that surrounds it but not so large as to overwhelm or intimidate him. The passions that flicker in her eyes and the dimple that plays about her mouth provide the pleasing variety and sense of movement integral to the Addisonian category of the beautiful—qualities which the flowing waters and flitting birds provide in the garden. This affinity between the gardener and her garden appears to be confirmed by the narrator's discovery that Miss Bruce is reading the passage from *A Midsummer Night's Dream* (1595-96) in which Titania instructs her attendant fairies to wait on the ass-headed Nick Bottom. Amory quotes the passage in full (4), reminding the reader of Titania's dominion over the creatures of the field and forest.[11] The "finest passions" animate Miss Bruce's face as she reads, for she is intuitively able to inhabit the role of the queen of the fairies. She too seems to the narrator to be a "fairy queen," presiding over an improbably lush and fertile domain hidden from the eyes of the mortal world in a remote corner of Northumberland.

The narrator associates Miss Bruce with the landscape by incorporating both the garden and its gardener in a single, extended verbal painting and by emphasizing the complementarity of Miss Bruce's personal charms and those of the garden in which he first beholds her. She and Hali-farm are sources of esthetic pleasure for the narrator, whose unperceived gaze embraces and takes symbolic possession of both garden and gardener. Addison argues that a "polite Imagination," a faculty which Amory's narrator possesses to an exemplary degree, gives a person "a kind of Property in every thing he sees" by allowing him to discern "a multitude of Charms, that conceal themselves from the generality of Mankind."[12] Amory literalizes Addison's metaphor; the charms of Hali-farm are hidden, not just from the eyes of the unperceptive or unimaginative but from all eyes but those of the narrator, who possesses those charms in a double sense—he is the only observer present to discern and appreciate the loveliness of Hali-farm and of Miss Bruce, and he asserts an additional claim to the farm and its charming resident by representing himself as their discoverer and by making them his narrative subjects.

Amory's narrator represents Miss Bruce as the tutelary spirit or "genius" of the paradisal garden that he discovers among the Northumbrian hills. The narrator's representation of Miss Bruce as a figure not only in but for the landscape reflects a persistent and widespread rhetorical habit among eighteenth-century writers on gardens and gardening. Pope, for example, counsels would-be gardeners to "consult the Genius of the Place in all" and to "treat the Goddess like a modest fair, / Nor over-dress, nor leave her wholly bare," while Richard Payne Knight, writing at the end of the century, compares an artfully designed garden to a "cunning nymph" who "with giddy cares / And wanton wiles, conceals her study'd air" as she "charms the sense, and plays around the heart."[13] While many seventeenth- and eighteenth-century writers associate women with nature as it appears improved by human art in the cultivated landscape of the field and garden, others associate women with the natural world in its uncultivated state—the enigmatic and vaguely threatening world over which Titania presides in *A Midsummer Night's Dream*. "Nature" can be represented as a female figure, but women can also be regarded as personifications of "nature"—and the natural world, untouched by the improving hand of man, inspired feelings of profound uneasiness in even the most candid observers at least until the second half of the eighteenth century, when popular enthusiasm for the picturesque led to the esthetic recuperation of the uncultivated landscape. The identification of women with the unimproved landscape had significant political and social implications. Milton brings such attitudes toward the natural world—and the value of human labor—into sharp focus in his representation of the Garden of Eden in *Paradise Lost* (1667). Adam and Eve perfect Paradise, he suggests, by lopping and pruning its luxurious foliage. He then associates this "luxurious" foliage, impatient of restraint and "Tending to wilde," with Eve, whom his rhetoric transforms into Eden's "fairest unsupported Flour," dependent on "her best prop," Adam, for strength and support.[14] By identifying Eve with the flowers that she both names and tends, Milton negates her distinctively human role as a cultivator of the garden and implies that she is properly an object of cultivation, to be nurtured, propped and restrained by the will of her husband and her God.

Milton's version of the biblical myth of origin anticipates Locke's secular myth about the origin of property. Cultivation, Locke claims, allows human beings to take possession of the natural world, for it is the labor of "improvement" that transforms the common property of humanity into private property. Locke's account of the origin of property retrospectively explains and helps to justify Adam's assertion of authority over Eve in *Paradise Lost*. As Eden's fairest flower, Eve is part of the paradisal landscape and is therefore a legitimate object of intellectual and spiritual cultivation, and Adam, by taking pains to cultivate her intellect, acquires a property in her, just as a farmer supposedly acquires as property the terrain that he tills and sows. Both God and reason, Locke argues, directed the first man "to subdue the earth, *i.e.*, improve it for the benefit of life, and therein lay out something upon it that was his own, his labour. He that in obedience to this command of God subdued, tilled, and sowed any part of it, thereby annexed to it something that was his property, which another had no title to, nor could without injury take from him."[15] Adam's "labour" in cultivating Eve anticipates the labor of parturition; both forms of work produce new beings, for Eve, like the landscape of Eden, is reborn as an object of property as a result of Adam's improving labor. The narrator of Amory's *Memoirs* reproduces Miss Bruce as an object of esthetic property through a different but related form of labor. By recreating her within his text as a mute and merely (albeit consummately) decorative object, he makes himself her author, just as God and Adam are Eve's authors and authorities in *Paradise Lost*.

The association between women and objectified—and appropriated—landscapes plays an important role in eighteenth-century thought. Simon Pugh, who maintains that eighteenth-century attitudes toward sexuality were at a "crossroads between understanding and control," argues that male consumers during this period viewed both women and landscape as "prototypical commodities" to be desired, idealized, violated and repressed.[16] This commodification was expressed on the symbolic level through personifications of nature which, as Carole Fabricant has shown, often encoded "statements about how power was conceived and wielded during this period" by men who sought imaginative and sensual pleasure in the enjoyment of both women and the natural world, which was conventionally represented as a female body (*e.g.*, "Natura" or "Mother Nature").[17] Both women and the landscape were subjected to concerted programs of "improvement" intended to confirm their status as objects of property, and the measures taken to restrain and discipline the "wanton" excrescences of the uncultivated landscape often recall the no less arduous educational and disciplinary regimes prescribed by an ever growing number of conduct books which, under the pretext of "cultivating" and "improving" the minds and morals of young ladies, sought, in Mary Wollstonecraft's words, "to hunt every spark of nature out of their composition" by "melting every human quality into female meekness and artificial grace."[18] Amory conflates these two forms of "improvement" in his description of Hali-farm by placing his highly cultivated heroine, a devoted student of Shakespeare who has benefited from an ambitious program of educational "improvement," within an artfully-designed and carefully tended garden which has also been the object of an extensive series of improvements. Miss Bruce and Hali-farm, as the narrator describes them, represent ideals to which "improvement" as both an educational and a horticultural practice aspired during the eighteenth century.

* * * * * *

Miss Bruce is not, however, merely an ornamental figure in the landscape. She is, rather, an accomplished artist in her own right, and she is employed in copying—and revising—two paintings by celebrated male artists, Coypel's *Crucifixion* and Poussin's *Arcadian Shepherds*.[19] Miss Bruce's artistic interest in the *Crucifixion* bears witness to a Unitarian piety which, like Amory's, regards Christ's sacrifice on the cross as an exemplary expression of spiritual love and self-abnegation. Her *Arcadia*, on the other hand, shows that she is "a master," on canvas as well as in the garden, "in the landskip way" (22). Miss Bruce displays her "mastery" of landscape as a pictorial genre by producing a painting that alludes to but differs significantly from Poussin's pastoral scene, in which a group of Arcadian shepherds contemplate a tomb inscribed with the epitaph "*Et in Arcadia ego*." The three male shepherds in Poussin's painting evince varying degrees of perplexity and concern as they contemplate the tomb and its enigmatic inscription, while the single female figure, distinguished, as Louis Marin has noted, by her "monumental stature, her presentation in profile, the position of her left arm and hand on her hip" and "her statuelike eye without vision," projects an air of calm and authoritative repose to which critics have repeatedly called attention.[20] The significance of the inscription on the tomb remains ambiguous; it may perhaps serve as a reminder to the painted shepherds and to the viewer of their own mortality ("Death is even in Arcadia"), or it may be an elegiac apostrophe "spoken" (from beyond the grave) by the deceased within the tomb ("I too lived in Arcadia").[21] Perhaps, as Marin suggests, it may even be Poussin's self-inscription within the allegorical scene ("I, in the utopian happiness of painting, Arcadia").[22] Amory and his heroine perceive an unrealized symbolic potential in the puzzled shepherds, the authoritative and statuesque woman and the tomb itself, startlingly situated in the midst of Arcadia.

Amory's heroine brings her fertile imagination and her extensive knowledge of the local landscape to bear in her revision of the French painter's landscape, blending elements of Poussin's idealized landscape with images drawn from the surrounding Northumbrian countryside. Like contemporary landscape gardeners, who constructed "Elysian fields" from the raw materials of the English countryside, Miss Bruce produces a distinctively English Arcadia—an imaginary space symbolically contiguous to but distinct from the happy valley that she herself inhabits. In order to give a more complete sense of the bliss of life in Arcadia, she also includes additional figures in her version of the scene. In her painting, "every day is delicious and serene, and an elysian temperature of sun-shine and shade for ever prevales." The Arcadians, "the happyest race of mortals," can be seen "in the valleys, and by the falling streams . . . plighting vows, and constant hearts to one another" or "footing it in country measure." These painted characters appear to the narrator to live and breathe: "The dancers really seem to trip it on the light fantastic toe, and in every countenance, love and laughter are inimitably expressed" (22). Miss Bruce and Poussin bring very different Arcadias to life on canvas. Miss Bruce's lifelike painting also possesses an energy lacking in the narrator's static verbal representation of Hali-farm. Miss Bruce responds to and explicitly challenges the pastoral ideals elaborated by Poussin and Amory's narrator by giving form on her canvas to the feminine, communal and celebratory qualities that she associates with life in Arcadia.

The principal figures in Miss Bruce's *Arcadia*, as in Poussin's, are a group of young Arcadians who are contemplating a tomb. Miss Bruce alters the tomb in Poussin's painting by adorning it with an effigy of the "beauty . . . snatched away in her prime" whose remains she imagines it to enshrine. By identifying the tomb in her painting as that of a young woman, Miss Bruce brings to the surface the implicitly feminocentric bias of Poussin's *Arcadian Shepherds*. She further emphasizes the importance of women in Arcadia by including several additional female figures in her painting: it is "*the youngest of the shepherdesses*" who "pulls off a garland of flowers, and with a finger of her other hand, points to the short inscription" which she "ponders with the most serious attention" while "opening her mouth to speak" (22-23, emphasis added). Miss Bruce, in a remarkable feat of ventriloquism, makes words proceed from this figure's open lips by "pitching her voyce on the picture, and keeping her own mouth and all her face as still and motionless during the time, as if it were marble" (23). Amory's heroine, as motionless as marble, becomes a living statue, while her painting comes to life and offers the narrator a pious sermon on human mortality and the transitoriness even of Arcadian pleasures. This "discourse from the charming little mouth in the picture" strikes the narrator to the quick, correcting his previous, over-enthusiastic encomiums of Hali-farm and prompting him to reflect that such a sermon, "on account of the singularity of the predication," would do more to reform the manners of his peers than interminable "descriptions of a heavenly spirit from the pulpit" (24-25). Poussin's powerful but oblique *memento mori* becomes, in Miss Bruce's rendition, the scene of a different sort of instruction, one in which the young shepherdess usurps the place of the male preacher by reminding her companions—and the narrator—of their impending dissolution and calling on them to cultivate the "*integrity* and *circumspection*" and "*prudence* and *pity*" that can alone prepare them "to appear before God's tribunal" (24).

Miss Bruce, whom the narrator initially presents as an ornamental figure in the landscape, proves to be an accomplished artist capable of re-envisioning Poussin's symbolic landscape in a way that privileges the female body and the female voice. She appropriates the French painter's Arcadian scene and uses it as a site within which to imagine a new form of community in which men and women who are "strangers to every care" pass their lives "in a fulness of pleasure" (22). She gives her own voice to the painted figure of the shepherdess in order to mount a wide-ranging critique of contemporary society, and she conscripts the narrator, who records her ventriloquized sermon *verbatim*, as her amanuensis, using his text, like her own painting, as a medium through which to address a diffuse and widely dispersed audience without sacrificing the safety and anonymity of her bucolic retirement. The painting and the *Memoirs* speak for—and in place of—Miss Bruce, who avoids exposing herself or her opinions directly by enlisting proxies, including the narrator and the Arcadian shepherdess, to speak on her behalf. Amory, the male author of the *Memoirs*, symbolically disclaims narrative authority by allowing his heroine to speak for herself, and in the process he suggests the possibility that other women both can and should abandon their position as silent objects of esthetic pleasure in order to speak, even if indirectly, in their own voices.

* * * * * *

The *Memoirs* is, of course, a male-authored text, and Miss Bruce, whatever her pretensions to artistic authority, is a projection of a male imagination.

Nevertheless, her story—told by one of the most astute, if idiosyncratic, observers of the relationship between sexual politics and artistic production in eighteenth-century Britain—offers an important insight into the artistic conditions and possibilities that shaped British women's writing during the middle decades of the eighteenth century. Miss Bruce's revision of Poussin's painting suggests that women who work within established genres, whether in literature or in the visual arts, need not be constrained by generic expectations that either elide or deny the possibility of female authority. The statuesque figure of the female shepherdess in Poussin's *Arcadian Shepherds* provides an opportunity for Miss Bruce to imagine an alternative story to the one that Poussin tells in his painting, and this alternative story reflects both Miss Bruce's personal beliefs and her extensive knowledge of the beauties of an English pastoral landscape. The concept of "disobedient" writing that Nancy A. Walker develops to describe the subversive rewriting of canonical narratives by twentieth-century American women provides a useful framework for analyzing Miss Bruce's fictional artistic activity. "Because of the way in which Western literary traditions have been formulated," Walker argues,

> most male writers who have appropriated and revised previous texts have worked within a tradition that included them and their experience, whereas women writers have more commonly addressed such texts from the position of outsider, altering them either to point up the biases they encode or to make them into narratives that women can more comfortably inhabit.[23]

Miss Bruce, a prototypically "disobedient" writer, alters Poussin's text and, in the process, makes it into a medium through which she can speak in her own voice. At least one critic has suggested that the boughs that appear to sprout from the figure of the female shepherdess in Poussin's painting symbolically identify her as a dryad, a divine spirit analogous to the Popean *genius loci*, who both personifies and animates the Arcadian landscape.[24] By re-envisioning Poussin's Arcadia, Miss Bruce gives voice to this "Genius of the Place," who represents the enigmatic—and silenced—female presence within landscapes constructed by an artistic tradition that treats both women and the landscape as objects to be appreciated—and exploited—for their superficial esthetic value.

The fictional Miss Bruce is an apt figure for the woman artist who struggles to speak in her own voice within a tradition that treats women as objects of artistic representation rather than as artists in their own right. Her "disobedient" reading of Poussin's painting, in turn, provides a useful model for interpreting the work of those eighteenth-century women novelists who rewrite canonical texts as a means of speaking about their own experiences and who reveal the range of opportunities available to women willing to challenge conventional expectations. Eliza Haywood, for example, uses the biblical creation narrative as a point of departure for a highly original fable about a "pre-Adamitic" princess in her pioneering science fiction novel *The Adventures of Eovaai, Princess of Ijaveo* (1736), which explores the problems and possibilities of female authority in a male-dominated world. Anne Finch, Countess of Winchilsea employs a similar strategy in her poems "Adam Posed" (1709) and "A Nocturnal Rêverie" (1713) by re-envisioning the circumstances surrounding the first humans' creation and fall from grace in order to call into question both the extent and the benevolence of patriarchal authority within the original human society. Sarah Robinson Scott, in her pastoral Utopian novel *A Description of Millenium Hall, and the Country Adjacent* (1762) also borrows freely from both classical and Judeo-Christian myths of origin in order to construct a fictional space, similar to the one that Miss Bruce envisions in her painting, in which women assume authority for their own lives and realize their full intellectual and spiritual potential.[25] Haywood, Finch and Scott read the biblical creation narrative against the grain in order to produce new, "disobedient" narratives that offer their readers—particularly their women readers—new ways of thinking about themselves and of leading their lives. The attention they devote to the biblical creation narrative reflects the importance of this particular narrative in the construction of gender roles in the western world. Other authors, including Lady Mary (Walker) Hamilton, offer "disobedient" readings of less canonical texts with equally fruitful results, as is the case in Hamilton's novel *Munster Village* (1778), which comments upon a disparate group of texts including Poussin's *Arcadian Shepherds* and Amory's *Memoirs* in order to explore the construction of gender roles in the landscape arts.

* * * * * *

Amory's narrator, delighted by Miss Bruce's *Arcadia*, exclaims that she has depicted "vales more charming than those of Juan Fernandez, with lawns like those of Tinian, and finer water-falls than Quibo has" (21-22). His enthusiastic outburst anticipates St-Preux's rhapsodic response to the Élysée in *La nouvelle Héloïse*, published five years after the *Memoirs*: "Surprised, stunned, transported by a spectacle so unexpected," Rousseau's hero declares upon entering Julie's garden, "I remained motionless for a moment, and cried out in spontaneous ecstasy: O Tinian! O Juan Fernandez! Julie, the ends of the earth are at your gate."[26] Tinian and Juan Fernandez, in turn, provide a verbal link between *Munster Village* and the two earlier novels. In Hamilton's novel, the heroine's brother, the young Lord Finlay, retires to a remote corner of Wales after incurring his father's displeasure by marrying his tutor's daughter. Lord Finlay and his new wife struggle to support themselves and are soon blessed—or afflicted—with a large family for which they are ill equipped to provide. Lady Finlay, who like Miss Bruce has "a fine genius for painting," contributes to the maintenance of her burgeoning family by painting "a *Crucifixion*, and an *Arcadia*" which she offers for sale.[27] The allusion to Amory's *Memoirs* is unmistakable, particularly when Hamilton describes Lady Finlay's *Arcadia*:

> In it there is exhibited a view of the most delightful region, with the grandest rural scenery in the world . . . . Her happy fancy, and the prospects in the country . . . supplied her with vales more charming than those of *Juan Fernandez*, with lawns like those of *Tinian*, and finer water-falls than those of *Quibo* . . . . The invention of the whole is extremely pleasing; and has been applauded by all who have seen it, as a master piece in the landscape way. (16-17)

Hamilton's description of Lady Finlay's painting echoes Amory's description of Miss Bruce's *Arcadia* almost word for word (Amory 21-22). Both paintings combine "happy fancy" with an extensive knowledge of the local scenery, both evoke and exceed the beauty of the islands that Amory's narrator and Rousseau's hero set up as standards of scenic beauty, and both are "master pieces in the landscape way." This apparent act of plagiarism, however, is more complex than it at first appears.[28] Hamilton reproduces Amory's description of Miss Bruce's *Arcadia* almost *verbatim*, evoking in the process that other great "master piece in the landscape way," Julie de Wolmar's Élysée, in order to raise specific expectations about the plot and narrative structure of her novel—expectations that she deliberately frustrates in order to call attention to the shortcomings of the form of community that Amory presents as an ideal in the *Memoirs*.

Amory and Rousseau derive their knowledge of the Pacific islands of Tinian (Tenian, in the Caroline Islands), Quibo (modern Coiba, in Panama) and Juan Fernández from Richard Walter's account of his circumnavigation of the globe between 1740 and 1744 with a squadron of British ships commanded by Commodore (later Admiral and Baron) George Anson (1697-1762).[29] Walter (?1716-1785), who served as chaplain aboard Anson's flagship, the *Centurion*, describes each of these islands in sensuous detail, representing them as paradisal gardens.[30] Walter and his shipmates aboard the *Centurion* respond enthusiastically to the verdant and fruitful landscapes of Coiba, Tenian and Juan Fernández because these green islands hold out the promise of relief from the hardships of life at sea. The lush vistas of Juan Fernández, Walter remarks,

> would, at all times, have been extremely delightful, but in our distressed situation, languishing as we were for the land and its vegetable productions, (an inclination constantly attending every stage of sea-scurvy) it is scarcely credible with what eagerness and transport we viewed the shore, and with how much impatience we longed for the greens and other refreshments which were then in sight.[31]

Like the weary and scurvy-ridden sailors aboard the *Centurion*, St-Preux and the narrator of Amory's *Memoirs* are ravaged by the sharp pangs of desire as they contemplate the idyllic landscapes that Julie and Miss Bruce have created. This longing takes an explicitly sexual form in *La nouvelle Héloïse*: the beauties of the Élysée become, for St-Preux, a symbolic representation of Julie herself, and this analogy allows him to enjoy an attenuated form of *jouissance* as he wanders in ecstasy through the garden: "I began to roam ecstatically through this orchard."[32] Amory's narrator approaches Miss Bruce's *Arcadia* with a different kind of hunger. He and Miss Bruce both seek friends sympathetic to their philosophical and religious beliefs—beliefs that Miss Bruce, in her ventriloquized sermon, attributes to the imaginary Arcadians, her only companions at Hali-farm. Amory's novel, like Walter's *Voyage round the World* (1748), chronicles a journey of exploration and discovery. After they leave Hali-farm, the narrator and Miss Bruce embark on a lengthy sea voyage during which they visit the Azores and the Outer Hebrides before arriving at a "Green Island" unlike any of those described in Walter's *Voyage*. On this improbably lush island situated "eleven leagues and a half to the south-west of St. Kilda" (406), a group of "reformed Recluses" (417), all of them women, have established a Unitarian religious community where they enjoy "the noblest, rational delights" by cultivating the arts and sciences in a landscape which, like those of Juan Fernández, Coiba and Tenian, has all of the advantages that "rendered the garden of Eden a paradice of charms" (414). The Green Island fulfills the yearning that Miss Bruce expresses in her *Arcadia* for an Edenic community of like-minded female friends.

The narrator's enthusiastic response to Miss Bruce's *Arcadia* invokes one aspect of the mythology of Juan Fernández, but Amory—and Hamilton—invite their readers to consider another, quite different aspect of that myth.

Walter's narrative helped to propagate the popular image of Juan Fernández as a mid-ocean paradise, but the island was also well-known as the site of the Scottish privateer Alexander Selkirk's solitary exile (1704-09), recounted by Sir Richard Steele in *The Englishman* (1713) and fictionalized by Defoe in *The Life and Strange Surprising Adventures of Robinson Crusoe* (1719). St-Preux, whom Rousseau represents as a participant in Anson's expedition to the South Sea, alludes to Selkirk's—or Crusoe's—lonely sojourn when he compares the Élysée to Juan Fernández.[33] Upon entering the Élysée, he feels a sense of isolation and solitude similar to that experienced by Defoe's protagonist: "I thought I was looking at the wildest, most solitary place in nature, and it seemed to me I was the first mortal who ever had set foot in this wilderness."[34] Miss Bruce's densely populated *Arcadia*, on the other hand, depicts an idyllic society, not an agreeable or melancholy solitude. Hali-farm, hidden among the hills of north Yorkshire, has more in common with the lonely but lovely island of Juan Fernández than does the painted Arcadia. Miss Bruce is, like Selkirk, the "monarch of all she surveys" at Hali-farm because, like the solitary castaway in William Cowper's version of the Selkirk story, she has no rival to dispute her title—and no comforting companion in her loneliest hours but religion, which, in the words of Cowper's castaway, "Gives even affliction a grace, / And reconciles man to his lot."[35] Miss Bruce's *Arcadia* expresses a loneliness as profound as that of any castaway on a South Sea island. She reveals this loneliness, however, not by depicting the solitude that she knows but by envisioning the community to which she yearns to belong. Miss Bruce longs for the companionship of other philosophical, devout and learned women, and she expresses this longing by painting a picture of the community of her dreams—dreams that come true for her on the Green Island.

Walter locates Juan Fernández, Coiba and Tenian precisely, noting their latitude and longitude and measuring the distance that separates them from known ports of call. His geographical specificity, however, belies the islands' shifting position in the geography of the eighteenth-century European imagination. Like the floating island of Laputa that Swift describes in the third part of *Gulliver's Travels* (1726), Walter's lovely but lonely islands hover above the fictional landscape of the eighteenth-century novel, offering a symbolic but unstable point of reference for authors who, like Amory and Rousseau, seek to transplant paradise from the South Sea to Northumberland or the shores of Lac Leman. Hamilton takes issue with the isolationist impulse that characterizes Amory's *Memoirs*, and she expresses her dissatisfaction by evoking these floating islands of the imagination in her novel, only to dismiss them as potential sites of intellectual or spiritual emancipation. Miss

Bruce revisits—and revises—Poussin's Arcadian landscape, and Hamilton follows her example by leading her characters over a fictional territory symbolically contiguous to Hali-farm, Clarens and Selkirk's desert island. She does so, however, in order to correct what she regards as Amory's misrepresentation of women's proper role in shaping the social and physical landscape.

Amory's novel describes the search for and eventual discovery of an Edenic community similar to the one that Miss Bruce depicts in her painting. Miss Bruce engages in an artistic dialog with Poussin about the role and status of women as she revises his painting, but neither she nor the "reformed Recluses" on the Green Island do anything to alter the balance of social or sexual power in contemporary society. Separatists rather than social reformers, the women in Amory's novel withdraw from a society in which they cannot live comfortably, but their self-imposed exile has no effect on the political, social and religious structures that preclude them from leading fulfilling lives among their peers. Amory's paradisal "Green Island" resembles Juan Fernández, Quibo and Tinian in more ways than one. Like the scurvy-ridden sailors aboard the *Centurion*, who fortuitously discover fruitful islands at crucial moments in their voyage, Miss Bruce and the narrator arrive on the Green Island by chance in their hour of greatest need, after being blown off course during a tour of the Hebrides. The "reformed Recluses" of the Green Island exercise an unprecedented degree of authority over their own lives, but their independence, like that enjoyed by Selkirk or Crusoe, is contingent upon their isolation from the rest of the human community.

Hamilton expresses her dissatisfaction with the ideal that Amory's Green Island represents by questioning the motives that lead individuals to choose lives of rural retirement. Lord and Lady Finlay retire to Wales not in order to enjoy the picturesque scenery but because they cannot afford to live anywhere else; extreme poverty, solitude and magnificent scenery, Hamilton reminds her readers, are often to be found in the same place. Hamilton reinforces the reader's sense of the futility of living in obscure retirement by associating Lady Finlay with Miss Bruce (and, implicitly, with that other great landscape artist, Julie de Wolmar) and then, almost immediately, narrating Lady Finlay's rapid decline in health and sudden death: "Lady Finlay's health decreasing she could no longer *exert this talent*" for painting. The "death of two fine children at last entirely subdued Lady Finlay's remaining spirits—She died" (17). Lord and Lady Finlay's decision to retire, like Miss Bruce, to the picturesque solitude of a remote and inaccessible valley represents a social and narrative dead end in *Munster Village*. The focus of Hamilton's novel quickly shifts to the real heroine, Lord Finlay's sister Lady Frances, who represents, both literally and figuratively, a collateral line in the narrative. Lord Finlay rapidly follows his wife to the grave, and Lady Frances takes charge of his family as well as of the property that soon devolves upon his children, transforming the family's ancestral estate in Shropshire into a garden Utopia by constructing a model town (the "Munster Village" of the title) in which she establishes an academy and a variety of artistic cottage industries. Instead of retiring to a distant island as Miss Bruce and Amory's "reformed Recluses" do, Lady Frances chooses to return to the familiar terrain of England, where she pursues an enlightened program of "improvement" and public benevolence that has positive and far-reaching effects on society at large.

* * * * * *

One of Lady Frances's first actions upon assuming management of the Munster estate is to invite the leading landscape architect of the day, Lancelot "Capability" Brown, to "improve" the grounds of the family's country seat by redesigning them in the current fashion: "The house and pleasure grounds" being in "great disrepair, from the late Earl's constant residence in London and the *environs*," Lady Frances sends "for Mr Brown," who discovers "great *capabilities* in the situation" and quickly transforms the estate into "one of the finest places in England" (21-22). Hamilton, eager to show that her heroine is familiar with the latest fashions and acquainted with the best-known and most widely respected practitioners of the various arts, has Lady Frances consult not only "Capability" Brown but also one of the Adam brothers ("Mr Adams," 22, 27), the playwright and orator Richard Brinsley Sheridan (25), and a student of the botanist Linnæus (28) for advice in constructing her Utopian village and regulating the plan of study for its fortunate citizens. At the same time, Hamilton breaks the traditional association between the objectified female body and the landscape, both of which are adorned and celebrated by male artists; rather than imitating and subtly altering the work of an old master, as Miss Bruce does, Lady Frances employs the most celebrated "new masters" to realize a vision of her own.

Hamilton's description of Lady Frances's garden-Utopia belies her attribution of the landscape to the celebrated "Mr. Brown" and suggests another line of influence, one that links the symbolic landscape of *Munster Village* to those of Amory's *Memoirs* and Poussin's *Arcadian Shepherds*. "[N]othing," Hamilton insists, "was ever more elegantly planned than Munster Village, the farm adjoining, and the pleasure grounds which lead to the house" (130). The distinguishing characteristics of this Utopian landscape, however, are not the broad and regular lawns, wide lakes and expansive, seemingly unbounded vistas that characterize Brown's mature style, but rather melancholy vales, meandering paths and unexpected juxtapositions of light and darkness, open and enclosed spaces, and practical and whimsical architecture[36]:

> in the farm, you wandered from variety to variety; buildings of great utility and much fancy, groves inspiring different sensations, from the lucid summits that wake the mind to gaiety, to the dark brown or *clair obscure* of trees crowding their branches in the vale, which possess the soul with home-felt contemplation. (130)

The landscape that Hamilton describes looks backward for inspiration to such early eighteenth-century gardens as those at Stowe and Stourhead, with their complex allegorical schemes, and forward to the artfully varied "picturesque" gardens championed at the end of the century by Richard Payne Knight and Uvedale Price. The tradition of allegorical and instructional pastoral painting exemplified by Poussin's *Arcadian Shepherds* and by Miss Bruce's fictional *Arcadia* also plays an important role in structuring Hamilton's description of the park surrounding Munster Village—a fact to which the concluding scene of the novel bears witness.

At the end of Hamilton's novel, Lady Frances surrenders control of the estate, now transformed into a flourishing Utopian community, to her nephew, who has achieved his majority, and at long last marries her lifelong love, Lord Darnley. Her nephew, the young Lord Munster, arranges an elaborate outdoor masquerade in the park at Munster Village, ostensibly to celebrate the first anniversary of his aunt's marriage, but also to thank her for her careful and enlightened stewardship of his estate and to pay tribute to her Utopian vision. For this purpose, he brings Lady Frances and her husband to the "Temple of Minerva," a classical "folly" located on an island which doubles as "Elysium" in the midst of "a fine piece of water" that figures for the purposes of the masquerade as the river Styx. A boatman disguised as Charon ferries the costumed guests to the island in several groups. The guests in the first group are disguised as eminent Greek poets, artists, orators and philosophers including Demosthenes, Artistotle, Phidias and Pindar. The guests in the second group represent such Roman worthies as Cicero, Lucretius, Virgil, Horace and Vitruvius and are followed in turn by parties of guests disguised as artists and poets of the Italian Renaissance and as British worthies of the Restoration including Dryden, Locke and Sir Edmund Waller. Each party in turn praises Lady Frances and her achievement at Munster Village, which they represent as the culmination of a tradition of artistic and intellectual achievement that stretches back through the Restoration and the Renaissance to classical antiquity.

The masquerade scene makes explicit the allegorical quality of Hamilton's Utopian landscape. The young Lord Munster's pretended "Elysium," surrounded by the gently flowing waters of the "Styx" and ornamented by a "Temple of Minerva," has no place within the expansive and generally unornamented terrain of a Brownian landscape park. They recall instead to the tradition of what Paulson denominates the "poetic" garden, in which various symbolic features including garden temples, historical statuary and inscribed texts created an explicitly symbolic landscape.[37] The garden created by Charles Bridgeman and William Kent for Richard Temple, Viscount Cobham, at Stowe in Buckinghamshire during the 1720s and 1730s offers an important analog to Hamilton's imaginary garden. At Stowe, contrasting temples honoring "ancient" and "modern" virtue pay tribute to the moral and intellectual achievements of the classical age while commenting obliquely on the depravity of contemporary mores. In *Munster Village*, Hamilton engages in the imaginative recuperation of contemporary morality in Lady Frances's garden Utopia, to which both ancient and modern worthies pay tribute inside a temple dedicated to Minerva, the female patroness of the arts and the fountainhead of wisdom.

Miss Bruce paints a similarly symbolic landscape, and Poussin depicts another in *Arcadian Shepherds*. The scene in *Munster Village* in which Lord Munster's guests praise Lady Frances's achievement also displays a "painterly" quality; the costumed guests, poised motionless in front of Lady Frances, deliver lengthy addresses in what appear to be a series of historical *tableaux vivants*. The difference between these carefully orchestrated allegorical scenes and other, more conventional *tableaux* is that the figures in Hamilton's *tableaux* speak. In Amory's *Memoirs*, the heroine creates a "speaking painting" in a ventriloquial *tour de force* in order to correct the narrator's misunderstanding of the relationship between women and the landscapes they inhabit, and in the process she claims a place for women as artists and moral teachers. In the masquerade episode which concludes *Munster Village*, Hamilton revisits this remarkable scene of instruction but alters Amory's assignment of gender roles. In the masquerade scene, the young Lord Munster is the artist, orchestrating a series of *tableaux* that celebrate Lady Frances's insight, creativity and leadership in founding the Utopian community that gives the novel its name. Lady Frances is also an artist, but she works in a different medium, producing neither a complex theatrical performance like the anniversary masquerade nor an imaginary Utopia such as the one Miss Bruce describes on canvas in her *Arcadia*.

Lady Frances's founds an actual community, one which exists for all to see within the fictional universe of Hamilton's novel. Unlike Miss Bruce, who withdraws into solitude to contemplate an imaginary Utopia that assumes concrete form only in isolation from society, on the enchanted "Green Island," Lady Frances intervenes in the social world of eighteenth-century Shropshire. Refusing to accept the romantic solitude of Tenian, Juan Fernández, Hali-farm or the Green Island as a substitute for the productive labor that alone can improve the condition of those unhappy swains and shepherdesses not fortunate enough to dwell in Arcadia, Hamilton's heroine instead sets about creating "Utopia" in the here and now, and her work challenges and ultimately transforms the fictional world described in *Munster Village*.

Hamilton rejects the separatism that Amory espouses in the *Memoirs*, but her imaginative revision of the opening scene of Amory's novel at both the beginning and the end of *Munster Village* places her within the same artistic tradition as Miss Bruce. Subversive—or "disobedient"—reading and revision, practiced by Miss Bruce in the *Memoirs* and by Hamilton in *Munster Village*, play an important role in the work of eighteenth-century artists in Britain, particularly those who were women or members of marginalized ethnic, religious or political groups. Writers as diverse as Aphra Behn, Eliza Haywood, Tobias Smollett, Olaudah Equiano, Mary Wollstonecraft and Maria Edgeworth employ similar strategies as they write in and through an artistic tradition and social milieu that at times threaten to deny them a voice. By re-envisioning Poussin's painting, Amory provides Hamilton with a model of the way in which marginalized artists can at the same time work both within *and* outside an established artistic tradition. Amory's imaginative revision of Poussin's painting and Hamilton's revision of Amory's *Memoirs*, understood within their broader cultural and literary context, offer a paradigm for interpreting the works of a wide range of other eighteenth-century writers who have only recently become the objects of critical efforts at "recovery" and, in the process, can help modern-day critics and scholars, influenced by Romantic notions of individuality and invention, to understand the function of the complex web of allusions and references that distinguish so many of these texts.

NOTES

1. Thomas Amory, *Memoirs: Containing the Lives of Several Ladies of Great Britain* (London: John Noon, 1755), 2-4. Subsequent references, given parenthetically in the text, are to this, the first edition of Amory's novel. A second edition of the *Memoirs* was published in London in 1769 by the firm of Johnson and Payne.

2. Carole Fabricant, "Binding and Dressing Nature's Loose Tresses: The Ideology of Augustan Landscape Design," *Studies in Eighteenth-Century Culture* 8 (1979): 111.

3. Katherine Esdaile, one of the few twentieth-century critics sympathetic to Amory, offers perhaps the best brief account of the plot and genre of the *Memoirs*: "the manner may be described as the picaresque in search of the Picturesque, with the important additions that the Picaro is a religious maniac, but a very learned one, and that he contrives to introduce a number of heroines of his favourite type . . . and to bring the hero into contact with other ladies, married and single, all as ready to tell their stories as Fielding's Man of the Hill." Esdaile, "The Real Thomas Amory," in *Essays and Studies by Members of the English Association* 26 (1940), comp. Arundell Esdaile (Oxford: Clarendon, 1941), 54-55.

4. William Hazlitt, "On John Buncle," from *The Round Table: A Collection of Essays on Literature, Men, and Manners* (1817), in *The Complete Works of William Hazlitt*, vol. 4, ed. P. P. Howe (London and Toronto: Dent, 1930), 51-52; Charles Lamb, Letter to Samuel Taylor Coleridge, 24 July 1797, in *The Letters of Charles Lamb, Newly Arranged, with Additions*, vol. 1, ed. Alfred Ainger (London: Macmillan, 1904), 80. Leigh Hunt numbers Amory among those "authors [who] retain, if not the highest, yet the most friendly and as it were domestic hold upon us during life, and sympathize with us through all portions of it." Hunt, *A Book for a Corner: Selections in Prose and Verse from Authors the Best Suited to That Mode of Enjoyment, with Comments on Each, and a General Introduction* (New York City: Derby & Jackson, 1859), 5.

5. James Mulvihill, "Amory's *John Buncle* and Wordsworth's *Excursion*," *Notes and Queries* 235 (1990): 25-26.

6. Ian Campbell Ross offers the most accurate information available about Amory's admittedly obscure biography. Campbell Ross, "Thomas Amory, *John Buncle*, and the Origins of Irish Fiction," *Éire-Ireland: A Journal of Irish Studies* 18 (1983): 71-85.

7. Amory appears, in particular, to rely upon Addison's theorization of the effects of the "greatness" and "beauty" in his description of the narrator's responses to the boundless prospect of the rolling Northumbrian hills and to the unexpected, fragile loveliness of Hali-farm. See Joseph Addison, *Spectator* 411 and 412, in *The Spectator*, vol. 6 (London: J. and R. Tonson and S. Draper, 1767), 93, 95-98, 101.

8. See Edmund Burke, *A Philosophical Enquiry into the Origin of our Ideas of the Sublime and Beautiful*, ed. James T. Boulton (1958; Notre Dame, IN, and London: Univ. of Notre Dame Press, 1968), 113-17.

9. Ronald Paulson, *Emblem and Expression: Meaning in English Art of the Eighteenth-Century* (London: Thames and Hudson, 1975), 20-22.

10. The narrator's description of Miss Bruce closely follows Hogarth's account of female beauty. See Hogarth, *The Analysis of Beauty: Written with a View of Fixing Fluctuating Ideas of Taste* (1753; New York City: Garland, 1973), 19-21, 39, 73.

11. "Be kind and courteous to this gentleman; / . . . / Nod to him, elves, and do him courtesies." William Shakespeare, *A Midsummer Night's Dream*, III.i.164-74, in *The Riverside Shakespeare*, 2nd ed., gen. ed. G. Blakemore Evans (Boston and New York City: Houghton Mifflin, 1997), 267.

12. Addison, *Spectator* 411; vol. 6, 92.

13. Alexander Pope, "Epistle to Burlington," *Moral Essays* IV, lines 57, 51-52, in *The Poems of Alexander Pope*, ed. John Butt (New Haven, CT: Yale Univ. Press, 1963), 590; Richard Payne Knight, *The Landscape, A Didactic Poem*, lines 288-89, 293 (London: W. Bulmer, 1794), 37.

14. John Milton, *Paradise Lost*, Book 9, lines 209, 212, 432-33, in *The Riverside Milton*, ed. Roy Flanagan (Boston and New York City: Houghton Mifflin, 1998), 590, 597.

15. John Locke, *The Second Treatise of Civil Government*, in *Two Treatises of Government, with a Supplement:* Patriarcha *by Robert Filmer*, ed. Thomas I. Cook (New York City: Hafner-Macmillan; London: Collier-Macmillan, 1947), 136-37.

16. Simon Pugh, "Loitering with Intent: From Arcadia to the Arcades," in *Reading Landscape: Country—City—Capital*, ed. Simon Pugh (Manchester and New York City: Manchester Univ. Press, 1990), 149-52.

17. Fabricant, 113.

18. Mary Wollstonecraft, *A Vindication of the Rights of Woman*, 2nd ed., ed. Carol H. Poston, 2nd ed. (New York City and London: Norton, 1988), 93. For a succinct account of the development and influence of female conduct books during the eighteenth century, see Nancy Armstrong, *Desire and Domestic Fiction: A Political History of the Novel* (Oxford and New York City: Oxford Univ. Press, 1987), esp. chap. 2 ("The Rise of the Domestic Woman"), 59-95.

19. The picture that Miss Bruce is engaged in copying is the second and better known of Poussin's two treatments of this subject; it was acquired by Louis XIV in 1683 and is now displayed in the Louvre. Amory does not make it clear whether the *Crucifixion* in question was painted by Antoine or Noël Coypel.

20. Louis Marin, "Towards a Theory of Reading in the Visual Arts: Poussin's *The Arcadian Shepherds*," in *Calligram: Essays in New Art History from France*, ed. Norman Bryson (Cambridge, Cambs., and New York City: Cambridge Univ. Press, 1988), 82. For other critical assessments of the role of the female figure in Poussin's painting, see Jerome Klein, "An Analysis of Poussin's *Et in Arcadia Ego*," *The Art Bulletin: An Illustrated Quarterly* 19 (1937): 314; Erwin Panofsky, "*Et in Arcadia Ego*: Poussin and the Elegiac Tradition," in *Meaning in the Visual Arts: Papers in and on Art History* (Garden City, NY: Doubleday, 1955), 313; John Berger, "*Et in Arcadia Ego*: Poussin," in *The Moment of Cubism and Other Essays*

(London: Weidenfeld and Nicolson, 1969), 84; Oskar Bätschmann, *Nicolas Poussin: Dialectics of Painting* (London: Reaktion Books, 1990), 61.

21. Erwin Panofsky argues that the grammatically correct interpretation of the inscription is "Death is even in Arcadia," making the painting a kind of *memento mori.* He also argues that this interpretation, familiar to seventeenth- and eighteenth-century commentators, was gradually displaced by the grammatically and syntactically impossible "I too lived in Arcadia," reflecting a Romantic and elegiac interpretation of the scene already implicit in Poussin's revision of his earlier treatment of the same subject in the version of *Arcadian Shepherds* (*c.* 1629-33) now preserved in the collection of the Duke of Devonshire at Chatsworth. For a perceptive critique of Panofsky's interpretation of the significance of the epitaph in the two versions of *Arcadian Shepherds*, see David Carrier, "Circa 1640," *New Literary History: A Journal of Theory and Interpretation* 21 (1990): 649-60, and *Poussin's Paintings: A Study in Art-Historical Methodology* (University Park, PA: Pennsylvania State Univ. Press, 1993), 29-35.

22. Marin argues that the "EGO" in the inscription assigns Poussin "to the place of painting himself when he paints them" while at the same time assigning the viewer who reads the inscription: "Yes, to be sure, even in Death, Arcadia can be . . . . I, the dead painter in the painted tomb; I, in the utopian happiness of painting, Arcadia." Marin, *Sublime Poussin* (1995), trans. Catherine Porter (Stanford, CA: Stanford Univ. Press, 1999), 119.

23. Nancy A. Walker, *The Disobedient Writer: Women and Narrative Tradition* (Austin, TX: Univ. of Texas Press, 1995), 3-4.

24. Berger, 84.

25. For a detailed analysis of the strategies employed by Finch and Scott to adapt and transform familiar stories and genres, see my "Eden Revisited: Re-visions of the Garden in Astell's *Serious Proposal*, Scott's *Millenium Hall*, and Graffigny's *Lettres d'une péruvienne*," *Eighteenth-Century Fiction* 9.2 (1997): 161-82.

26. *"Surpris, saisi, transporté d'un spectacle si peu prévu, je restai un moment immobile, et m'écriai dans un enthousiasme involontaire: 'O Tinian! ô Juan-Fernandez. Julie, le bout du monde est à votre porte.'"* Jean-Jacques Rousseau, *Julie ou la nouvelle Héloïse: Lettres de deux amants habitants d'une petite ville au pied des Alpes*, ed. Michel Launay (Paris: Garnier-Flammarion), 353. The English translation in the text of this essay is taken from *Julie, or the New Heloise: Letters of Two Lovers Who Live in a Small Town at the Foot of the Alps*, trans. Philip Stewart and Jean Vaché, *The Collected Writings of Rousseau*, ed. Roger D. Masters and Christopher Kelly, vol. 6 (Hanover, NH, and London: Univ. Press of New England, 1997), 387.

27. Lady Mary (Walker, *née* Leslie) Hamilton, *Munster Village*, introd. Sarah Bayliss (London and New York City: Pandora-Routledge, 1987), 16. Subsequent references are to this edition of Hamilton's novel.

28. Alessa Johns claims that Hamilton "plagiarizes" a passage from Defoe's *Political History of the Devil* (1726) in *Munster Village*. Hamilton's debt to Amory is far more explicit than her debt to Defoe, but "plagiarism" is perhaps not the most

appropriate term for Hamilton's (or Amory's or Miss Bruce's) complex reworking of earlier texts, a practice which in fact reflects a greater degree of originality than Johns concedes. Johns, "Mary Hamilton, Daniel Defoe, and a Case of Plagiarism in Eighteenth-Century England," *English Language Notes* 31 (1994): 25-33.

29. Walter's role as the sole author of *A Voyage round the World* was disputed during the eighteenth century by James Wilson, who claimed that much of the narrative was composed by Benjamin Robins, an engineer and mathematician employed by the East India Company. Robins's role in the composition of the *Voyage* remains a matter of dispute. See Richard Walter and Benjamin Robins, *A Voyage round the World, in the Years MDCCXL, I, II, III, IV. By George Anson*, ed. Glyndwr Williams (London and New York City: Oxford Univ. Press, 1974), xxi-xxv.

30. See, *e.g.*, Walter, 119, 202, 280.

31. Walter, 112.

32. "*Je me mis à parcourir avec ecstase ce verger*" (Launay, 354; Stewart and Vaché, 388).

33. Milord Edouard Bomston uses his influence to secure St-Preux a position as an "Engineer of the landing force [*ingénieur des troupes de débarquement*]" with Anson's expedition (Launay, 292-93; Stewart and Vaché, 324-26), and St-Preux describes his travels to Mme d'Orbe upon his return (Launay, 307-11; Stewart and Vaché, 338-41).

34. "*Je crus voir le lieu le plus sauvage, le plus solitaire de la nature, et il me semblait d'être le premier mortel qui jamais eût pénétré dans ce désert*" (Launay, 353; Stewart and Vaché, 387).

35. William Cowper, "Verses: Supposed to Be Written by Alexander Selkirk, during His Solitary Abode in the Island of Juan Fernandez" (1782), lines 1, 55-56, in *The Complete Poetical Works of William Cowper*, ed. Humphry S. Milford (1905, 2nd ed., 1906; London: Oxford Univ. Press, 1913), 311-12.

36. Dorothy Stroud provides well documented and copiously illustrated descriptions of several of Brown's better-known gardens in her biography of Brown, and Roger Turner devotes a chapter in his more recent critical study to Brown's style and techniques as a landscape architect. Stroud, *Capability Brown*, introd. Christopher Hussey (1950; rev. ed. London: Faber & Faber, 1975); Turner, *Capability Brown and the Eighteenth-Century English Landscape* (New York City: Rizzoli International Publications, 1985), 68-91.

37. Paulson, 19-34.

John Marsh and the Ancient-Modern Polemic

HOWARD IRVING

The writings of musical amateur John Marsh offer one of the most extensive eye witness accounts known of late eighteenth century English musical life. Marsh's importance rests, however, on two very different contributions that researchers have often considered in isolation. This is regrettable, since the two sources were written for different purposes and different audiences and consequently reveal something about Marsh's thinking when read together that is less readily apparent when they are considered separately. The purpose of this essay is to connect disparate threads of research on Marsh and in the process to shed some light on the ideologies that shaped musical thought during a crucial period in the creation of the institutions and values we now associate with the phenomenon of classical music.

Recent attention on Marsh has focused mainly on what he called his *History of My Private Life*.[1] This massive autobiography offers an invaluable record of provincial musical life and of the complex web of social customs and rituals that were important to a gentleman of modest fortune in the southern cathedral cities in which Marsh lived. Marsh began the process of recasting daily diaries he had kept since early adolescence into a formal life history as he reached his forty-fourth year in 1796. The result eventually grew to some thirty-seven volumes spanning the years from 1765 to a point very near his death in 1828. A large part of this manuscript, which was once believed lost in its original, unedited form, was recently published as *The John Marsh Journals* from a complete copy obtained by the Huntington Library in 1990.

Long before the reappearance of his original autobiography, Marsh received some scholarly notice for his work as a minor composer and for an abridged version of his life history, but also for two important works that stand out among his handful of published contributions to music criticism and pedagogy.[2] One is a long essay published anonymously in the *Monthly Magazine* in 1797 that Marsh called "A Comparison Between the Ancient and Modern Styles of Music in Which the Merits and Demerits of Each are Respectively Pointed Out." The other is a related slender volume entitled *Hints to Young Composers of Instrumental Music, Illustrated with 2 Movements for a Grand Orchestra in Score* (London, ca. 1807) from around a decade later, in which Marsh reprised many of the ideas of the earlier essay and acknowledged its authorship. Together, these two sources are among the most important historical documents known that describe a pervasive cultural schism in England between proponents of so-called "ancient" and "modern" music.

Since these two musical species might be defined in several different ways at different points in the eighteenth century some clarification is in order. At the time Marsh wrote his essay, the expression "ancient music" was often understood to mean music of Handel, Corelli, and Geminiani plus a select repertory of madrigals, earlier sacred music, and a very limited sampling of Italian opera. The expression "modern style," on the other hand — at least in the limited way Marsh understood it — referred to instrumental music written in what is sometimes called the mid-century homophonic style, including such figures as J. C. Bach, Ignaz Pleyel, and Haydn.[3]

Marsh completed the first draft of his *Monthly Magazine* essay in the spring of 1796, shortly before beginning the long project that resulted in the *History of My Private Life*. The *Hints to Young Composers*, on the other hand, dates from a point a few years after Marsh had brought his life history up to date and consciously scaled back his journal-keeping activities.[4] The two published works, then, frame the important parts of the autobiography that concern the late eighteenth century and date from roughly the same time, but they were written for very different purposes and addressed to different audiences. The autobiography was intended to be read by family and friends who crossed many of the social and ideological lines that define Marsh's own place at crossroads of British society. Marsh was a moderate Anglican whose mother was a Dissenter as were many in his social circle. He was politically a supporter of the government with notably main-stream views to the extent they are known, but at the same an individual whose writing has been shown occasionally to betray innocent hints of sympathy for radicals like John Wilkes and William Godwin and for the Republican cause.[5] Finally, he was a land owner by virtue of an inherited estate but one whose income and personal interests were incompatible with the life of a country squire and who therefore remained poised socially between the gentry and the middle classes.

The *History of My Private Life*, in keeping with its domestic purposes and diverse audience, avoids controversy and minimizes — but does not avoid entirely — overt expressions of ideology. The anonymously-published "Comparison Between the Ancient and Modern Styles of Music" and later *Hints*, by contrast, were intended to be read by the musically literate and to expose cultural divisions important to that audience in particular. With fewer constraints on expression, both the essay and the *Hints* confront directly the value systems of ancient and modern music and in the process reveal aspects of the ideologies of the two musical parties that neither Marsh's autobiography nor any other source of the period shows as clearly.

When the ideas expressed in Marsh's relatively candid essay are the starting point for a reading of his *History of My Private Life*, the origins of the essay's critical position with regard to ancient music emerge from the details of his half-a-lifetime of musical experiences with the old music community. At the same time, Marsh's autobiography clarifies his interests in the essay and reveals the depth and complexity of the ideology that informs his critical writing. A superficial reading of the essay might conclude that it, like the autobiography, was motivated by a need to promote reconciliation between contending parties. Its stated purpose is to advocate concerts mixing the two musical species as opposed to what Marsh views as regrettably one-sided events by the important London concert associations. The essay does not minimize controversy in the way the autobiography does, however, and accordingly presents the ancient-modern polemic as a persistent cultural schism with some three decades of history behind it and with its own set of sensitive issues and simplistic characterizations.

Marsh does not describe ancient and modern music in specifically ideological or political terms, but his remarks in the essay clearly point to sharply different value systems or ideologies. These ideologies are worth examining because elements of the values of both ancient and modern music were eventually incorporated into the developing notion of classical music as that idea-complex began to take shape in the decades surrounding the end of the eighteenth century.[6] At the same time, there are few in Marsh's time who speak openly of an ancient-modern rift and still fewer who try to illuminate both sides by the deliberate opposition of two ways of thinking about music and its legitimate purposes. What sources of this kind there are were written by extremists like Tory ideologue and ancient-music advocate William Jones of Nayland, and, on the other side, by poet, Opposition figure, and champion of modern music, the reverend William Mason of York Minster. Both of these individual's writings show the influence of strong political interests, however, that urge caution in accepting them as representative of the culture at large, especially by comparison with Marsh's notably moderate views.[7] Marsh shows by his example that even though a strong connection may exist between politics and the ideologies of ancient and modern music it is still entirely possible for an individual to be a progressive in the arts but a political conservative.

Marsh tends to be viewed as a neutral in the ancient-modern polemic in much the same way the *History of My Private Life* presents him has a determined non-combatant in a celebrated musical dispute that erupted in Salisbury after the death of Salisbury music festival director James Harris.[8] Marsh's apparent neutrality has resulted in his being viewed as a kind of prototypical provincial gentleman amateur of they period. He is seen, in other words, as an individual who stood above the overtly politicized concerns of a few contentious and unrepresentative voices and who can therefore be accepted as a kind of spokesman for the majority view among contemporary music lovers. This perception is encouraged by the reconciliatory theme of the *Monthly Magazine* essay and by the fact that in the provincial setting that formed the backdrop of much of Marsh's musical activity the calculated exclusivity of organizations like London's famous Concerts of Ancient Music was not a conspicuous fact of musical life. A perception of Marsh's neutrality may also be encouraged by a view of the ancient-modern polemic itself, which acknowledges the existence of ancient-modern tensions but interprets them as a relatively minor phenomenon in the musical life of the period and, accordingly, rejects the binary opposition of ancient and modern music as an important factor in the evolution of musical classicism.[9] In other words, if amateurs on both sides of the ancient-modern divide could in fact have worked together as closely and as amicably as seems to have been true in Marsh's peaceful world, the dispute itself cannot have been the pivotal controversy that somewhat later observers maintain it was.

I believe, however, that while Marsh exhibits a characteristically moderate position with regard to the ancient-modern polemic, to view him as completely neutral is to misunderstand the issues of ancient versus modern music. First, a close reading of Marsh's essay, the source in which he could speak most freely, puts him on the modern side of the aesthetic issues that were most important to the debate. But more important for the present purposes, I contend that within what might be called the ideology of modern music the eclecticism and tolerance for old music Marsh exhibits should not necessarily be viewed as am indication of neutrality; such qualities are instead virtues the modern side normally assigns itself and finds lacking among partisans of ancient music. From the modern perspective, the ancient-modern polemic was to a very significant extent about the intolerance and exclusivity of the elite social classes controlling ancient music and the reluctance of this segment of society to accept innovation. This was true even though it is undeniable that a prominent segment of the modern-music audience consciously imitated the style of this same social elite and engaged in its own calculated exclusivity.[10]

The most musically sophisticated figures who might generally be assigned to the modern side of the ancient-modern divide — including Charles Burney, Burney's friend and frequent correspondent Thomas Twining, and even the most vituperative modern voice of the period, William Mason — all display a genuine appreciation for ancient music at some level. Most of these men also found it possible to attend ancient music programs, sometimes regularly, and to relish certain examples of the type. All three of the individuals named, however, might have argued that progress had left this music behind and each might also have described forces sympathetic to ancient music as motivated not by consistent aesthetic principle but by bigotry and the mistrust of innovation. This perception is confirmed by Marsh's own recorded experiences, in which advocates of modern music are, perhaps of necessity, conspicuously more receptive to ancient music than ancient partisans are to modern.

Music and Ideology

The ideological underpinnings of the movement for ancient music have been described in detail by William Weber.[11] A central tenet of this value system, which Weber has called "musical Toryism," is a belief in the integrity and even moral superiority of ancient music by contrast with more recent music that is viewed as the ingenious but insubstantial product of a degenerate popular culture.[12] William Jones of Nayland, a "leading conservative ideologist and musical theorist" of the period before the turn of the century,[13] praised ancient-music composers Handel and Corelli for being "distinct in their Ideas, and clear in the design of their accents and measures." "As for *Haydn* and *Boccherini*," however, "who merit a first place among the Moderns for *invention*,"

> they are sometimes so desultory and unaccountable in their way of treating a Subject, that they may be reckoned among the wild warblers of the wood: And they seem to differ from some pieces of *Handel*, as the Talk of the Tea-table (where, perhaps neither Wit nor Invention are wanting) differs from the Oratory of the Bar and the Pulpit.[14]

Thus, recent music is not merely trite and fashionable but discursive and lacking in the all-important virtue of "connexion." Such flaws, combined with a dangerous and wanton sensuousness resulting from modern music's too-close association with Italianate melody and from its apparent rejection of solid learning in preference for passion and feeling, are often cited when the moderns are damned with the ultimate late eighteenth-century musical epithet "effeminate."[15]

It is not ancient music's presumptions about learning and musical sophistication that are most important to the situation of Marsh, however, but its exclusivity. The Concert of Ancient Music, formed in 1776 by a group composed mostly of nobles and led by John Montagu, 4th Earl of Sandwich, evolved into one of the London's most restrictive social arenas. As a later observer wrote, "to go with your money in your hand was no passport; your social position had to be as carefully vouched for as for a ball at Almacks."[16] The exclusivity of the "Antient Concert," as it often styled itself, was imitated by other, less-elegant concerts,[17] but the Concert of Ancient Music always retained first place among the socially ambitious. Marsh's *Journals* reveal his distaste for snobbery,[18] but the exclusivity that concerned him most was the Ancient Concert's well known policy restricting most kinds of music performed at its prestigious programs to examples at least twenty years old.

There are two components of the restrictive mind-set that accompanies the Ancient Concert's programmatic constraints and they are often at odds with each other in a way that the friends of modern music liked to interpret as evidence of bigotry. The first is a strong reflex against innovation, which tends to be viewed as an arbitrary change of style in the service of fashion and not, as a modern-music advocate might argue, as actual refinement or improvement in the art resulting from inevitable progress. Modern-music sympathizer Charles Burney writes of a regrettable social *faux pas* on his part at the home of the Duke of Portland, in which he unthinkingly launched into a few indiscrete remarks about modern music in the presence of the Lord and Lady Darnley without first cautiously exploring their preferences:

> Something was s^{d} ab^{t} styles in music; when I soon found that I was talking with determined exclusive admirers of Handel & old music[.] The expression of modern refinements happened to escape me, when boldly my Lord and my Lady wth the most consummate contempt — repeated: "Modern refinem^{ts} indeed" — we'll call it modern changes of style and taste — but what one party calls refinement^{s}, the other side constantly calls corruption and deterioriation.[19]

Not surprisingly, suspicion of innovation is typically accompanied by the fear of being swept up in a tide of easy enthusiasm that can lead lesser audiences to embrace impressive-sounding products that lack substance. This, in turn, is the driving force behind a general rejection of music featuring technical display.[20]

But even though advocates of ancient music were predisposed to accept age as a defining quality of their developing canon of acknowledged musical masterpieces, they also applied certain stylistic criteria that were partially independent of age and therefore liable to the appearance of contradiction and inconsistency. In particular, ancient music had a reverence for Renaissance and Baroque counterpoint as a musical approach with its own kind of scholarly tradition and its own cachet of intellectual respectability. Music in the Baroque tradition was still being written late in the eighteenth century, however, by figures like blind organist John Stanley. Stanley's name is often cited respectfully alongside the legendary figures of ancient music even though the Ancient Concert's policies banned it from their prestigious concerts.[21] Still another problem with the first musical canon was the fact that non-polyphonic music and even music with stylistic roots in the theater — a domain ancient music characteristically viewed with suspicion — had already made its appearance in England at the end of the seventeenth century and thus qualified for the Ancient Concert on the basis of age but not necessarily style. Even some die-hard enemies of ancient music like William Mason found it possible to embrace selected examples of this type.[22]

Opposing a learned, elitist, aristocratic conception of ancient music is an alternative voice in British criticism that rejects musical learning and argues instead for a passionate, melody-centered music that can move the common man.[23] Accordingly, in his *Essays Historical and Critical, on English Church Music* (York, 1795; London, 1811) Mason objects to the "abstruse harmonical Proportions" of Renaissance counterpoint "which had neither common sense, nor, in this case a better judge, the approbation of the common ear, for their

Support."[24] He concludes that it is only

> misapplied art, which combines a variety of parts in various intricate manners, and gives to the different voices that perform those parts, different words to express at the same time, which occasions this confusion; a confusion which constantly perplexes the common ear, and which the most practised in harmony cannot always easily develop.[25]

Mason was an enthusiastic proponent of the music of Haydn and of Haydn's contemporary and former student Ignaz Pleyel, and even tried to adapt their music for church use.[26] At its most extreme, however, the critical voice of the moderns can reject kind of any cultivated music — including that of composers like Haydn, Pleyel, and Mozart — in favor of a nationalistic primitivism that held up Celtic music as an ideal in much the same way other British men of letters viewed the legendary music of the ancient Greeks as an art of perfect simplicity but at the same time remarkable power.[27]

The philosophy Marsh reveals in the *Journals* does not conform completely to either of the musical ideologies sketched briefly above but contains elements of each. In many ways, in fact, Marsh resembles Charles Burney in his ability to appreciate both sides of the ancient-modern polarity and in his combination of progressive aesthetic values with conspicuously Church and King politics. His *Journals* document how this remarkably balanced position evolved.

The John Marsh Journals

In general, Marsh emerges from his *Journals* as an amateur string player of better-than-average ability who was often prepared to walk several miles at night and in winter weather for the opportunity of an evening of ensemble playing. The presence of a congenial group of instrumentalists was also a matter of sufficient import to be a major influence on the town in which Marsh chose to live. At the same time, the *Journals* reveal that the music Marsh was able to play was often dictated by other performers, and that those other performers often had interests that were more narrow and abilities more limited than his own. From the earliest such references in the mid-1760's, when Marsh was barely thirteen years old, restrictions on repertory do not typically take the form of militant supporters of modern music who refuse to try Corelli or Handel but lovers of ancient music who were either unable or unwilling to play modern music.

For example, Marsh describes private musical parties he attended in Gosport near Portsmouth in 1768. The company included a Mr Ducket, whom Marsh describes as "an elderly gentleman who play'd a very good fiddle in the old style of playing" and a Mr Clarke, "an elderly & very respectable man, tho' but a moderate performer upon the fiddle." Although the group included more capable and more adventurous semi-professional musicians such as a Mr McArthur, who was "then principal 2d. fiddle at Portsmouth Concert" and Mr Chapman, "apprentice (or assistant) to Mr Hawker, organist of Portsmouth," both of whom were more open to the modern style, Marsh observes that because of a preponderance of old music enthusiasts they "frequently play'd Corelli, Handel & Geminiani's concertos compleat." He adds, pointedly commenting on both his own developing performance skill and the limited demands of older music, that he "now began playing the ripienos at sight."[28]

These remarks are consistent with Marsh's later words in the essay and the *Hints to Young Composers of Instrumental Music*, where he depicts ancient music as a music for the elderly and the unskilled and modern as a more challenging species for the young and capable. "I have always observed that *elderly* people are generally the most attached to the ancient, and *young* people to the modern music" Marsh writes, noting that

> people who have been long accustomed or confined to a particular system (as elderly people must formerly have been), especially if they are performers, find the modern music more difficult in its execution from the mere novelty of the style, and the rapidity with which its allegros and prestos are required to be performed.[29]

This characterization is not entirely reasonable since, as Marsh acknowledges elsewhere, the relative difficulty of either type would have depended considerably on the particular part an amateur played. Ancient music offered players of limited ability the chance to play ripieno or filler parts. As Marsh observes in the essay,

> [f]ormerly if a good leading first and second violin, and principal bass, could be procured, very indifferent players were competent to make up the rest of the orchestra, the principal parts being generally played single, whilst the repienos were doubled or even trebled. In modern music, however, all the violins and basses are generally obliged to take principal parts.[30]

In the *Journals* Marsh does not mention that the wind parts of modern symphonies, which in his limited circle had to be played by a violinist since there were no wind players available in Gosport, were no more challenging than ripieno playing. Accordingly, Marsh's narrative in his autobiography continues with the observation that

> The modern symphony or overture with hautboy & horn parts instead of ripieno violins having been introduc'd not long before this time, Mr McArthur soon brought the two first setts of Bach & Abel to our meetings as a valuable addition & variation of style, which he used to lead with great spirit & rapidity. It was however some time before he could bring over any but Mr Chapman to his opinion, as Mr Ducket used to twist about in playing the 2d.fiddle & wanted to rest at the end of every quick movement. Little Wafer [organist at Gosport and Marsh's first teacher] too grumbl'd at the reiterated quavers upon one note for several bars together, which not being used to, he co'd hardly manage to play at sight, & did not like quitting Corelli, Handel etc. most of which he was well acquainted with, the basses of which were also of much more consequence than those of the modern symphony.[31]

Others in this group including Marsh himself expressed concerns about the modern music in question, and their various objections are instructive. Clark and a Mr. Phillips — both of whom Marsh identifies as partial to ancient music — complained "of the quickness of the allegros, & last movements in particular (in w'ch they used to say they co'd scarce get a note in edgeways).[32] Marsh himself, however, was concerned about something else. As the youngest participant he was relegated to playing the indispensable wind instrument parts on his violin. He thus protests at playing "the long holding notes for several bars together, but rather wishing for something more to do with the bow." He also didn't like the fact that "the middle strains being almost always mark'd *tacet* for the hautboys," he "by no means wish'd to be unemploy'd with a fiddle in my hands."[33]

Marsh was less troubled about the specific concerns raised by his older colleagues. "As to the quickness of the prestos etc.," he writes,

> that I did not at all care about but felt myself rather flatter'd in being able to keep up with them (& leaving the old gentlemen behind) in the few notes I had to play. Indeed the only parts that had any execution in them were the 2 fiddle parts (which were very brilliant) & the tenor which had much more to do than in the old concertos (in which it was

> a mere ripieno) as a great part of it in Bach & Abel's symphonies was in unison or octave with the bass.[34]

Though basically a modest individual by nature, Marsh often takes the opportunity in the *Journals* to cite his own prowess. When he does this, he most often emphasizes his superiority in the area of modern music in particular, as in the quotation above. Thus, when a Mr Watson, who was "recon'd a capital old style player upon the violin for an amateur" was appointed to the Free School at Romsey, Marsh met and immediately became acquainted with him. Marsh observes that "as we became better acquainted I found he excell'd me in the ancient music & also in Campioni's Trios [Carlo Antonio Campioni 1720-1793] (of which he produced 3 or 4 sets) & such other music as he had formerly practic'd at Oxford. With regard however to the more modern music of Bach, Abel, Stamitz etc, (which he was unacquainted with) I found the superiority of performance to be on my side."[35]

Soon after he relocated to Chichester, Marsh was introduced to Charles Lennox, 3rd Duke of Richmond, and through this connection came into contact with a higher caliber of player where the modern style was concerned. The band of Lord Lennox's 25th Regiment, which at the time numbered around 9 players and included strings in addition to the usual contingent of winds, often played at the Duke's country seat Goodwood some three miles north of Chichester. Marsh describes an officer named Rose, a violinist and recent addition to the band, who joined him and others for musical party. "I found Mr Rose far to excell me in taste & neatness of execution as to modern music," Marsh observes, "but as to that of the old school he seem'd to know little about it. As therefore we co'd not think of leaving out Corelli, it was settled that I sh'd lead in that & he in what modern music we played."[36]

Marsh's statement implies that the Duke's band mostly performed modern music. It is revealing that Marsh makes no direct mention of any such preference even though he does not hesitate to call attention throughout his *Journals* to any exclusive partiality to ancient music. A better indication of the band's repertoire is given in Marsh's description of an incident at Goodwood. Marsh observes that Hyler, a German cellist in the Duke's band, "sent to me for some ancient music (viz. Handel's overtures, Corelli's concertos etc.), to play in the even'g to Lord Campden who was staying there & did not like modern music."[37] This seems to indicate that the Duke's library did not include sufficient ancient music for the evening. In fact, Marsh ended up playing with the Regimental band that evening because of his familiarity with ancient music. He reports — possibly sneering a little at a common affectation within the ancient community over its claimed sophistication — that Ld. Campden "had before tried to puzzle us by requesting the Overture in Semele of Handel, one of his most difficult ones & that *we* happen'd to be least acquainted with, for w'ch we therefore substituted that in *Otho* [i.e., the opera seria *Ottone* by Handel]."[38]

If the Duke himself was partial to modern music, the above indicates that this was not always true of his guests and acquaintances. Another incident with a visitor to Goodwood is also revealing. Marsh had, in time, become leader of a subscription concert series in Chichester by virtue of his accommodating personality and willingness to compromise. He could not lead every concert, however, and in December of 1788 was forced to turn over the reins to the Duke's guest, a Major Goodenough:

> [T]he following pieces chosen by Maj'r Goodenough (who led) were done, viz the Overtures to Sampson & Ariadne [i.e., Handel's opera *Arianne in Creta*] Corellis 1st Concerto & Stanley's 6th. Thinking however there sho'd be one modern piece I chose one for the last piece, but the horn parts happening to be left behind the Major immediately chose the Overture in Otho instead, so that *every* full piece was this evening of the ancient style, in which I must confess I much differ'd from the Major as tho' I was always fond of Handel, Corelli etc. yet I thought it the best plan to contrast the 2 styles with each other & not to have an entire concert of either. He however it seem'd was determin'd to be master this evening & wo'd hearken to no proposal in favor of a little modern music, in w'ch I did not think he altogether behaved very civilly in regard to me, who had usually had the principal management of the Concert & went thro' all the drudgery of attending rehearsals, settling with the performers etc.[39]

It should be noted that this is a rare mood indeed for Marsh, who seldom calls attention to the rudeness of others in his *Journals*.

A few years later, Marsh was obliged to spent considerable time in London trying to help his son John become established in the law. He repeatedly remarks in the *Journals* of having to play or attend evenings consisting mostly or exclusively of ancient music in his dealings with this august society. Perhaps not surprisingly, he does not make similar observations concerning modern music. Thus he had some music at the home of a "Captain H." at which they played mostly ancient music, though here Marsh makes a point of remarking that they tried out "the 1st. of Haydn's Symphonies composed for the late Hanover Square concerts." Shortly thereafter, he met with a Mr Cook of upper Titchfield Street, who invited Marsh to a musical party at which Marsh's own concerto in D was the only modern piece played, "all the rest being either Handel or Geminiani."[40]

Ideology and Marsh's *Journals*

If the *Journals* occasionally reveal a certain frustration with the intransigence of the old music movement, many other aspects of Marsh's ideology that occasionally emerge from his long autobiography suggest a definite establishment philosophy that is closer to Weber's ideology of ancient music than to its binary opposite. Marsh was incensed, for example, at the sight of a rock-throwing mob accosting the King on his way to the houses of Parliament in 1795 and complains of "the democrats & disaffected who had taken advantage & incited the rabble to these acts of insurrection."[41] He is concerned because

> there being at this time a great spirit of republicanism & levelling prevalent all over the kingdom kept up by the corresponding Society & their emissaries there were great apprehensions of riots & tumults in London, on w'ch account the Tower was fortified & the guard at the bank doubled etc.[42]

But this point of view did not, however, prevent Marsh from sympathizing with his friend

> Mr Williams, who had been rather imprudent in uttering his democratic sentiments, & fearing he had gone too far & might be recon'd a *mark'd* man put himself in as conspicuous a part of the hall as he co'd & warmly supported the resolutions [against sedition] joining the cry of God save the King etc., with great vociferation as he inform'd us the next day when hecame over to spend a day or two with us.[43]

Marsh associated just as easily with Dissenters and had a sister who married one.[44] At the same time, he speaks against Dissent on occasion — mostly, it should be noted, on aesthetic rather than doctrinal grounds. He describes hearing a Sunday night lecture in 1772, for example, in which he "by no means liked his manner so well as that of his predecessor or many other Dissenting ministers that I have heard he having rather too much of the cant for me."[45]

Because Marsh had three brothers who fought with the Royal Navy, it is probably not surprising that he should take a strongly establishment position on the American war. In 1776 he refused to attend a musical party at the home of a Mr Beaumont (who Marsh says was "rather lax in his religious opinions") because it was scheduled on a fast day set aside to pray for success in the war.[46] Indeed, Marsh saw to it that his family and servants attended church twice that day.

Marsh's reaction to radicalism is almost invariably negative. His *Journals* reveal a wide assortment of reading material, including William Godwin's radical novel *Things as they are; or The Adventures of Caleb Williams*, which he describes only as "eccentric."[47] Marsh has much more to say about Thomas Paine, whose:

> rights of Man, or Answer to Burke being now lately come out & much talked of, we got it in our society & on Monday the 25th. I began reading it, but was much disgusted with the author's treason, impudence & scurrility.[48]

He was less offended by radicalism that was expressed during a dinner at a Mr. Southby's house with "the celebrated Mr Wilkes" in March of 1782, though he notes that the company "had a good dish of politics." Political discussion was something that

> Mr. S. seem'd to enjoy as much as his guest of whom I afterwards heard several anecdotes relating to his freethinking & Blasphemous conversation, when amongst those of the same way of thinking as himself. At Mr Southby's however I found [Wilkes] to be much of a gentleman in his manner, & very pleasant & entertaining in his conversation.[49]

Marsh rarely expresses points of view with regard to music that are consistent with the ideology of ancient music. He does, however, relate one such instance in which his brother objected to the levity of sacred music in the Italian style. William Marsh had recently returned to England from America in September of 1777. John Marsh remarks that he

> went with him to a rehearsal of some anthems at Mr Harris's, adapted by him to old Italian music, which were to be done at the ensuing [Salisbury] Music Festival. They however, perhaps for want of the musical simplicity of that species of music were not altogether to the taste of Will'm who told me afterw'ds that he had heard better. He

> also ridiculed the concluding Amen of one of them which had very light fiddling accomp'ts the music of w'ch would certainly have done for the finale of a comic opera.[50]

The "old Italian music" to which William Marsh objected probably included sacred music by Neapolitan composers, a common variety at the Salisbury festival.[51] It should be noted that the Concert of Ancient Music itself later came to be known for a judicious blend of the this style with a more severe contrapuntal approach.[52]

There is, however, one instance in the *Journals* in which John Marsh was confronted with an extreme form of the modernist ideology in 1786 in the person of Joseph Cooper Walker, author of the above-mentioned *Historical Memoirs of the Irish Bards*. With characteristic tolerance, Marsh remarks that

> This Mr Walker tho' a very pleasant & agreeable man & certainly very eminent in his profession, was I found very singular in his opinions as to religion, politics & music; as if it was necessary that as a man of sense & abilities he sho'd make a point of thinking for himself in every thing & differ *at any rate* from the vulgar in all common receiv'd opinion. Accordingly as to religion, he was a deist, laughing at all religious establishments & abusing the clergy of *all* denominations for their pretended infallability.[53]

"As to politics," Marsh remarks, "he of course sneer'd at the existing Governm't as if he knew much better than any of the ministry to manage the helm of state."[54] In the same breath — suggesting Marsh's awareness of a connection between a disaffection for Handel's music and radical politics — he remarks thereafter that

> [i]n music his chief singularity appear'd in his indiscriminate abuse of Handel, whom he wo'd not allow to have excelled in any thing, except the art of making a great noise. And tho' I mention'd parts of his works in which the piano, or more delicate parts prevailed, such as 'I know that my Redeemer liveth' 'The flocks shall leave the Mountains' the Minuet in Ariadne etc. yet in none of these co'd he discover any particular merit. I therefore observ'd that I hardly supposed he went to the Commemoration of Handel at the Abbey. 'Oh, yes he said he co'd not but go there once because it was the *fashion* to do so, but met with very little entertainment except as to the spectacle,' which *for once* he allowed was worth going to.[55]

Marsh concludes with an observation with which Burney would have agreed. Walker, he notes, "seem'd to wish to bring down all excellence in the art to level of his own knowledge of it & execution, as supposing a quartetto to be the extent of a modern instrumental composition, he co'd by taking a tenor or bass (if not however too difficult) take always a principal part in it himself."[56]

Marsh's "Comparison of the Ancient and Modern Styles of Music"

With these kinds of experiences in mind, we turn now to the essay Marsh wrote immediately after he transcribed the last of the diary entries cited above from his diary to the *History of My Private Life* in 1796. The essay, it should be noted, begins more provocatively than the decade-later *Hints to Young Composers*. "Since the great revolution in instrumental music," Marsh observes in the former, "it has been too much the custom in England for musical amateurs to be prejudiced in favour of one of the two styles, either the ancient or the modern, and to reprobate the other."[57] The *Hints*, however, softens this image of a musical Glorious Revolution to begin with a milder "[f]rom the great change, which took place in the style of instrumental music about forty years ago," etc.[58]

Though Marsh's purpose in the essay is to encouraged mixed concerts, his specific objections are directly toward the aristocratic Concert of Ancient Music rather than any modern music organization. Marsh views the modern-music bias of series like J. P. Salomon's famous Haydn concerts not as a matter of prejudice but as a misinterpretation of public demand, which, if properly gauged, would, he thinks, have resulted in the mixed concerts he advocates and might in fact have prevented Salomon's eventual failure. Marsh suggests, however, that the exclusive programs of the Concert of Ancient music are not the result of a reasonable and legitimate preference but of the deliberate intention to injure the modern style. Marsh observes,

> I cannot but remark that if the managers of the Concert of Ancient Music wish to discountenance the *modern* style of composition, and to encourage the *ancient*, by suffering no piece of music to be performed that has not been composed within a limited number of years, they entirely frustrate their own design. What composer, however, attached to, or capable of writing in the ancient style (of which there are doubtless many in the metropolis) can have the least encouragement to do so, whilst his works must necessarily be rejected at both the above

> mentioned concerts [i.e., Salomon's and the Ancient Concert]; at those of modern music, on account of its antique style, and at those of ancient music, because recently composed.[59]

It should be noted that Marsh himself was a composer of works in the ancient style that were excluded from the ancient concert's prestigious programs.

With the perception of ancient bigotry in mind, Marsh's essay arrives at its stated purpose of systematically tallying the merits and demerits of the ancient and modern styles only after a lengthy opening defense of modern music that by itself ought to be sufficient to place him on the modern side. But it is the ultimate conclusion of his essay that is most revealing. A cornerstone of ancient music's claim of superiority over the modern style is its supposed greater reliance on "contrivance" and harmony. These qualities are supposed to give old music a kind of integrity and moral authority lacking in modern music. Marsh, for example, is sure that lovers of ancient music will attribute its supposed appeal to the elderly — an assertion that he assumes in this case will be conceded without question — to the fact that "people of experience and mature judgment will naturally prefer the good solid harmony of the ancient system to the light and trifling music of the new."[60]

Marsh is strangely conflicted — as are many others, including Charles Burney — over the place of musical contrivance. He allows that the complex choruses of Handel oratorios "are apt to please less at first than after a few hearings; and they constantly improve in their effects on repetition, as the ear then frequently discovers new beauties or excellences that had before escaped it."[61] This statement articulates a position that precisely mirrors the ideology of ancient music. At the same time, Marsh also praises Haydn's "ingenious modulation, and contrivance" and — curiously in the light of his basic argument — tries to show that in its own way Haydn's music is as complex and sophisticated as any ancient music.[62] But in the end, Marsh's argument is that "perhaps the proper test of excellence in [music] should not be, that it affords pleasure to professors and connoisseurs only, but to the greatest number of *amateurs* indiscriminately taken."[63] His main complaint about Haydn and Pleyel is that they have "in a great measure departed from that simplicity which alone is capable of giving *general* pleasure."[64] Marsh concludes that "it would therefore be well for the state of music in general, if subsequent composers would adhere at all times to *simplicity*, and not attempt to imitate those very elaborate and extravagant compositions, which were merely designed to exhibit the powers of a modern orchestra."[65] This point of view might be in line with a common sentiment of writing that is expressly favorable to the modern point of view.

To conclude, if the above tends to support a view of Marsh as a voice for the modern side of the ancient-modern polemic, the consequences of such a view are significant. First, to conceive Marsh as a modern is to reinterpret the terms of the debate to make musical tolerance — or, to be more accurate, its absence — a central issue. Further, Marsh is as close to a moderate voice as anyone of the period could be. With this relatively unbiased and presumably more reliable status in mind, Marsh's finding in his 1796 essay that a pervasive ancient-modern split was not only a dominant feature of the British musical community at the end of the century but had in fact been developing for some two or three decades prior, suggests that ancient modern tensions deserve to be viewed as the compelling issue in contemporary musical life that some later figures believed them to be.

NOTES

1. The manuscript Marsh calls his *History of My Private Life* was recently published by Brian Robbins as *The John Marsh Journals: The Life and Times of a Gentleman Composer (1752-1828)* (New York: Pendragon Press, 1998). Recent studies of Marsh that are based on this book include Brian Robbins, "John Marsh and Provincial Music Making in Eighteenth Century England" *Royal Musical Association Research Chronicle* 29 (1996): 96-142 and "An Introduction to the Journals of John Marsh" *Huntington Library Quarterly* 59 (1997): 125-144; William Weber, "The Fabric of Daily Life and the Autobiography of John Marsh" *Huntington Library Quarterly* 59 (1997): 145-169 and John Brewer, "John Marsh's *History of My Private Life 1752-1828*" in T. C. W. Blanning and David Cannadine, eds. *History and Biography: Essays in Honour of Derek Beales* (Cambridge University Press, 1996), 72-87.

2. Some of these contributions are now lost. Marsh describes a volume of "Musical Definitions" (*The John Marsh Journals*, 598) that was finished on 11 March 1796, but which does not survive and an an essay he calls his "Thoughts on the abuse of Cathedral Music" from 1785, which also has not been located. Brian Robbins reports (*The John Marsh Journals*, 47), on the other hand, that an *Instruction Book for the Tenor*, which Marsh published in 1821, remained in use throughout the nineteenth century. The two surviving critical works of interest here are [John Marsh], "A Comparison Between the Ancient and Modern Styles of Music in Which the Merits and Demerits of Each are Respectively Pointed Out" *Monthly Magazine* supplement to vol. II, (1796): 981-98, reprinted by C. L.

Cudworth as "An Essay by John Marsh" *Music and Letters* 36 (1955): 155-164; and John Marsh, *Hints to Young Composers of Instrumental Music, Illustrated with 2 Movements for a Grand Orchestra in Score* (London, n.d.), reprinted by C. L. Cudworth as "John Marsh, *Hints to Young Composers of Instrumental Music*" *Galpin Society Journal* 18 (1965): 57-71.

3. Howard Irving, *Ancients and Moderns: William Crotch and the Development of Classical Music* (Aldershot: Ashgate Press, 1999), 75-81, offers a critique of Marsh's conceptions of the ancient and modern styles and more inclusive definitions of both musical species.

4. John Brewer describes the process by which Marsh created his autobiography in "John Marsh's *History of My Private Life 1752-1828*" 72-73. Marsh had recast the contents of his diaries up to the current date in his autobiography by 1802.

5. This point is made by Weber in "The Fabric of Daily Life and the Autobiography of John Marsh," 154.

6. See Howard Irving, *Ancients and Moderns*, especially 102-129.

7. See William Mason, *Essays Historical and Critical, on English Church Music* (York, 1795; London, 1811), William Jones (of Nayland), *A Treatise on the Art of Music, in which the Elements of HARMONY and AIR are Practically Considered . . .* (Colchester, 1784), and William Jones, *Physiological Disquitions; or Discourses on the Natural Philosophy of the Elements* (London, 1781).

8. *Journals*, 229. A sensitive treatment of Marsh's role in this dispute is found in John Brewer, *The Pleasures of the Imagination: English Culture in the Eighteenth Century* (New York: Farrar, Straus and Giroux, 1997), 544.

9. This, for example, is the conclusion of William Weber in *The Rise of Musical Classics in Eighteenth-Century England: A Study of Canon, Ritual, and Ideology* (Oxford: Clarendon Press, 1992).

10. Simon McVeigh *Concert Life in London from Mozart to Haydn*, (Cambridge: Cambridge University Press, 1993), 11-13.

11. Weber, *The Rise of Musical Classics*, especially chapter 7, "The Ideology of Ancient Music," 198-222, and the same author's "The Intellectual Origins of Musical Canon in Eighteenth-Century England" *Journal of the American Musicological Society* 47 (1994): 488-520.

12. William Weber, "The 1784 Handel Commemoration as Political Ritual" *Journal of British Studies* 28 (1989): 51. Weber finds that ancient music advocates like William Jones of Nayland attacked modern music by "drawing on the language of the Tory critique of commercialism at the start of the century" but stresses that "musical Toryism" was "a matter of cultural values more than political party."

13. Weber, "The 1784 Handel Commemoration as Political Ritual": 51.

14. William Jones (of Nayland) *A Treatise on the Art of Music, in which the Elements of HARMONY and AIR are Practically Considered . . .* (Colchester, 1784), 49.

15. Jones, *A Treatise on the Art of Music*, iv: In modern music "Novelty and custom . . . have given sanction to degenerate Harmony, wildness of Air, effeminacy, tautology and affected difficulties, inconsistent with the powers

and beauties of Expression." Jones of Nayland's complaints are not unlike a familiar critique of Italian opera — ultimate the source of the modern instrumental style — that appears in *The Dunciad.* As Pope points out in a footnote: "Every Reader will see, that from this verse to the 68th is a detach'd piece. . . . The Attitude given to this Phantom represents the nature and genius of the *Italian* Opera; its affected airs, its effeminate sounds, and the practice of patching up these Operas with favourite Songs, incoherently put together. These things were supported by the subscriptions of the Nobility." See *The Twickenham Edition of the Poems of Alexander Pope* 6 vols. ed. John Butt; vol. 5 *The Dunciad* ed. James Sutherland (New Haven: Yale University Press, 1963), 345.

16. James E. Matthew, "The Antient Concerts, 1776-1848" *Proceedings of the Royal Musical Association* 33 (1906): 57.

17. In *Concert Life in London from Mozart to Haydn*, 11-13, Simon McVeigh shows that elitism was a factor at all of the concert series since the same social classes dominated the management of all of the concerts.

18. Weber, "The Fabric of Daily Life and the Autobiography of John Marsh": 152. Discomfort with the social life of a country squire was one of the factors that caused Marsh to move from his inherited estate Nethersole to a less socially demanding life in Chichester.

19. From an unpublished page of Burney's fragmentary memoirs for 1805 in the Osborn Collection, Beineke Library, Yale University (no shelf mark).

20. Weber's analysis of the repertoire of the Concert of Ancient Music (*The Rise of Musical Classics*, 174-176) shows, for example, that when Italian opera appeared on the program display arias were deliberately avoided in favor of slower, more contemplative types.

21. Thus William Jones of Nayland writes in *Physiological Disquisitions; or Discourses on the Natural Philosophy of the Elements* (London, 1781), p. 350: "most of the pieces of Coreli, Geminiani, Handel, Martini, Stanley, etc, have a character of their own: their several pieces are distinct and original, so that each in new in respect of the other. But with much music of a modern date this not the case, because the genius and style of it renders it in a great measure incapable of true variety."

22. In *Essays Historical and Critical, on English Church Music*, 344, Mason speaks in favor of the music of Purcell. "[W]ere they cleared of their scientific modulation, which they might be in many passages without prejudicing their general harmony," Mason argues, "they would certainly be the best models of that style, which ought to prevail in Church Music." By way of example, Mason asserts (p. 345) that there is "little learning or ingenuity in that very plain and Simple harmony which Purcell has set to [the anthems] *Peace be within thy walls*, and to *O visit me with thy salvation*; yet the expression and pathos of these passages have a greater effect on even the learned ear, than any complicated contrivance in fugue or imitation which that sublime genius ever produced."

23. This alternative voice is more difficult to identify because it appears characteristically in the writing of literary men who were not practicing musicians

and because musicians themselves could not afford to risk an important source of partonage by speaking publicly against the old music movement. See Irving, *Ancient and Moderns*, 102-140. Among the more important sources point to an ideology of modern music are [Benjamin Stillingfleet] *Principles and Power of Harmony* (London, 1771), Mason's *Essays Historical and Critical, on English Church Music*, and Alexander Molleson, "Melody, the Soul of Music" in *Miscellanies in Prose and Verse* (Glascow, 1806).

24. Mason, *Works*, 381.

25. Ibid., 333.

26. Charles Burney's review of Mason's *Essays, historical and critical on English Church Music* in *Monthly Review* 20 (1796): 401, objects strenuously to Mason's suggestion. Though he was a champion of modern music, Burney felt that introducing it into church would "instantly carry the minds of many hearers from the church to the opera, concerts, and playhouses."

27. For example, Joseph Cooper Walker's *Historical Memoirs of the Irish Bards* (Dublin, 1786). Charles Burney wrote in his review of this book [*Monthly Review* 77 (1787), 433] that Walker's "knowledge of music [is] as small, as his credulity in Hibernian antiquites is great." Similar works from the period include Philip Yorke's *The Royal Tribes of Wales*, Edward Jones's *Musical and Poetical Relics of the Welsh Bards* and Charlotte Brooke's *Reliques of Irish Poetry*, along with Alexander Molleson's slender pamphlet *Melody the Soul of Music* cited above.

28. *Journals*, 47.

29. Essay, 981. See also *Hints*, 1.

30. Ibid., 981-982.

31. *Journals*, 48.

32. Ibid.

33. Ibid.

34. Ibid.

35. Ibid., 81-82.

36. Ibid., 141.

37. Ibid., 500.

38. Ibid., 501.

39. Ibid., 442.

40. Ibid., 679-680.

41. Ibid., 587.

42. Ibid., 528.

43. Ibid.

44. Ibid, 285.

45. Ibid., 102.

46. Ibid., 153. The date in question was December 13, 1776.

47. Ibid., 602 and n. 20.

48. Ibid., 492. The date is April, 1791.

49. Ibid., 262.

50. Ibid., 165.

51. See Douglas Reid and Brian Pritchard, "Some Festival Programs of the Eighteenth and Nineteenth Centuries: 1. Salisbury and Winchester" *Royal Musical Association Research Chronicle* 5 (1965): 51-79. The 1777 festival included what is described (p. 59) as "Te Deum and Jubilate, and two Anthems" including "pieces which are accommodated to the much admired church of the Italian masters."

52. Some later observers found the Concert of Ancient Music's acceptance of the Neapolitan style a contradiction to its expressed value system. Charles Burney's friend and correspondent Thomas Twining remarks in a review of Burney's *An Account of the Musical Performances in Westminster Abbey. . . in Commemoration of Handel* in *Critical Review* 59 (1785): 130, "the writer of this article remembers a time, not very distant, when [Neapolitan opera composer] *Pergolesi*, who is now adopted as an *Ancient*, and whose works are become of *age* to merit *preservation*, was regarded with a jealous eye by the *Handelomaniacs*, and one of the chief fountains of *modern* degeneracy and corruption."

53. *Journals*, 362-363.

54. Ibid., 363.

55. Ibid.

56. Ibid.

57. "Comparison," 981.

58. *Hints*, 1.

59. "Comparison," 981.

60. Ibid.

61. Ibid., 985.

62. Ibid.

63. Ibid.

64. Ibid.

65. Ibid., 986.

Revising Rousseau: Young, Legrand d'Aussy, and the Challenge to Enlightenment Constructions of the Peasantry, 1787-1794

AMY WYNGAARD

> Toujours des voyages de Suisse, d'Angleterre, d'Italie, de tous les états du monde enfin et jamais des voyages de France! Nous recherchons, nous lisons avec avidité tout ce qui concerne les pays étrangers; et le nôtre, qui, dans ses diverses provinces, offre des mœurs, des usages, des productions, des montagnes . . . qu'il serait pour nous si utile et si intéressant de connaître, le nôtre, dont la description bien faite deviendrait un travail si sûr d'être accueilli par des Français, nous ne le connaissons pas![1]

Thus laments Pierre-Jean-Baptiste Legrand d'Aussy in the introduction to his *Voyage dans la haute et basse Auvergne*, which he undertook in 1787 and 1788. Certainly, for most of the eighteenth century, French travelers of both the adventurer and armchair types had their eyes turned toward foreign lands and their exotic inhabitants: the Persia of Chardin and Montesquieu, the Tahiti of Bougainville and Diderot, the Peru of La Condamine and Graffigny, just to name a few. In the years preceding the Revolution, however, the voyage in France became popular among scientists and philosophers, professional and amateur, who, in the spirit of the Enlightenment quest for knowledge, set out to explore and document the different customs, climates, and soils of the nation.[2] Following the models of Rousseau and Buffon, voyagers such as the comte de Guibert, the abbé Papon, Jean Dusaulx, François Marlin, and Horace de Saussure, among dozens of others, documented the details of their travels for a French public increasingly interested in reading about the terrain and population of its own country.[3]

The voyage of Legrand d'Aussy is representative of this burgeoning interest in travel for scientific and philosophical inquiry in late eighteenth-century France. A Jesuit traveling in Auvergne recounting his discoveries in letters to his friend the abbé de Fontanay, editor of the *Journal général de France*, Legrand d'Aussy was primarily interested in geology and mineralogy, although a later, three-volume edition of his *Voyages*, published in 1794, expanded upon the ethnographic aspects of his work in response to criticism directed at his 1788 edition charging that he was more interested in rocks than people.[4] The voyage of Arthur Young, an Englishman who set out to study French agriculture in order to bring ideas and improvements back to England, was largely inspired by the interest in the reform of French farming techniques generated by the writings of the physiocrats and the agronomists in the second half of the eighteenth century. Although their primary objects of inquiry differed, both authors shared an interest in documenting the condition of the contemporary peasantry, providing lengthy and moving testimonies to the tragic state of farming, the heavy burden of taxes, and the overwhelming poverty and misery that plagued the inhabitants of the French countryside.

As I will argue in this essay, the works of these two travelers are significant not only because of the historical and cultural information they contain, but also because they expose the critical pretensions of Enlightenment travel literature, fictional and documentary. Containing the most detailed descriptions of the state of the French peasantry ever before published in the eighteenth century, the *Voyages* of Young and Legrand d'Aussy reveal the extent to which eighteenth-century notions of national identity were based not simply on the construct of the foreign other, but more importantly on the exclusion of the native peasant from French society and consciousness. The writings of Young and Legrand d'Aussy define a key moment in French history, when the public was forced—by both the texts and the events they documented—to confront the realities of peasant existence with the fictional representations propagated by Enlightenment authors, artists, and thinkers. In the pages that follow, I will provide a comparative reading of their texts within the context of eighteenth-century cultural production, showing how the two authors both prepare and prefigure the social and political crises of self-definition faced by the French nation in the years surrounding the Revolution. As I will suggest, if the peasantry is ultimately freed from earlier fictions, it is only to be re-inscribed by emerging Republican mythologies.

I

When the texts of Young and Legrand d'Aussy revealed to the public the tragic state of the French peasantry, many readers may have been unaware of the extent of contemporary rural misery. Although peasants represented approximately two-thirds of the French population, the absent aristocratic landlord and the middle- or upper-class city dweller had little understanding of their way of life.[5] After the writings of Vauban, Boisguillebert, and Fénelon at the end of Louis XIV's reign, lamenting the poverty and misery found in the countryside and adamantly calling for reforms, the realities of peasant life were increasingly eclipsed by literary and artistic representations that had little or nothing to do with actuality.[6] While early eighteenth-century critics such as the abbé Dubos, the marquis d'Argens, and Saint-Mard set the scene for the production of more realistic images of village life by attacking the pastoral genre typified by Fontenelle and calling for portrayals of the peasantry that were verisimilar, the representations that developed out of these theories elevated the "natural," or that which appealed to the sentiments, over the "real," seen as vulgar.[7] Over the course of the century, writers and painters, Rousseau, Rétif de la Bretonne, Greuze, and Fragonard most prominent among them, advanced sentimentalized portrayals of virtuous and happy peasants, creating an idealized vision of the countryside and its inhabitants as the repository of all that was good in society, in direct contrast to the corruption and decadence found in the city and the court.

As critics such as Harvey Chisick and David Denby have pointed out, these sentimental representations served an important social and political function. Valorizing portraits of peasant simplicity and goodness served to cultivate feelings of commonality and universality in the public, helping to foster an imagined community of French citizens that saw themselves as sharing the same patriotic values of virtue, humanity, and charity.[8] At the same time, however, these portrayals served to dissimulate—and thereby ensure the continuation of—a troubling and potentially explosive reality. Robert Mauzi sees the eighteenth-century peasant vogue as based in a cynical social conservatism, suggesting that it allowed members of the bougeoisie to forget about the peasantry in good conscience while at the same time serving to advance their cause by celebrating the moral superiority of the non-noble:

> [Le bourgeois] ne peut abandonner le peuple qu'en étant bien convaincu qu'il n'existe aucune urgence à modifier son état. D'où l'importance de cette littérature, moins "littéraire" qu'on ne le croit, qui célèbre avec transport le bonheur campagnard et l'oppose au martyre doré des gens du monde. . . . Bien loin de modifier la condition des humbles, il faut les fixer dans leur essence, les enfermer dans le halo magique de la frugalité heureuse. Ils sont trop précieux, tels qu'ils sont, comme justification mythique des revendications bourgeoises.[9]

As with the bourgeoisie, the social and political agendas of the enlightened nobility were similarly advanced by idealized representations of the peasantry and farming. Beginning in the 1760s, the physiocrats, champions of agricultural reform, propagated rose-colored portraits of village life that ultimately ran counter to the improvement of the peasantry's lot. Seeing the revivification of the traditional social order as essential to the health of farming and the wealth of the nation, they sought to inspire aristocrats to return to their lands and take a renewed interest in agriculture and the peasantry.[10] Presenting images of rural life that focused on the happiness the nobility could derive from its contacts with the simple, loving villager, physiocratic publications consistently blurred the lines between theory and propaganda.[11] Their journal, *Les Ephémérides du Citoyen* (1765-1772), served as an advertisement for contemporary literature and art that promulgated visions of harmonious, happy relationships between peasant and seigneur, featuring enthusiastic reviews of works such as Favart's *Les Moissonneurs* (1768), Saint-Lambert's *Saisons* (1769), and Marmontel's *Silvain* (1770).[12] Indeed, if peasant poverty was mentioned by the physiocrats, it was most often within the context of emotional tales of seigneurial beneficence geared toward making the prospect of rural life more appealing to an aristocracy searching to redefine its role in society and justify its claims to the leadership of the nation.[13] Significantly, the eventual demise of the physiocratic movement can in part be traced to this unsettling disregard for the condition of peasantry and the lower classes.[14]

The increasing focus on the colonialist project in the eighteenth century, I would suggest, also contributed to the dissimulation of peasant realities: to concentrate on the savage within instead of outside national boundaries was potentially to put into question theories of the supremacy of French civilization and the nation's progress, upon which notions of conquest and exploitation were largely founded.[15] Further, to develop the obvious comparisons between colonial slaves and French peasants was to risk igniting humanitarian debates and shaking the very basis of the nation's political economy.[16] While these are oversimplifications for the sake of argument, the fact remains that the condition of the peasantry was sublimated for a number of economic, political, and social—not to mention purely aesthetic—reasons over the course of the eighteenth century. As the 1763-1789 debates on educating the peasantry show, it was in the interest of the nation to overlook peasant ignorance and backwardness; for, as it was commonly feared, to do anything about it would raise class consciousness and discontent, as well as increase the desire for upward mobility, and France would be left without a food source.[17]

The writings of Young and Legrand d'Aussy are interesting precisely because they bring the condition of the peasantry to light just before and during the crises of the Great Fear and Revolution, when the peasantry not only had an important role in the actual events, but was also held up as a symbol of the oppressed Third Estate in the abbé Sieyès's January 1789 pamphlet "Qu'est-ce que le Tiers Etat?" and in the propagandistic imagery surrounding the meeting of the Estates-General in May 1789.[18] Both authors were aware of the importance of their works as a documentation of the class troubles and inequities that led to the Revolution, and Legrand d'Aussy took pains to emphasize and justify this pre-Revolutionary conflict in his 1794 edition. His expanded edition contains a number of patriotic and anti-aristocratic exclamations vindicating the rights of the oppressed and glorifying the Republican cause:

> L'Auvergne, devenue libre par la grande révolution qui a régénéré la France, va changer aussi; et c'est alors que le patriotisme, brisant le joug qui l'écrasait et ranimant son courage éteint, verra naître ces jours de bonheur et de prospérité que depuis si longtemps il ne lui était plus permis d'espérer (I: 85-86).

In contrast to Legrand d'Aussy's text, Young's work poses a direct challenge to notions of French nationalism and patriotism. Young writes from a position of perceived superiority—the England he portrays is a land of agricultural wealth, social harmony, and parliamentary representation, whereas France suffers from poor leadership, insufficient mastery of agricultural techniques, and a shocking disregard for the misery of the populace. For Young, then, the French peasant is the «other» that serves to measure and affirm English cultural dominance, a notion certainly troubling to contemporary French readers, who had access to the English edition as early as 1792 and a French translation in 1793.[19] Timely and opportunistic, the texts of Young and Legrand d'Aussy were written and published during a critical period when France was becoming increasingly aware of its national space and citizens. Confronting the public with unsettling truths from within France and abroad, the two authors attest to the shift in the social and political imaginaries being effectuated on the eve of the French Republic's advent, suggesting that their travels may have played a role in the re-scripting of cultural paradigms.

II

In the course of three voyages undertaken between 1787 and 1790, Young traveled through most of France. During his first trip, from May 15 to November 15, 1787, he visited central, southwestern, and western France, including the regions surrounding Clermont, Toulouse, Cahors, Bordeaux, Poitiers, and Tours. During his second journey, from August 1 to October 15, 1788, he concentrated on Normandy and Brittany. On his last and longest voyage, from the beginning of June 1789 to the end of January 1790, he focused on the eastern part of France, or the triangle formed by Paris, Strasbourg, and Moulins, including the regions surrounding Nancy, Strasbourg, Dijon, and Besançon, as well as Aix, Marseille, and Chambéry; this trip was framed by longer stays in Paris during which Young witnessed important Revolutionary events. Young's account of his trips takes two distinct forms, inspired by his desire to combine the pleasurable and the didactic: the first, a journal, where he recounts his impressions and experiences on an almost daily basis; the second, a treatise on the state of French agriculture, where he summarizes what he saw and incorporates information taken from other written sources.

Of the two, Young's journal provides the most vivid account of the state of the peasantry before the Revolution. He is consistently struck by the misery, hunger, and ignorance he encounters in almost every region of France. Hosted and guided by the political and economic elite, enjoying the best that Parisian and provincial society have to offer, Young has every opportunity to remark on the contrast between rich and poor:

> Quel miracle que toute cette splendeur et cette richesse des villes en France n'aient aucun rapport avec l'état de la campagne! Il n'y a pas de transitions graduelles: la médiocrité aisée et la richesse, la richesse et la magnificence. D'un bond vous passez de la misère à la prodigalité, de mendiants dans leur hutte de boue à mademoiselle Saint-Huberti,

> dans des spectacles splendides de 500 livres par soirée (I: 158).

Particularly disturbed by the juxtaposition of rural desolation and the splendors of Chantilly and Versailles, Young suggests that France's socio-economic inequities derive from the government's lack of understanding that national prosperity is based on the happiness of all individuals (I: 23, 129). Page after page, Young critiques the French government for going to war so often ("des guerres éternelles qui arrêtent tous les travaux utiles et répandent la désolation là où les efforts privés tendaient à appeler le bonheur" (I: 82)), for promoting theories of agriculture but not putting them into practice ("le progrès d'une agriculture nationale demande autre chose que des académies et des mémoires" (I: 94)), or for grossly misappropriating funds in building grand bridges to impress foreign travelers while ignoring the state of its people ("quel voyageur . . . ne souhaitera moins d'apparente splendeur et plus de bien-être réel" (I: 69)). In Languedoc, faced with what he sees as yet another misuse of government funds, Young's indignation turns to satire:

> Des femmes sans bas, beaucoup même sans souliers; mais si leurs pieds sont pauvrement couverts, il leur reste la *superbe* consolation de les poser sur une chaussée grandiose; la nouvelle voie a cinquante pieds de large, plus cinquante autres déblayés pour lui faire place (I: 53; Young's emphasis).

A gifted rhetorician, Young provides moving accounts of his discussions with the peasantry. (throughout his text) At one point he recounts a conversation with a poor woman from the area surrounding Metz who bitterly complains about the burden of taxes and feudal rights:

> Elle me dit que son mari n'avait qu'un coin de terre, une vache et un pauvre petit cheval; cependant il devait comme serf à un seigneur un frauchard (42 lb.) de froment et trois poulets, à un autre, 4 frauchards d'avoine, un poulet et un sou, puis venaient de lourdes tailles et autres impôts. . . . Dieu nous vienne en aide, ajouta-t-elle, *car les tailles et les droits nous écrasent* (I: 235; Young's emphasis).

Young goes on to give a jarring description of the woman: "Même d'assez près on lui eut donné de 60 à 70 ans, tant elle était courbée et tant sa figure était ridée et endurcie par le travail; elle me dit n'en avoir que 28." For Young, the physical appearance of French peasant women is a clear sign of the superiority of England. There women maintain their beauty and femininity, as they are not forced to work as hard as men:

> Un Anglais qui n'a pas quitté son pays ne peut se figurer l'apparence des paysannes en France: elle annonce, à première vue, un travail dur et pénible; je les crois plus laborieuses que les hommes, et la fatigue plus douloureuse encore de donner au monde une nouvelle génération d'esclaves venant s'y joindre, elles perdent toute régularité des traits et tout caractère féminin. A quoi attribuerons-nous cette différence entre la basse classe des deux royaumes? Au gouvernement (I: 235-36).

In a series of lengthy passages, Young attributes the majority of the social ills he witnesses to the abuses of the feudal system. According to Young, aristocratic landowners are much more interested in living a life of luxury than in doing anything to help their peasant subjects or advance the agricultural wealth of the nation: "Les seigneurs ont une malheureuse préférence à s'entourer de forêts, de sangliers et de chasseurs, au lieu de germes propres et bien cultivées, de chaumières avenantes et de gais paysans" (I: 91). Once again, the state of French civilization is put directly into question in his description of the town of Combourg, a passage of particular interest because of his criticism of the brother of the Romantic author François de Chateaubriand:

> Le pays a un aspect sauvage; la culture n'est pas beaucoup plus avancé que chez les Hurons, ce qui paraît incroyable au milieu de ces terrains si bons. Les gens sont presque aussi sauvages que leur pays, et leur ville de Combourg est une des plus ignoblement sales que l'on puisse voir. . . . Il y a cependant un château, et qui est habité. Quel est donc ce M. de Chateaubriand, le propriétaire, dont les nerfs s'arrangent d'un séjour au milieu de tant de misères et de saletés? (I: 146-47).

If the living conditions of the peasantry evoke visions of "savage" Native Americans rather than picturesque scenes, Young believes that the French nobility and monarchy are to blame. Continually faced with the spectacle of abandoned lands and starving peasants, he challenges French leaders to act: "Ah! Si pour un jour j'étais le législateur de la France, comme je ferais sauter les grands seigneurs!" (I: 84).

Highly cognizant of increasing class tensions, Young predicts revolution throughout his accounts of 1787 and 1788. Witness to the riots surrounding the grain shortages and the events of the Great Fear in the summer of 1789, Young sides with the peasantry despite his avowed aversion to violence: "Quel malheur que la noblesse, au lieu d'être le soutien, la bienfaitrice de ses pauvres voisins, devienne son tyran par ces exécrables droits féodaux! N'y a-t-il donc que les révolutions qui, en brûlant ses châteaux, la forcent à céder à la violence ce qu'elle devait accorder à la misère et à l'humanité?" (I: 329). He even goes so far as to suggest that the beleaguered aristocracy is not worthy of compassion, but deserves what it gets (I: 272). Eager to show his affinity for the French underclass when faced with a menacing crowd, Young delivers a speech comparing the state of affairs in France and England. Praising his nation's tax system, he proclaims: "Nous avons, messieurs, un grand nombre de taxes qui vous sont inconnues en France; mais le *tiers état*, les pauvres n'en sont chargés, ce sont les riches qui paient. . . . le pauvre fermier en est exempt, bien mieux, le riche, en Angleterre, contribue au soulagement du pauvre" (I: 254-55; Young's emphasis).

Significantly, Young reveals that his performance is predominately guided by an instinct for self-preservation, a gesture that evokes the bad faith implicit throughout his account. Despite the didactic and humanitarian emphasis he initially ascribes to his project, he proves to have little interest in helping ameliorate the state of French agriculture. At one point he notes that it is a waste of time for him to suggest improvements to members of agricultural societies, as they have only committed "sottises" (blunders) in the past (I: 188, 274). Further, he dismisses French peasants as ignorant and stubborn, believing them to be unwilling or unable to recognize the benefits of fertilizer, crop rotation, enclosures, and irrigation. Although he does express hope that the creation of a new government will help to improve French farming conditions, his account essentially shows that there are only negative lessons to be learned from France (I: 345). For Young, the state of agriculture and the peasantry in France only points to English enlightenment and superiority, and in the end he holds up his nation's social, political, economic, and agricultural model for the new French Republic to follow.

III

Like the *Voyages* of Young, Legrand d'Aussy's work documents the destitute state of the French peasantry, although his account differs sensibly from Young's due to his professed emotional ties to his fellow citizens. Throughout his text, he describes at length the problems faced by the Auvergnats. According to Legrand d'Aussy, poor soil, backward farming techniques, high taxes, frequent natural disasters, and high rates of birth and mortality destroy their patience and courage, causing many to become lazy, alcoholic, and resigned to ignorance. Struggling to support their families, many are forced to migrate annually to find work in other regions or countries (I: 78-89). Legrand d'Aussy sees this migration as particularly tragic, summarizing his thoughts in an acerbic critique of government officials who argue that the migrations are good for the economy:

> Quel avantage, grand Dieu! Que celui qui annuellement chasse de leurs foyers une grande partie des habitants; qui rend désertes des communes entières, n'y laisse que les infirmes, les enfants et les femmes . . . qui enlevant à l'agriculture une quantité infinie d'hommes utiles, ne les renvoie à leurs familles que corrompus par des vices étrangers, ou gangrenés par les suites du libertinage; tandis qu'un grand nombre, ou renoncent à leur patrie . . . ou meurent loin d'elle (III: 291-92).

In describing these devastations, Legrand d'Aussy plays to the reader's emotions by emphasizing the destruction caused to the family, at several points providing vivid descriptions of the ravages brought about by venereal disease: "Malheureusement, il en est beaucoup qui rapportent dans leurs foyers les germes de maladies infames, qu'ils ont prises dans leurs caravannes; et par eux sont infectées des épouses honnêtes, qui bientôt languissent, ou périssent, comme eux, des suites d'un mal qu'elles ignorent" (I: 81). His account is interspersed with sentimental interjections designed to appeal to the reader's sympathy: "le pauvre habitant, sans ressource et sans espoir malgré son travail excessif, est devenu aussi malheureux qu'un être humain puisse jamais le devenir. Faut-il s'étonner après cela s'il fuit sa terre natale! Où pourrait-il être aussi à plaindre?" (I: 331). Careful to combine this pity with admiration, he praises at length the work ethic that compels the Auvergnat to leave his home: "Forcé de quitter sa terre natale, [l'Auvergnat] ne va point, comme d'autres peuples, mendier sans pudeur dans les départements voisins. Né laborieux, s'il abandonne son pays et ses parents, c'est pour chercher ailleurs du travail; et voilà, selon moi, qu'un écrivain honnête ne saurait trop louer" (II: 31).

Consistently appealing to the power of emotion, Legrand d'Aussy sees his account as fulfilling an important social function. He wants to show the rest of France the unfortunate state of this "canton ignoré" and generate public concern and government action. With false modesty, he posits himself as the advocate of the poor Auvergnat natives:

> on trouve un pays pauvre, un sol détestable, enfin des habitants malheureux, mais intéressants par leur travail et leur misère; et, à ce titre, dignes d'occuper une place honorable dans un ouvrage comme le mien. Il est si doux d'avoir à parler pour des humains qui souffrent! Le sort de ceux-ci m'a touché. Je dois plaider leur cause. Que n'ont-ils un avocat plus éloquent! (I: 329).

His account is so repetitive, in fact, that at one point he chides himself for his incessant harangues and promises his reader he will focus his account on the character and customs of the people rather than on their miserable condition: "Mais c'est trop m'arrêter sur ces lamentables et monotones tableaux d'expatriation, de misère, de villes pauvres, de manufactures ruinées par l'excès ou le mode erroné des impôts. Les Auvergnats ont dû m'occuper avant tout" (II: 39).

In spite of this professed respect and compassion, Legrand d'Aussy reveals his disdain and prejudice throughout the text. On several occasions he portrays the peasantry as subhuman savages, suggesting that the Auvergnat is less physically developed than other Frenchmen: "Robuste et nerveux, il est lent et lourd. Ses formes sont grossières, sa stature médiocre, sa physionomie sans traits, ses mouvements sans grâce. . . . ce n'est qu'une masse pesante" (III: 279). Further, when he learns that mountain villagers beat each other with sticks when angry, he admits that his indignation is somewhat alleviated by the fact that the injured parties rarely die, as their skulls are thicker than in other regions of France (III: 277). Similarly, he notes that mountain families have the disturbing practice of living with their animals in the stables during the cold winter months (II: 182-83). But for Legrand d'Aussy, the clearest sign of their barbarity is their savage treatment of women, described in a passage that evokes Buffon's theories on the condition of women as the measure of civilization:

> Ces rustres montagnards ont, pour les femmes, ce profond mépris et ce dédain despotique, qui est propre à toutes les peuplades sauvages ou demi-barbares. Ils les regardent comme des esclaves, destinées à tous les travaux qu'ils réputent vils et qu'ils dédaignent (II: 179-80).[20]

Although such passages may appear to work against Legrand d'Aussy's proclaimed goals, exposing the public to these unflattering details of peasant life fulfills a greater critical purpose. Throughout the text, the author claims that he aims to combat the pastoral vision of the peasantry propagated by literary and artistic representation, which he suggests has impeded rural progress and development. In describing a particularly picturesque mountain scene, for example, he attacks his reader's idealized images of rural life:

> D'après ce tableau brillant, tu vas te faire sans doute l'idée la plus avantageuse des cantons qui possèdent ces bestiaux nombreux. Tu vas comparer le paysan qui les habite à ces patriarches anciens que leur opulence rendait si puissants, quoiqu'ils ne fussent riches qu'en troupeaux. Détrompe-toi, mon ami. Jamais rapprochement ne fut plus erroné (II: 385-86).

Later, he criticizes the authors who have contributed to the proliferation of these "mensonges" (lies): «Il ne tiendrait qu'à moi d'y trouver les mœurs de ce prétendu siècle d'or, qui né dans le cerveau des poètes, est devenu la chimère de tous les peuples et celle même de presque toutes les religions. . . . je puis t'assurer . . . qu'il n'est guère possible d'avoir à la fois et un séjour plus affreux, et une vie plus malheureuse» (II: 394). However, Legrand d'Aussy ultimately shows himself to be profoundly ambivalent, expressing disappointment when he does not find the same idyllic scenes in real life as in Rousseau («Combien de détails rustiques nous charment sous la plume d'un écrivain agréable, qui, vus de près, rebutent et ne sont que dégoûtants!» (II: 395)), and tearfully rejoices when he does come across a scene worthy of *Julie* or *Emile*. Describing the moral perfection of the family commune of the Quittards in the hamlet of Pinon, he proclaims: «A Pinon, le vœu de Rousseau est accompli» (I: 483).

In fact, despite protestations to the contrary, Legrand d'Aussy contributes to the corpus of sentimental peasant imagery in his descriptions of the patriarchal, egalitarian commune of the Quittard-Pinon. Adding his portrayal to earlier evocations of the family published by the marquis de Mirabeau, the abbé Rozier, and Rétif de la Bretonne, among others, he praises the community's quasi-socialist organization: "Dans Pinon, l'administration est paternelle; mais elle est élective. . . . Tous travaillent, en commun, à la chose publique. Logés et nourris ensemble, habillés et entretenus de la même manière et aux dépens du revenu général, ils ne sont plus, en quelque sorte, que les enfants de la maison" (I: 477). He also describes their dedication to their community and humanity, emphasizing the generosity and hospitality they show in training their dogs not to bite a poor beggar who comes in search of food and shelter: "Quelle bonté réfléchie, quelle âme humaine et compatissante . . . ! Ah! Puissent-ils prospérer à jamais ces honnêtes gens, si dignes d'être heureux!" (I: 486). He sees the Quittard-Pinon as a microcosm of the ideal Republican state:

> Ces égards, cet accueil, le spectacle de cette famille patriarchale, composée de tous les âges depuis la vieillesse jusqu'à la plus tendre enfance, auraient suffi seuls pour m'intéresser. Mais ce que je ne pus voir sans émotion . . . c'était surtout le tableau de concorde et d'union, de bonheur et de santé, que me présentait cette république de parents (I: 487-88).

The representational shift that Legrand d'Aussy operates in these passages is highly significant. Reshaping sentimental images of the peasantry to fit an emerging Republican agenda, his portrayal is representative of a larger recasting of peasant imagery taking place at the time. Authors such as Le Bouvier-Desmortiers, in his 1789 *Coup d'œil sur l'Auvergne*, and Republican visionaries such as Cambacérès and Maréchal, similarly draw upon descriptions of the Quittard-Pinon in their works, seeing in their egalitarian organization and self-sufficient economy the reflection of hoped-for social and political reforms.[21] The appropriation and diffusion of portrayals of the Quittard-Pinon by Legrand d'Aussy and his contemporaries attest to the power of mythic images of the peasantry and rural life in the (re-)formation of ideas of self and nation in eighteenth-century France, particularly during the Revolutionary period. In many ways, the proliferation of portrayals of the Quittard-Pinon can be seen as the triumph of peasant reality over fiction, designating an historical moment when peasant imagery, although idealized, was used to foster not social immobility, but progress.

The difficulty that Legrand d'Aussy experiences in reconciling peasant reality and representation is indicative of the challenges that faced the French public confronted with the accounts of both travelers. He makes reference to these difficulties when addressing a number of criticisms directed at his 1788 edition. In mounting his defense, Legrand d'Aussy refers to the attacks launched against "l'homme véridique et courageux qui entreprendra d'écrire sur notre France":

> Ce n'est plus en lui un historien erroné qu'on critique; c'est un ennemi qu'on dénonce. De toutes parts, les haines s'éveillent; les coteries s'ameutent; et les sots, criant vengeance, lui cherchent partout des adversaires. Peut-être lui eût-on pardonné ses erreurs; on ne lui pardonne pas sa véracité (III: 155-56).

Above all, Legrand d'Aussy feels vindicated by the fact that he has recounted the truth, however difficult it may be for the public to bear. Most importantly, he claims, he accomplished what he set out to do by calling attention to the condition of the Auvergnats, noting that his 1788 edition was instrumental in alerting the government to the devastation caused by excessive taxation and rural exodus (III: 158-59).

By exposing the condition of the contemporary French peasantry and challenging the status quo, the *Voyages* of Young and Legrand d'Aussy are both testimonies to and one of the forces behind the moment of cultural crisis and redefinition when France was forced to come to terms with the savage within its borders at the end of the eighteenth century. While Young shows that the reality of the peasant condition put into question notions of French cultural superiority, Legrand d'Aussy demonstrates the extent to which peasant fictions were essential to notions of both individual and national identity, and just how difficult it was to let go of these constructions. Although both Young and Legrand d'Aussy are optimistic that the events of the Revolution and the actions of a Republican government will improve the lot of the contemporary peasantry, Young notes in a 1792 addendum to his text that very little had actually changed (II: 465).

Reforms such as those undertaken by the abbé Grégoire in 1790 attempted to address some of the most evident problems, trying to unite city and country in France and to civilize the peasant through the standardization of language and education. However, these reforms revealed the same desire to control and subjugate the peasantry through the manipulation of sign and representation manifested throughout the eighteenth century. Aiming to quell any counter-revolutionary sentiment present in the countryside, Grégoire and his advocates essentially wanted to teach the peasantry enough French to be able to assimilate Republican propaganda. Following on the Republican peasant mythologies established by Legrand d'Aussy and others, these reforms contributed to the advancement of yet another ideologically motivated image of the peasant in the early 1790s. Reinvented as the innocent, virtuous embodiment of the primitive roots of all French citizens, in a gesture that drew upon the role the rural population played in bringing about the establishment of a new political order, the peasant of representation was again used to cover a thinly veiled reality that soon emerged in the violent events surrounding the 1793 Vendée counter-revolution.[22] Ironically, it was only in the late nineteenth century, some 80 years after the failure of Grégoire's project, that the condition of the peasantry was meaningfully addressed by government officials and humanitarians alike.[23] In the end, the peasant remains one of the major paradoxes of the Enlightenment project, showing the extent to which the philosophical ideals of inquiry and observation were based on a refusal to see or make seen the majority and least enlightened of French citizens.

NOTES

1. Pierre-Jean-Baptiste Legrand d'Aussy, *Voyage fait en 1787 et 1788 dans la ci-devant Haute et Basse Auvergne.* 3 vols. (Paris: 1794), I: v-vj. I have modernized the French in all citations.

2. Jean M. Goulemot, Paul Lidsky, Didier Masseau, eds., *Le Voyage en France. Anthologie des voyageurs Européens en France, du Moyen-Age à la fin de l'Empire.* 2 vols. (Paris: Robert Laffont, 1995), I: i-xxvi, 589.

3. See, for example, Jacques-Antoine-Hyppolyte Guibert, *Voyages dans diverses parties de la France et en Suisse, faits en 1775, 1778, 1784, 1785* (Paris: d'Heutel, 1806); Jean-Pierre Papon, *Voyage de Provence* (1787), ed. Godard de Donville (Paris: La Découverte, 1984); Jean Dusaulx, *Voyage à Barège et dans les hautes-Pyrénées* (Paris, 1788); François Marlin, *Voyages en France et pays circonvoisins depuis 1775 jusqu'en 1807.* 4 vols. (Paris: Guillaume, 1817); Horace Bénédict de Saussure, *Voyage dans les Alpes* (Paris, 1834).

4. Pierre-Jean-Baptiste Legrand d'Aussy, *Voyage fait en 1787 et 1788 dans la ci-devant haute et basse Auvergne*, ed. Pierre-François Aleil (Roanne/Le Coteau: Editions Horvath, 1982), p. 5.

5. See Emmanuel Le Roy Ladurie, "De la crise ultimà la vraie croissance, 1660-1789," in *Histoire de la France rurale*, ed. Georges Duby and Armand Wallon (Paris: Seuil, 1975), II:577.

6. See Pierre le Pesant, sieur de Boisguillebert, *Le Détail de la France* (1697), in Eugène Daire, *Economistes financiers du XVIIIe siècle* (1851; Paris: Slatkine Reprints, 1971), pp. 163-247; François de Salignac de la Mothe Fénelon, *Lettre à Louis XIV* (1694) (Paris: Séquences, 1994); Sébastien le Prestre, seigneur de Vauban, *Projet d'une dîme royale* (1707), in Daire, *Economistes financiers*, pp. 33-148; see also Paul Hazard, *La Crise de la conscience européenne, 1680-1715* (Paris: Fayard, 1961), pp. 264-66.

7. See Jean Ehrard, *L'Idée de nature en France dans la première moitié du XVIIIe siècle* (Paris: Albin Michel, 1994), pp. 255-328; see also Daniel Mornet, *Le Sentiment de la Nature en France de Jean-Jacques Rousseau à Bernardin de Saint-Pierre* (1907; New York: Burt Franklin, 1971), pp. 292-352.

8. See Benedict Anderson, *Imagined Communities: Reflections on the Origin and Spread of Nationalism* (New York: Verso, 1983), pp. 41-49; Harvey Chisick, *The Limits of Reform in the Enlightenment: Attitudes Towards the Education of the Lower Classes in Eighteenth-Century France* (Princeton: Princeton University Press, 1981), pp. 215-38; David Denby, *Sentimental Narrative and the Social Order in France, 1760-1820* (New York: Cambridge University Press, 1994), pp. 95-96.

9. See Robert Mauzi, *L'Idée du bonheur dans la littérature et la pensée françaises au XVIIIe siècle* (Paris: Albin Michel, 1994), p. 168.

10. Elizabeth Fox-Genovese argues that while the physiocrats were torn between advocating traditional hierarchies and promulgating what can retrospectively be identified as a bourgeois social model, they were essentially interested in maintaining the monarchy and the status quo. See Elizabeth Fox-Genovese, *The Origins of*

Physiocracy: Economic Revolution and Social Order in Eighteenth-Century France (Ithaca: Cornell University Press, 1976), pp. 15, 27-29, 61, 212-13.

11. Throughout *L'Ami des hommes* (1756), sometimes considered the founding text of the physiocratic movement, the marquis de Mirabeau tearfully evokes the emotional gratification he derives from looking after his peasant subjects. For example: "Les larmes me viennent aux yeux, quand je songe à cette intéressante portion de l'humanité, ou quand, de ma fenêtre, comme d'un thrône, je considère toutes les obligations que nous leurs avons, quand je les vois suer sous le faix, et que me tâtant ensuite je me souviens que je suis de la même pâte d'eux." See Victor Riqueti, marquis de Mirabeau, *L'Ami des hommes*. 6 vols. (Paris, 1759-1760), I: 171-72.

12. See *Les Ephémérides du citoyen*, v. 2, part 3 (1768); v. 3, part 2 (1769); v. 4, part 2 (1769), v. 5, part 2 (1769); v. 1, part 2 (1770). For a discussion of physiocratic propaganda techniques, see Georges Weulersse, *Le Mouvement Physiocratique en France de 1756 à 1770*. 2 vols. (1910; New York: Johnson Reprint Corp., 1968), I: 91-241, II: 151-70.

13. See Roland Bonnel, *Ethique et esthétique du retour à la campagne au XVIIIe siècle* (New York: Peter Lang, 1995), pp. 1-4, 191-231; see also Sarah Maza, *Private Lives and Public Affairs: The Causes Célèbres of Prerevolutionary France* (Berkeley: University of California Press, 1993), pp. 75-76.

14. See Weulersse, *Le Mouvement physiocratique en France*, II: 572-625.

15. Michèle Duchet describes the challenge to notions of progress caused by Voltaire's assertion that the peasants of Westphalia and the Jura were just as savage and barbarous as the indigenous peoples of the Americas. See Michèle Duchet, *Anthropologie et Histoire au siècle des Lumières* (Paris: Albin Michel, 1995), pp. 307-8.

16. See Duchet, *Anthropologie et Histoire*, pp. 163-64; see also Anthony Pagden, "The Effacement of Difference: Colonialism and the Origins of Nationalism in Diderot and Herder," in Gyan Prakash, *After Colonialism: Imperial Histories and Postcolonial Displacements* (Princeton: Princeton University Press, 1995): 135-36.

17. See Chisick, *The Limits of Reform*, pp. 106-9.

18. In the weeks before the meeting of the Estates-General in May 1789, images circulated showing peasant figures carrying members of the aristocracy and clergy on their backs; portrayals depicting avenged and triumphant peasants being carried on the backs of the aristocracy and clergy were also popular. See *Images de la Révolution française*, ed. Laure Beaumont-Maillet. Laserdisk. (Oxford: Pergamon Press, 1990), in particular images 2458-69, 2523-35.

19. In fact, despite the credit immediately given to his work as a document of the state of France in 1789, the affront to the French national ego posed by Young was still close to the surface as late as 1860, when the editor of a new translation, Léonce de Lavergne, insisted on systematically pointing out all of the errors in Young's critical assessment of French agricultural techniques. See Arthur Young, *Voyages en France pendant les années 1787, 1788, 1789*, trans. M. Lesage. 2 vols.

(Paris: Guillaumin, 1860), I: xi-xxxvi.

20. Buffon writes: "Ce n'est que parmi les nations civilisées jusqu'à la politesse que les femmes ont obtenu cette égalité de condition, qui cependant est si naturelle et si nécessaire à la douceur de la société; aussi cette politesse dans les mœurs est-elle leur ouvrage, elles ont opposé à la force des armes victorieuses, lorsque par leur modestie elles nous ont appris à reconnaître l'empire de la beauté." Georges-Louis Leclerc, comte de Buffon, *Histoire naturelle de l'homme. Œuvres complètes.* 44 vols. (Paris: Verdière et Ladrange, 1824-32), XIII: 160-61.

21. For a discussion of eighteenth-century historical and literary texts treating the Quittard-Pinon, see Irmagard Hartig, "Révolution et communautés familiales. Témoignages et représentations," *Annales historiques de la Révolution française* 54 (1) 1982: 59-70.

22. See Michel de Certeau, Dominique Julia, Jacques Revel, *Une Politique de la langue. La Révolution française et les patois: L'Enquête de Grégoire* (Paris: Gallimard, 1975), pp. 9-81, 105-9, 114-16, 124-30, 152-60.

23. Certainly, it could be argued that the reforms and improvements brought to the countryside in the late nineteenth century were just as unenlightened as the eighteenth-century sublimation of the peasant condition. See Eugen Weber, *Peasants into Frenchmen: The Modernization of Rural France, 1870-1914* (Stanford: Stanford University Press, 1976).

Contributors to Volume 31

Daniel J. Ennis is Assistant Professor of English at Coastal Carolina University in Conway, South Carolina. He is the author of *Enter the Press-Gang: Naval Impressment in Eighteenth-Century British Literature*, and of recent articles about Colley Cibber, John Dryden and Christopher Smart. He is currently at work on a book about the 1779 London theater season.

James E. Evans, Professor of English at the University of North Carolina at Greensboro, is the author of *Comedy: An Annotated Bibliography of Theory and Criticism*, as well as numerous articles on Fielding, Congreve, and early British periodicals. Evans was a winner of the 1999-2000 ASECS Teaching Competition.

Howard Irving is Professor of Music at the University of Alabama at Birmingham. His recent publications include *Ancients and Moderns: William Crotch and the Development of Classical Music*, published by Ashgate Press in 1999. His paper was presented at the 2000 SEASECS meeting.

John R. Iverson is Assistant Professor of French at the University of Missouri–Columbia. He has written primarily on Voltaire, including an article on celebratory poetry and the battle of Fontenoy published in volume 28 of *Studies on Eighteenth–Century Culture*. He is currently preparing a study of heroic discourse and the concept of glory in eighteenth–century France. He will also be contributing to the edition of Voltaire's *Complete Works* at the Voltaire Foundation.

Joe Johnson is Assistant Professor of French at Georgia Southwestern State University. His essay is part of a larger project on depictions of idealized male friendship in French narrative from the Middle Ages through the Enlightenment.

Catherine Keohane recently earned her Ph.D. from Rutgers University. She is working on a project which considers eighteenth-century didactic and literary depictions of the charitable exchange in order to gain insight into gender ideology and the work of literature. She has published examinations of the way debt combines with stereotypes of the poor to confuse the moment of charitable giving and of the contradictions between one text's prefatory material and actual content.

J. David Macey, Jr. teaches Restoration and eighteenth-century British literature at the University of Puget Sound. He is currently working on a book-length study of the strategies that writers including Eliza Haywood, Samuel Richardson, Henry Fielding, Frances Burney, and Jane Austen employ to interrogate the widespread representation of women, the rural poor, and Britain's colonial subjects as figures in—and for—the culturally constructed landscape.

Leanne Maunu received her PhD in English in 2001 from Indiana University and is currently teaching at San Diego State University. Her research interests center on nationalism and women writers of the late eighteenth and early nineteenth centuries, and her current research project is entitled "Women Writing the Nation: Nationalism and Female Community in Late Eighteenth-Century Britain."

Reginald McGinnis is Associate Professor of French at the University of Arizona. He has written several articles on eighteenth- and nineteenth-century French literature and culture, as well as a book on Baudelaire: *La Prostitution sacrée* (Belin, 1994).

Brijraj Singh taught at St. Stephen's College, Delhi, and North-Eastern Hill University, Shillong, and was Professor of English at Delhi University in India before coming to live in the United States, where he is currently a professor of English and Chair of the Department at Hostos Community College of CUNY. He is the author, most recently, of *The First Protestant Missionary to India: Bartholomaeus Ziegenbalg (1683-1719)*, and has published over forty scholarly and academic articles in India, the U.S. and Britain.

Beth Kowaleski Wallace is the author of *Consuming Subjects: Women, Shopping, and Business in the Eighteenth Century* (Columbia University Press, 1997). Her new project concerns contemporary representations of the eighteenth-century slave trade. She is an Associate Professor of English at Boston College.

Amy Wyngaard, an Assistant Professor of French at Syracuse University, has published essays on Marivaux, Watteau, and Rétif de la Bretonne. She is completing a book entitled *From Savage to Citizen: The Invention of the Peasantry in the French Enlightenment.*

Executive Board 2001-2002

President: **Daniel Brewer,** Professor of French, University of Minnesota
First-Vice President: **John Bender,** Director, Stanford Humanities Center and Meier Family Professor of English and Comparative Literature, Stanford University
Second-Vice President: **Joan B. Landes**, Professor of Women's Studies and History, Pennsylvania State University
Past President: **Keith Baker,** Cognizant Dean for the Humanities, J.E. Wallace Sterling Professor in the Humanities, Stanford University
Treasurer: **Catherine Lafarge,** Professor of French, Bryn Mawr College
Executive Director: **Byron R. Wells,** Professor of Romance Languages, Wake Forest University

Members-at-Large
Kevin Berland, Professor of English and Comparative Literature, Pennsylvania State University
Marshall Brown, Professor of English and Comparative Literature, University of Washington
Julie Candler Hayes, Professor of French, University of Richmond
Alan Charles Kors, Professor of History, University of Pennsylvania
Mary Lindemann, Professor of History, Carnegie Mellon University
Mary Vidal, Professor of Art History, University of California at San Diego

Administrative Office
Office Manager: **Vickie Cutting,** Wake Forest University
Website Manager: **Jay Bates**, Wake Forest University

For information about the
American Society for Eighteenth-Century Studies, please contact:
ASECS
P.O. Box 7867
Wake Forest University
Winston-Salem, NC 27109-7867
Telephone: (336) 727-4694
Fax: (336) 727-4697
E-mail: asecs@wfu.edu
Web Site: http://asecs.press.jhu.edu

Patron Members 2001-2002

Paul Alkon
Mark S. Auburn
James G. Basker
R. Bernasconi
Barbara Becker-Cantarino
Peter M. Briggs
Joseph A. Byrnes
Michael J. Conlon
Brian A. Connery
Margaretmary Daley
Marlies K. Danziger
Joan DeJean
Julia Douthwaite
William F. Edmiston
Frank H. Ellis
Roger J. Fechner
Charles N. Fifer
Bernadette Fort
Christopher Fox
Monika Greenleaf
Joan R. Gundersen
Basil Guy
Wolfgang Haase
Martha Hamilton-Phillips
Robert D. Hume
Lynn A. Hunt
Malcolm Jack
Margaret C. Jacob
Annibel Jenkins
Claudia Johnson
Gary Kates
Shirley Strum Kenny
Charles A. Knight
Alan Charles Kors
Paul J. Korshin
David H. Koss
Thomas W. Krise
Catherine Lafarge
Susan Lanser
J. Patrick Lee
Nancy M. Lee-Riffe
Elizabeth Liebman
Robert P. Maccubbin
H.W. Matalene
Marie E. McAllister
Christine McDonald
James C. McKusick
Donald C. Mell, Jr.
John H. Middendorf
Michael Mooney
Dennis Moore
Mary Ann O'Donnell
Frank Palmeri
Ruth Perry
R.G. Peterson
J.G.A. Pocock
Adam Potkay
Ruben D. Quintero
John Radner
Richard Sher
Eleanor Shevlin
Kazuko Shimizu
Doughlas Smith
Barbara Stafford
Susan Staves
Joan Koster Stemmler
Ruud N.W.M. Teeuwen
Bertil Van Boer
David Venturo
Howard D. Weinbrot
Byron R. Wells
James Winn
Karin E. Wolfe
Servanne Woodward
James Woolley
Karin Wurst
Lisa M. Zeitz

Sponsoring Members 2001-2002

Paula Backscheider
Joseph E. Bartolomeo
Jerry C. Beasley
David Blewett
Carol Blum
Thomas P. Bonnell
Martha F. Bowden
Gay W. Brack
O.M. Brack, Jr.
Leslie Ellen Brown
Chester F. Chapin
Thomas M. Columbus
Brian Corman
Howard J. Coughlin, Jr.
Alix S. Deguise
Robert DeMaria
JoLynn Edwards
A.C. Elias, Jr.
Antoinette Emch-Dériaz
Clarissa C. Erwin
Timothy Erwin
David Fairer
Brandon Brame Fortune
Diana Guiragossian-Carr
Roger Hahn
Elizabeth Harries
Karsten Harries
Phillip Harth
Donald M. Hassler
Daniel Heartz
Charles H. Hinnant
Stephen Holliday
J. Paul Hunter

Adrienne D. Hytier
Thomas Jemielity
Loftus Townshend Jestin
Gwin J. Kolb
Joanna Lipking
Lawrence Lipking
April London
Steven Walton Lynn
Robert Markley
David McNeil
Heather McPherson
Linda E. Merians
Kathryn Montgomery
Dewey F. Mosby
Maureen E. Mulvilhill
Malcolm H. Murray
Felicity Nussbaum
John H. O'Neill
Douglas Lane Patey
Virginia J. Peacock
Stuart Peterfreund
James Pollak
Shirley McNerney Rendell
John Richetti
Betty Rizzo
Raymond Rizzo
Wendy Wassyng Roworth
Peter Sabor
J.T. Scanlan
Mona Scheuermann
Barbara B. Schnorrenberg
Gordon Schochet
Frank Shuffelton
Donald T. Siebert
Jeffrey Smitten
Patricia Spacks
James L. Thorson
Dennis Todd
Randolph Trumbach
Peter Wagner
Myron D. Yeager

Institutional Members 2001-02

American Antiquarian Society
Arizona State University
Brown University
John Carter Brown Library
University of Calgary
University of California
University of California Science Library
Carleton University Library
Colonial Williamsburg Foundation
John D. Rockefeller, Jr. Library
Emory University
Robert W. Woodruff Library
University of Evansville Library
Florida Atlantic University
Wimberly Library
Folger Institute
Fordham University Library
Harvard College Library
Holy Cross College *Dinand Library*
Indiana University
Kings Library Science/English
University of Kentucky
Young Library
McMaster University Library
Metropolitan Museum of Art
Thomas J. Watson Library
University of North Carolina
Davis Library
University of Notre Dame
Ohio State University Libraries
Omohundro Institute for Early American History - *Kellock Library*
University of Pennsylvania Libraries
University Press of Kentucky
University of Rochester Library
SUNY at Binghamton Library
Smith College
Neilson Library
University of South Carolina
College of Liberal Arts
University of Southern California
English Department
University of Tennessee Library
University of Texas at Austin
General Library
Thomas Jefferson Memorial Foundation
University of Tulsa
McFarlin Library
University of Victoria
McPherson Library
Waddesdon Manor Collection Department
Washington University
Olin Library
William Andrews Clark Memorial Library
Yale Center for British Art
Reference Library
Yale University Library
York University
Scott Library

Index

Every effort has been made to include references to all identifiable persons living before or during the long eighteenth century, as well as to often cited twentieth-century critics and commentators, and to provide a selective listing of relevant concepts and keywords. Readers may also wish to consult the endnotes of each essay for more comprehensive information.